Simple Statistics

Applications in Criminology and Criminal Justice

Terance D. Miethe

University of Nevada, Las Vegas

New York   Oxford
OXFORD UNIVERSITY PRESS

Oxford University Press, Inc., publishes works that further Oxford University's objective of excellence in research, scholarship, and education.

Oxford   New York
Auckland   Cape Town   Dar es Salaam   Hong Kong   Karachi
Kuala Lumpur   Madrid   Melbourne   Mexico City   Nairobi
New Delhi   Shanghai   Taipei   Toronto

With offices in
Argentina   Austria   Brazil   Chile   Czech Republic   France   Greece
Guatemala   Hungary   Italy   Japan   Poland   Portugal   Singapore
South Korea   Switzerland   Thailand   Turkey   Ukraine   Vietnam

Copyright © 2007 by Oxford University Press, Inc.

Published by Oxford University Press, Inc.
198 Madison Avenue, New York, New York 10016
http://www.oup.com

Oxford is a registered trademark of Oxford University Press

ISBN 978-0-19-533071-7

Printed in the United States of America
on acid-free paper

Contents

Preface

This book was written in large part out of frustration and necessity. The frustration derived from my experience with other "stats" books that provide technically accurate information about various statistical procedures but fail to inspire students because they are written in an obtuse and jargon-ridden manner. These textbooks are also expensive to buy because they contain elaborate graphics and glossy photos, and feel compelled to cover nearly every possible statistical technique for qualitative and quantitative data. For purposes of teaching a basic statistics course in a distance education format, it was necessary for me to have a textbook that "stands alone" (i.e., enabling students to learn without outside instruction). These dual concerns were the motivation for this book.

My goal in this book is to provide an accurate, no-frills, and interesting introduction to basic statistics for students in criminology and criminal justice. Compared to other textbooks, this stats book is different in the following ways:

- This book is written in a more conversational tone than most statistics books. Compared to other books with a similar goal, the current book does not attempt to "dumb down" the material. Rather, it attempts to show the value of statistical thinking and reasoning for both users and informed consumers of this information.

- The text places social statistics within their proper context. Chapter 2 is especially important in illustrating the various ways that "garbage in, garbage out" operates to affect the substantive conclusions from statistical analyses.

- It shows how verbal statements and other types of information become converted into statistical codes, measures, and variables. Most books don't talk about this process of operationalization and measurement, so most students do not have a clue how research methods and statistics are related or how to conduct statistical analysis from the bottom up.

- The chapters provide answers to both "how to do" and "why we do" these statistical procedures. Most statistics books emphasize the "how to" to the neglect of the "why we do" questions. The problems at the end of each chapter focus exclusively on "applying what you have learned" to provide more context for "why we do" these procedures. The term *informed consumer* is used throughout the book to convey the importance of understanding social statistics for being a better employee/student and concerned citizen.

- The book covers "essential" statistical techniques. It does not try to cover all statistical procedures. The reader is directed to other sources to learn how to use other techniques (e.g., logistic regression, gamma/lambda, and tau).

- The author attempts to use humor and everyday "street" lingo at numerous places to further demystify the phobia or panic surrounding statistics courses.

- The book uses hand computation methods to demonstrate how to apply the various statistical procedures. However, each chapter contains an optional section on how to do these procedures in SPSS and/or Microsoft Excel spreadsheets. If students have access to these programs, they can apply what they have learned to these computer programs, but such applications are not necessary for understanding the statistical methods described in this book.

- Several examples are used to illustrate each statistical procedure to help understand and apply them. Rather than overwhelming students with too many examples, the book tries to reach a balance between computation methods and examples of how to do them.

- Detailed summaries are provided at the end of each chapter to further highlight the major points. The specific problems at the end of each chapter serve to further illustrate and apply these principles.

Several people have reviewed this book and made helpful corrections and suggestions for improving it. I especially appreciate the comments by Jane Gauthier, Clay Mosher, Jared Shoemaker, and Jon Goodman. Maxine Franks and the rest of the staff of the Campus Computing Services at the University of Nevada, Las Vegas (UNLV) have provided technical assistance in developing the graphs, charts, and tables in this book. The faculty in the Department of Criminal Justice at UNLV has also been extremely helpful in providing a sounding board while I tried to figure out what to include and exclude in this book.

Finally, the author would like to acknowledge the helpful comments and suggestions made by various other reviewers of this book. These reviewers include John Stuart Batchelder, North Georgia College and State University; Jeb A. Booth, Northeastern University; Brian Forst, American University; Lior Gideon, John Jay College of Criminal Justice; Paige H. Gordier, Lake Superior State University; Shanhe Jiange, University of Toledo; Kent R. Kerley, University of Alabama at Birmingham; Teresa LaGrange, Cleveland State University; and Wayne J. Pitts, University of Memphis. However, any errors of omission and/or commission in this manuscript are my sole responsibility.

Terance D. Miethe

1

Introduction to Statistical Thinking

Sex offenders are often viewed as the most prolific and active criminals in American society. They are considered sexual predators with an uncontrollable sexual compulsion that leads to persistent and specialized forms of sex offending.

A recent study of about 10,000 sex offenders released from U.S. prisons, however, questions this conventional wisdom about them. In fact, the authors of this study (Miethe, Olson, and Mitchell 2006) found that sex offenders have an average of about 7 different arrests over their entire criminal "career," but most of them (61%) had only 1 arrest for sex offenses. Burglars, in contrast, averaged 13 arrests, and most of them (56%) had more than 1 burglary arrest in their criminal history. Based on these findings, the authors concluded that sex offenders are neither specialist nor persistent offenders when compared to other criminals.

As a public consumer of this type of information, what do think about the results of this study? Do they make sense to you? Is there some major flaw in this study that severely undermines its basic conclusions? Are community notification laws going to protect the public from sexual predators when the typical sex offender in this study seems to desist in sexual offending once he is arrested the first time for these offenses?

I think most of you would conclude that there is something wrong with this study and the numbers (i.e., statistics) that derive from it. Guess what? You are correct. In fact, here are a couple of major problems with this study:

- It is based on sex offenders who were released from prison—such sex offenders may be quite different in their criminal histories from sex offenders who aren't released from prison or are not caught at all.

- All sex offenders are combined in the same category. Maybe there are clear differences between rapists, child molesters, and exhibitionists that are blurred by combining all sex offenders into one category.

- Both the level of repeat offending for sex crimes and the frequency of offending are based on arrests. If most sex offenses are not reported to the police, using arrests to measure repeat offending patterns may bias these conclusions.

So, what does all this mean? Well, it means that you have gotten your first exposure to the type of "statistical thinking" that will be used throughout this book. As you will soon discover, the calculation of statistical numbers (like 61% or an average of 7 arrests) is fairly easy. The more difficult task is interpreting them within the context in which they are computed. In this example, I have confidence that 61% of the sex offenders in this study had only 1 sex offense arrest in their criminal career. However, I don't know whether sex offenders are actually less likely to repeat their crimes or have shorter criminal records than other types of offenders because of the problems mentioned above. In short, "simple statistics" do not necessarily translate into simple answers about the profile of sex offenders and other important substantive questions within criminology and criminal justice.

SOME DEFINITIONS AND BASIC IDEAS

Statistics involve a set of tools and measures to describe, classify, and summarize information. This information is called **data** and the things we try to describe with it are called **variables**. When there is not very much data (e.g., less than 25 observations or people and only 1 or 2 variables to describe or summarize), most basic statistical analyses can be done in your head and by counting on your fingers and toes. For more complex problems with more variables and more observations per variable, computer software programs have been developed to analyze or "crunch" the numbers and visually or graphically represent the patterns that underlie them. Both hand and computer calculations will be used to illustrate the statistical methods described in this book.

Regardless of the method we use to crunch the numbers, the two primary goals of statistical analysis are (1) data description and reduction, and (2) estimation and inference. These two goals correspond to the two primary branches of statistics: descriptive and inferential statistics.

Descriptive statistics are used for the goal of data description and reduction. The primary descriptive statistics involve summary measures of centrality or location (e.g., means, medians, and modes), dispersion (e.g., ranges, variances, and standard deviations), and association between variables (e.g., correlations). These statistics offer a useful way to reduce or boil down an entire set of observations into one single number. Take, for example, the following descriptive statistics derived from criminological research and other sources. Notice how they provide a very succinct summary of crime and criminal justice practices in contemporary American society:

- Nearly 250,000 pounds of cocaine were recovered in federal drug seizures in 2003 (*Sourcebook of Criminal Justice Statistics 2003*).

- An estimated 83% of Americans will be a victim of a violent crime in their lifetime (Koppel 1987).

- The average bail amount set for persons charged with murder in large U.S. counties was $575,000 (Cohen and Reaves 2006).

- 34% of American adults think that marijuana should be legal (Gallup Poll 2004).

- The average minimum salary for an entry-level police office in large cities is $33,900 (Hickman and Reaves 2003).

- The estimated lifetime chances of going to prison is 32% for black males compared to 6% for white males (Bonczar 2003).

- 38% of Americans are afraid to walk alone in their neighborhood at night (Gallup Poll 2006).

- The average maximum prison sentence given to convicted murderers is about 10 years (Durose and Langan 2004).

- About 15% of Americans report having driven while under the influence of drugs and/or alcohol in the past 12 months (DHHS 2004).

- Only 2% of applications for firearm transfers or permits are rejected on background checks (Bowling et al. 2005).

Inferential statistics involve these same statistical measures except that the goal is to use these summary values to make estimates and inferences about characteristics of a wider population. These summary population values (called **population parameters**) are often unknown, and we draw a random sample from this population and then compute **sample statistics** (e.g., means and percentages) to get the most reasonable estimate of these population values. Don't worry if these terms sound a bit strange. We will discuss them in great detail in later chapters. For now, just try to get the general idea surrounding these concepts.

For example, let's suppose you wanted to know what percent of juveniles in Nevada smoke pot (marijuana). To estimate this unknown population value, we would have to do the following: (1) Develop a list of all juveniles in Nevada, (2) select a large **random sample** of them from this list, (3) ask them discreetly if they smoke dope, and (4) compile the collected data and crunch out some statistical numbers. If 65% of your sample said they use marijuana, then your best estimate is that about two-thirds of juveniles in the state are users. Unfortunately, if only drug users answered your survey (i.e., your sample is a biased, nonrandom one) or juveniles simply lie about their drug use, your estimate of the state's level of dope-smoking juveniles is going to be pretty worthless. The major point, however, is that this is the process we use to develop sample statistics to estimate population parameters.

This ability to use descriptive statistics from sample data to estimate and infer population values is an incredibly powerful aspect of statistical thinking. How, when, and why we compute these descriptive and inferential statistics are the primary topics of this book on statistical thinking in criminology and criminal justice.

With the exception of math courses, there is no class in the undergraduate careers of social science majors that is more misunderstood, feared, and surrounded with horror stories than the dreaded, mind-numbing "stats" course. This incredible trepidation over taking "stats" is attributed to two primary factors: (1) math phobia and (2) the inability of course instructors to convince students of the value of statistical skills and reasoning in both their professional careers and personal lives. How this book addresses these impediments to understanding and appreciating statistical thinking is summarized below.

MATH PHOBIA, PANIC, AND TERROR IN SOCIAL STATISTICS

Based on the titles of many introductory books on statistics, there is an obvious "image problem" with this subject matter that is perpetuated by many book authors and students. Whether these books are entitled *Statistics Without Tears*, *Statistics for Dummies*, or *Sadistic Statistics*, students are initially confronted with this fear-invoking title and then told not to worry because "the math really isn't that bad in this stats class." Yeah, right—just as painless as a root canal!

After making this "not bad" comment, however, the typical stats instructor will then rattle off a laundry list of class prerequisites that will presumably help you on this journey through this ominous math maze. The math-prone statistics instructor will navigate this terrain by requiring of you at a minimum a working knowledge of college algebra, matrix algebra, calculus and differential equations, and much of the Greek alphabet. In contrast, the typical instructor who teaches **social statistics** will also cover basic mathematical functions and operations, but the course will emphasize the substantive applications and interpretations of this statistical information. Unfortunately, math-challenged or math-phobic students often freak out in both types of stats courses, and this stress is even more severe and chronic in advanced courses, where stronger math skills are required for computational and estimation purposes.

Given high phobias and feelings of mathematical incompetence among most students in the social sciences, the primary challenge for both teaching and learning social statistics is to demystify its hype and stereotypical portrayal as "complex stuff." The easiest way to debunk this image is to confront it directly by clear articulation of the particular math skills that are necessary for understanding this material. Accordingly, Table 1.1 provides a list of the mathematical functions and operations used throughout this book. Is this complex stuff? I don't think so.

TABLE 1.1	Basic Mathematical Operations and Functions		
Operations	**Example**	**Functions**	**Example**
Addition	$4 + 5 + 3 = 12$	Square	$4^2 = 16$
Subtraction	$6 - 5 = 1$	Square Root	$\sqrt{4} = 2$
Multiplication	$10 \times 15 = 150$		
Division	$210 \div 10 = 21$		

In addition to mastering a little basic math, you will also need to know a couple of characters in the Greek alphabet. Greek symbols are often used in statistics to refer to **population parameters** or values (e.g., the Greek symbol for mu, μ, is the population mean), whereas Latin characters are used to symbolize **sample statistics** or values (e.g., $\bar{x}$ refers to the sample mean). The most commonly applied Greek symbols in introductory statistics courses, and their Latin counterparts, are summarized in Table 1.2.

TABLE 1.2 Greek and Latin Characters Used in Basic Statistical Methods

Descriptive Measure	Greek Symbol (population)	Latin Symbol (sample)
Mean	μ (mu, lowercase)	$\bar{x}$ (x bar), $\bar{y}$ (y bar)
Standard Deviation	σ (sigma, lowercase)	s, s_x, s_y
Variance	σ^2 (sigma, lowercase)	s^2, s_x^2, s_y^2
Chi-Square Values	χ^2 (chi, lowercase)	X^2
Eta-Square	η^2 (eta, lowercase)	R^2
Pearson's Correlation Coefficient	ρ (rho, lowercase)	r, r_{xy}, r_{yx}
Standardized Regression Coefficient	β (beta, lowercase)	B, B_{yx}, B_{xy}
Y-intercept Term in Regression Model	α (alpha, lowercase)	a
Probability of Type I Error	α (alpha, lowercase)	alpha, $p =$

When the mathematical operations and functions are combined with the different characters in the Greek and Latin alphabets, it should be clear that these basic math and language prerequisites are not complex or extensive. If you know these math functions and a few Greek symbols, you should have no problems with the computational aspect in any basic social statistics course. Specific applications of these functions and symbols, their substantive meaning, and underlying statistical properties will be discussed throughout this book.

So, take three small breaths, relax, and cleanse your mind of that dastardly math phobia, panic, and/or fear. You won't need calculus or an intensive language course to pass an introductory course in social statistics. Comforting thought? I hope so.

THE PRACTICAL VALUE OF SOCIAL STATISTICS AND STATISTICAL REASONING

A very common question asked by students in criminology and criminal justice is "Why do I have to take a stats class?" Most of you probably gravitated to this major, or the social sciences in general, because of math fear and failure. Escaping the dreaded calculus series in business and economics by switching majors, you are now rudely confronted with another math course that is subtly disguised by the title *statistics* or *quanti-*

tative analysis. Both frantic and inquisitive minds want to know, "Why do I need this stuff?"

The standard answer to this "why" question is some version of the infamous "You will be a better person if . . ." reply. However, in this particular case, this overused and abused cliché is actually true. Before you consider this claim to be totally absurd, think about the following arguments about the practical value of being statistically informed.

By all indications, the modern world is an increasingly quantitative one. Our daily lives are totally saturated with numbers. Some numbers (like telephone and Social Security numbers) give us our unique identities and/or make other *qualitative* distinctions (e.g., the code words #1 or #2 for kids' bathroom behavior). Other numbers represent *quantitative* differences in the order, magnitude, intensity, or duration of human activity. Crime rates, unemployment levels, police expenditures, yearly salaries, baseball batting averages, car insurance premiums, and the lifetime risks of criminal victimization are all examples of these types of numbers. Graphs and charts are often used as an alternative visual representation of numerical data. However, the ultimate way we create these visual images is through some type of statistical manipulation of qualitative attributes or quantitative variables.

The pervasiveness of numbers and statistics in everyday life is easily demonstrated. All you have to do is read any daily newspaper, surf the Web, look at your home utility bills, or watch news programs or professional sporting events on television. You will see statistics everywhere in various shapes, sizes, and forms. If you read or use technology, you can't avoid statistics even if you want to. Under these conditions, why not learn how they are abused, misused, and correctly used to convey information about our world?

Most of you already have a good working knowledge of statistical thinking and data analysis even if you have totally repressed it. By the time you have passed the sixth grade, most Americans have learned how to compute measures of central tendency (e.g., means and medians), draw charts and graphs, and calculate slopes (i.e., "the rise over the run") and intercepts in a linear equation. This statistical stuff was also covered again in your basic and intermediate algebra course(s) in high school. Guess what? You will get it again in this book!

As a functioning human in the modern world, you have also already acquired the skills necessary to interpret visual representations of statistical data. If you don't believe me, look at the following charts and graphs and describe the major trends in them. This should be easy.

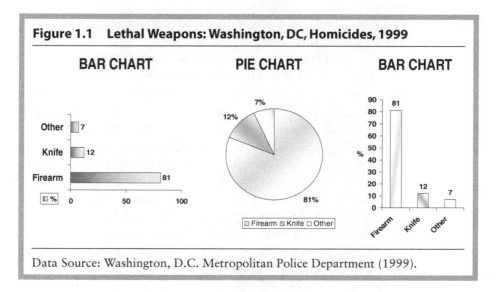

Figure 1.1 Lethal Weapons: Washington, DC, Homicides, 1999

Data Source: Washington, D.C. Metropolitan Police Department (1999).

Based on your daily experiences with statistics, you should have come up with something like this as substantive conclusions about crime from these statistical graphs and charts:

- The vast majority of homicides in Washington, DC, involve firearms.

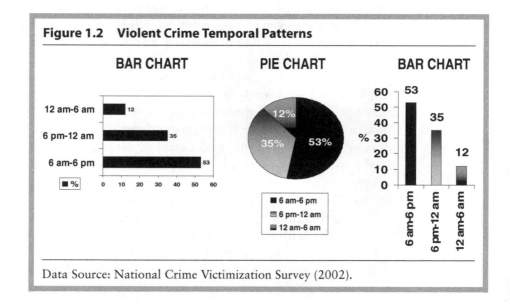

Figure 1.2 Violent Crime Temporal Patterns

Data Source: National Crime Victimization Survey (2002).

Figure 1.3　Multiple Offenders in Sexual Assaults

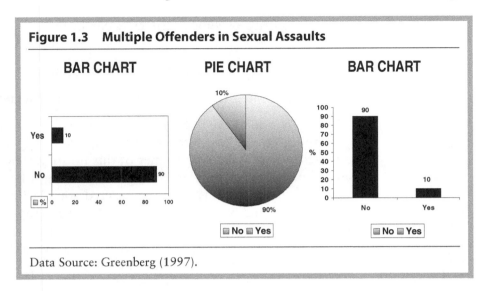

Data Source: Greenberg (1997).

Figure 1.4　U.S. Homicide Rates, 1900–1999, Yearly Trends

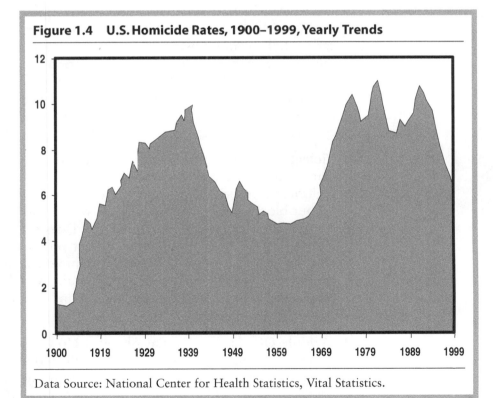

Data Source: National Center for Health Statistics, Vital Statistics.

- The majority of violent crimes occur in the daytime (6 a.m. to 6 p.m.).

- Almost all sex offenses involve a single offender.

- Homicide rates in the United States have varied widely over time.

While you don't have to be a trained statistician to reach these conclusions about crime, basic statistical training will help you become a more informed and critical consumer of this information. In fact, there are several problems and major assumptions that must be addressed before these substantive claims can be considered even the least bit credible. Hopefully, by the end of this book, you will be able to say, "Yes, but . . ." to each of these claims and offer a more informed interpretation of this information. Some of the types of statistical and methodological questions that you will learn to consider before accepting these presumed crime "facts" include the following issues:

- **Washington, DC, Homicides:** Are these statistics based on arrests or all known offenses? What percent of homicides are known to the police? Do known offenses accurately represent all D.C. homicides? Maybe deaths due to drug overdoses, poisoning, suffocation, falling, and drowning are routinely classified as accidents, thereby dramatically decreasing their prevalence in homicides and increasing the apparent prevalence of guns as the lethal method. Is 1999 representative of all years? Is it just handguns (not rifles or shotguns) that are the primary lethal weapon in this city? How are "missing persons" counted?

- **Violent Times:** What counts as a violent crime? Is there some hidden reason why daytime is expressed in a 12-hour block, but the nighttime categories cover only 6-hour periods? Converting to a 6-hour block for all temporal periods would make the most violent time between 6 p.m. and midnight. Does the bias in victimization surveys of undercounting violent offenses against other family members adversely affect substantive conclusions about the presumed dangerousness of particular times of the day? Is this conclusion only true of stranger attacks and serious assaults involving acquaintances?

- **Multiple Offenders in Sexual Assaults:** How does one evaluate the merits of the information in this graph? No mention is made of the original data source, the year of the study, the number of sexual assault cases in the sample or population, and what constitutes multiple offenders or sexual assaults. Who are these offenders? Does the study involve primarily or exclusively pedophiles, gang rapists, and/or acquaintance rape situations? Is this a clinical sample, a prison sample, or a self-report of sexual assaults by college students? Without this fundamental information, the visual representation and the substantive conclusions that derive from them are basically worthless.

- **U.S. Homicide Rates Over Time:** What population figures are used in the calculation of these rates? What counts as a homicide (e.g., most official statistics on homicide in the United States for the year 2001 do *not* include the nearly 3,000 deaths associated with the 9/11 attacks on the World Trade Center and Pentagon— aren't these homicides?)? Also, are adjustments made for missing data in national reports and for medical advances and faster emergency medical response over time that turn potential homicides into offense categories (e.g., attempted murders or aggravated assaults)? How does the pattern in the graphs change when yearly intervals are replaced by other time frames (e.g., 5-year increments or 10-year increments)?

The typical consumer of statistical information does not have the training or substantive expertise to know all of these particular nuances about data quality, its method of collection, the representativeness of the sample(s), and the inherent limitations and errors in social data. However, being an **informed consumer** of statistics requires a basic understanding of (1) statistical computations, (2) the substantive area in which they are applied, and (3) research methods that are used in the collection and measurement of the data. As will be discussed in detail in Chapter 2, the phrase "garbage in, garbage out" **(GIGO)** represents the consequence of having bad measurement, bad sample(s), bad theory, and generally bad research skills and no common sense. Hopefully, this book will help you develop and refine your skills as an informed consumer and user of statistics.

The bottom line about the practical value of statistical training and reasoning is simply stated. The best consumers, the most challenging and best students, the most valuable employees, and the most engaging and critical citizens are those who have a fundamental understanding of the basic principles, limitations, and computational assumptions underlying the world of social statistics. From my perspective, you *will* be a better person (and the world a better place) if you take the time and effort to master the material in a basic course in social statistics. It will provide you with the basic skills to critically challenge many of the statistical "facts" that are a major part of modern American society. It will also give you the basic training for impressing your friends, boss, or teachers by your informed "Yes, but . . ." reply to the various truth claims about social facts that are provided in the daily newspaper, television news, Internet blogs, and government reports.

TYPES OF STATISTICAL METHODS

Even within an introductory statistics book, there are an incredibly large number of statistical methods and techniques that could be discussed. The ultimate selection of topics to include in a book, however, is often tied to one's disciplinary training and perspective. Mathematically in-clined statisticians will often focus on a wider array of techniques than is typically covered in a course on social statistics. Within the social sciences, psychologists seem to be a bit more inclusive of techniques and methods than their colleagues in other related disciplines.

As a sociologist and criminologist, my focus in this book will be re-stricted to the particular statistical methods that are most commonly used within these disciplines. They include both **descriptive** and **inferential statistics**, **univariate analysis** and **bivariate analysis**, and a brief overview of statistical techniques for **multivariate analysis**. The specific topics and statistical methods that will be described and applied in this book are summarized in Table 1.3. Don't worry if these terms and phrases make no sense to you at this time. You will learn what is meant by all of them in later chapters.

TABLE 1.3   Topics and Statistical Methods Described and Applied in This Book

General Topic	Chapter	Statistical Method/Technique/Procedure
Research Methods and Threats to Statistical Conclusions	2	Measurement Validity, Causal Validity, Generalizability, Sampling Issues, Theory, and Political Issues
Data Preparation	3	Operationalization, Level of Measurement, Coding and Recording Data, and Statistical Analysis Packages (SPSS and Microsoft Excel)

(continued)

TABLE 1.3   Topics and Statistical Methods Described and Applied in This Book (continued)

General Topic	Chapter	Statistical Method/Technique/Procedure
Univariate Distributions for Qualitative Variables	4	Frequency and Percent Distributions for Attributes, Bar Charts, and Pie Charts
Univariate Distributions for Quantitative Variables		Frequency and Percent Distributions for Variables, Cumulative Frequency and Percent Distributions, and Histograms
Measures of Central Tendency and Location	5	Mode, Median, Refined Median, Mean, and Weighted Means
Measures of Dispersion and Variation	6	Range, Interquartile Range, Variance, and Standard Deviation
The Normal Curve and Sampling Distributions	7	Standard Normal Curve, Binomial Distribution, t-Distribution, χ^2 Distribution, and F-Distribution
Parameter Estimation and Confidence Intervals	8	Confidence Intervals for Population Means and Proportions (σ known)
		Confidence Intervals for Population Means and Proportions (σ unknown)
Introduction to Hypothesis Testing	9	Basic Concepts: Null and Alternative Hypotheses, Critical Values, Zone(s) of Rejection, and Type I and Type II Errors
Hypothesis Testing of Means and Proportions	10	z-Tests of a Single Population Mean or Proportion, t-Tests of a Single Population Mean or Proportion, z-Tests of Differences in Population Means or Proportions, and t-Tests for Population Means and Proportions
Measures of Association Between Two Attributes	11	Contingency Tables (Crosstabs), and Chi-Square (χ^2) Tests of Independence
Multiple Comparisons of Group Means	12	Analysis of Variance (ANOVA), Coefficient of Determination (η^2), and F-Ratios
Measures of Association Between Two Variables	13	Scattergrams, Correlation Coefficients, Linear Regression, and Regression Coefficients
Multivariate Analysis and Statistical Control	14	Multivariate Tabular Analysis, Partial Correlation, and Multiple Regression

PEDAGOGICAL (TEACHING) APPROACHES

There are various ways to teach social statistics. Some use exclusively hand-calculation methods, some only use computer software packages, and many offer a combined or hybrid approach. The approach used here also combines hand-computation and computer applications.

Rather than having students purchase expensive computer software (that may have 1-year expiration dates for the student versions of them), the current book places primary emphasis on simple hand calculations for illustrating the computational methods underlying each statistical procedure. However, for students who have access to some of these computer packages (e.g., **SPSS** or **Microsoft Excel**), the commands (called *syntax*) and other relevant computer language are provided to show how to do the various statistical procedures with these programs.

Your successful mastery of introductory statistics does not require access to these computer software packages. In fact, it is my strong belief that you will actually learn a lot more about the logic, assumptions, and limitations of particular statistical procedures and the data used within them by doing these simple hand computations. However, by providing the specific codes and commands to perform statistical operations within these software programs, students with access to these programs can use the syntax commands and codes to apply what they have learned to more comprehensive data files.

Another pedagogical device used in this book involves the standard format for covering material within each chapter. In particular, each chapter will cover three separate questions about the various statistical procedures: (1) *When* do you use a particular statistical procedure, (2) *Why* is this procedure the best statistical approach for this type of problem, and (3) *How* do you compute and apply this statistical procedure or technique through hand computations and computer software packages? By using this format, it is anticipated that students will be less inclined to approach statistical methods with fear, terror, and the "Why do we need to know ____" attitude that often accompanies the subject matter.

SUMMARY OF MAJOR POINTS

- Statistics involve a set of tools and techniques for describing, classifying, and summarizing information.

- The two primary goals of statistics are (1) data description and reduction, and (2) estimation and inference. The two major branches of statistics (i.e., descriptive and inferential statistics) are linked to these two goals.

- You don't have to be a math whiz to understand basic social statistics. Being a logical and/or critical thinker is more important for understanding social statistics and their use and abuse.

- The modern world is totally saturated with statistical information that is presented in a variety of forms (charts, graphs, and/or numbers). To be an informed consumer and user of this statistical information, you need to know both what underlies these numbers (e.g., how they were collected, what samples were used, and the motivation for the original study) and how they are crunched and analyzed.

- You will be a more confident person and a more productive and useful citizen and employee if you understand the logic of statistical thinking.

KEY TERMS (*SEE GLOSSARY FOR DEFINITIONS*)

Bivariate Analysis	Population Parameters
Data	Random Sample
Descriptive Statistics	Sample Statistics
Inferential Statistics	Social Statistics
Informed Consumer	Univariate Analysis
Multivariate Analysis	Variable

APPLYING WHAT YOU HAVE LEARNED (*SEE APPENDIX E FOR THE ANSWERS*)

1. What is the difference between descriptive and inferential statistics?

2. What is the difference between a sample statistic and a population parameter?

3. A Gallup poll in 2004 reports that 34% of American adults think that marijuana should be legal. What does this statistic tell you about Americans' support for legalizing marijuana? (*Hint:* Answer this question from the perspective of an informed statistical consumer.)

4. At what grade have most students learned about descriptive statistics like the mean, mode, and "rise over the run"?

5. Watch the nightly news on TV for one hour and report the most interesting statistic that you saw during this broadcast. Describe what the news reporter said about this statistic or number *and* then describe what you think it means from the perspective of being an informed consumer.

6. Greek symbols (e.g., α, β, and σ) are used to represent population parameters. True or False? ✦

2

Garbage In,
Garbage Out (GIGO)

According to national police data (FBI 2004), the average "take" from a street robbery or mugging is $898. Most people will logically conclude from this statistic that the typical U.S. mugger gets about $900 per incident.

Unfortunately, any inference about the typical behavior of muggers from police data is fundamentally flawed in several ways. Here are four immediate problems:

1. Many, if not most, muggings are not known to the police, especially those that occur when the victim is engaged in illegal activities (e.g., drug dealers don't call the police to report someone for stealing their drugs, and prostitutes don't typically file police reports against "johns" who rip them off).

2. Victims of attempted street robberies may also not report them (because they were not injured or didn't lose anything).

3. Different police departments may not count robberies the same way (e.g., some departments may count them as assaults, investigations, or larcenies).

4. The $900 average may be inflated because of a couple of "big-money" street mugging incidents.

Depending upon the overall direction of the biases in official data and statistical computations involving them, the typical "take" from street muggings may be substantially higher or lower than the $900 reported by the FBI. This number is only as good as the sources from which it derives. This is the basic message of the current chapter.

Statistical numbers are not omniscient. Instead, data analysts and their informed critics are required to decide when, where, and how these statistics are applied appropriately. Statisticians widely recognize that even their best analytic tools can't fully compensate for poorly designed and faulty research studies. Unfortunately, the mystical aura surrounding some statistical computations, their visual representation, and the prestige of the data sources (e.g., FBI reports or U.S. Census data) often gives public consumers a false impression of their omniscient quality and infallibility.

The phrase **"garbage in, garbage out"** (i.e., **GIGO**) aptly describes the adverse consequences of uninformed, misguided, nefarious, and otherwise dubious statistical analyses. The incoming garbage derives from various sources (e.g., bad measures or bad samples), whereas the outgoing garbage is the substantive conclusions that we attempt to make based on our statistical analysis. The primary sources of GIGO and their remedies are described below.

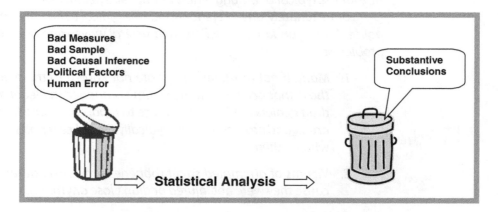

MEASUREMENT INVALIDITY

Validity is a fundamental property of any type of measurement. It asks the simple question "Are we measuring what we think we are measuring?" When the chosen measures are indicative of the particular substantive concepts (e.g., criminality, love, power, and alienation), **measurement validity** is assumed. Otherwise, we have the problem of measurement invalidity.

Most introductory texts in research methods will describe the various ways to evaluate whether measurement validity exists in any scientific study. Previous research, existing theory, common sense, the consistency of findings across studies and different measures, and the predictive value of chosen variables are the most common methods of validity assessment. Whatever method of validation is used, however, statistical analyses will yield "garbage" as substantive conclusions when measurement validity is lacking.

Claims of measurement invalidity are a possible criticism of virtually every study in the social sciences. Notice how this criticism applies in the following examples of basic criminological research:

- Police reports of known crime incidents are widely used to measure the nature and volume of crime in particular jurisdictions and the sociodemographic profile of criminals. However, it has long been recognized that (1) police reports are a more accurate measure of police activities rather than the true nature and extent of crime, and (2) the characteristics of persons arrested are a poor indication of the sociodemographic profile of all criminals because crimes committed by rich people (e.g., corporate crimes) are rarely contained in these reports and police patrol low-income areas more extensively. Although these problems with measurement invalidity are known to criminologists, we still continue to use police incident reports as the primary measure of crime and criminality in American society (see also Mosher, Miethe, and Phillips 2001).

- Contrary to their typical media portrayal as specialized and persistent offenders, a recent study found that sex offenders released from prison actually have less extensive criminal histories and exhibit less specialization than other types of convicted felons (see Miethe, Olson, and Mitchell 2006). However, this study can be criticized on the grounds of measurement invalidity (e.g., arrest histories are not a good measure of criminality). Although the authors address this concern, it remains the case that alternative measures (e.g., self-reported offenses) may yield dramatically different conclusions about the level of specialization and persistence of criminal behavior in sex offenders.

- For research on crime rates and economic conditions, the unemployment rate is often used as a measure of economic opportunities. The U.S. unemployment rate is computed on the basis of the percent of the civilian labor force who are actively seeking work and did not work in the last week. However, serious questions about measurement invalidity have been raised in this context because this measure grossly underestimates the actual unemployment rate by excluding from the ranks of the unemployed and those who are receiving unemployment benefits (1) persons whose unemployment benefits have run out and (2) persons who are so frustrated with their inability to find work that they have given up their job search and are no longer included in the count of the civilian labor force.

The obvious solution for measurement invalidity and its adverse effects on our conclusions is to use and develop more accurate measures of substantive concepts. This may involve using multiple measures of these concepts and checking the convergence of findings across these different indicators. Unfortunately, because of the costs and practical problems with collecting new data sources with better measures, this solution is easier said than done. Nonetheless, by paying greater attention to the process of **operationalization** (i.e., the decisions we make when trying to measures substantive concepts), informed data analysts can minimize one of the most fundamental sources of "garbage" in social statistics.

SAMPLING PROBLEMS

Most research studies can be criticized on the basis of their sampling design and the extent to which the selected subsets of individuals/objects are representative of their wider population of cases. Similar to measurement invalidity, errors in sampling have major consequences on the substantive conclusions that we can legitimately derive from statistical analyses. The term **sampling bias** is used to describe situations in which sample statistics will not provide accurate estimates of population parameters because of flaws in the sampling process.

Sampling bias comes from several sources. For example, sampling frames (i.e., a finite list of population members from which the sample is drawn) may be incomplete or outdated. A good example of this type of sampling bias involves the use of telephone directories to draw public samples. The obvious problem with samples drawn from telephone directories is that they exclude (1) people without telephones, (2) residents with unlisted phone numbers, and (3) recent movers (i.e., those who get new phone service or change their existing numbers after the directories are published). The sampling bias in this case is due to the fact that people with unlisted phone numbers and recent migrants are qualitatively different from those with listed numbers (e.g., unlisted residents are generally younger, more mobile, home renters, and single).

While methods of random digit dialing (RDD) overcome many of the problems with telephone directories (e.g., they contact people with unlisted numbers and recent movers), samples derived from RDD are still susceptible to sampling biases due to (1) the exclusion of residents without any telephone service and (2) nonresponse bias from the failure to contact many residents in the sampling frame (because they were not home at the time, screen their calls with answering machines or caller ID, or refuse to participate in the telephone survey or interview). Elaborate statistical procedures and modeling approaches are sometimes used to make adjustments for nonresponse and sampling bias (see Regoeczi and Reidel 2003). Unfortunately, these types of sampling bias are largely ignored in most criminological research.

The magnitude of sampling bias and its impact on substantive conclusions are even more serious in cases of **nonprobability sampling**. By selecting sample elements on the basis of convenience, availability, and/or "snowball" procedures (like chain letters and pyramid schemes), we really have no idea about the sample's representativeness. While nonprobability sampling techniques are widely used in exploratory and qualitative research, it is the inability to estimate **sampling error** and the strong likelihood of sampling bias that make statistical estimates from nonprobability sampling designs especially vulnerable to criticisms of GIGO. It is for these reasons that statisticians are adamant about using **probability sampling**. When there is a known probability of being selected in a sample (i.e., the key feature of probability sampling), the selection of large, random samples will allow for clearer substantive inferences about population values because the magnitude of sampling error can be estimated.

For most criminological research, probability sampling is not used. So, the only real way to check whether sampling bias is a serious threat to the external validity (i.e., **generalizability**) of your findings is to compare them with previous studies. However, because most public consumers of statistical information will lack this knowledge of previous research, they must rely on the "good faith" of the data analysts and reporter to disclose the various caveats about the sampling design.

The importance of providing the reader with the content of the sampling approach before drawing any substantive conclusions cannot be overstated. To illustrate this point, check the magnitude of your possible "shock and awe" reactions to the following statistical "facts" of American life:

- 30% of males have had sexual relations with animals (Kinsey 1953). Such offenses often fall under the legal categories of bestiality and buggery under most criminal codes.

- The average child molester admits to having about 120 illegal sexual contacts with 14 different children (Weinrott and Saylor 1991).

- The average "salary" for a street-level drug dealer is estimated at $27,000 per year (tax free) (Plate 1975).

Before you tell your friends about these strange numbers, you should recognize that all of them are susceptible to serious sampling bias that makes them nearly worthless as estimates of population parameters about these aspects of human behavior. The particular sources of sampling bias include the following:

- Kinsey's sex research was based on volunteers, and the method he used to collect this information involved personal interviews. People who agree to talk candidly to a stranger about their sexual behavior (e.g., having sex with animals) are probably far more sexually liberated and active than "normal" Americans. This sampling bias is especially acute in the 1950s, when talking about sex or taking sex surveys was considered by most people to be vulgar and socially inappropriate.

- This conclusion about the prevalence of self-reported sex offenses against children is based on a small sample of 67 institutionalized male child molesters in a sex offender treatment program. Sample selection bias is due to (1) the sampling of sex offenders in a treatment program (who may not represent all sex offenders), and (2) the use of volunteer subjects (who may not represent even the sex offenders in this particular treatment program). Under these conditions, it is an enormous inferential leap to assume that these people will honestly report their participation in illegal sexual activity, and those who do are probably quite different than the typical sex offender. The large average rate of child molestation among the offenders in this sample is also susceptible to inflation due to the inclusion of a few highly prolific sex offenders (called statistical **outliers**) who dramatically increase the average rate. For example, one incest offender in this sample admitted to over 1,000 sexual encounters with his two daughters (Weinrott and Saylor 1991, 291).

- The estimated average salary of street-level drug dealers is based on a small convenience sample. Those people who are actively engaged in criminal activities and tell people about it are probably different than those who keep quiet about their illegal behavior. It is also likely that drug dealers in a particular city who talk about their criminal enterprise are different from similar offenders in other cities and rural areas. The use of convenience sampling and selective biases within this group of drug dealers places severe limits on the generalizability of this reported sample statistic about the profitability of drug dealing.

As was true of issues of measurement validity, sampling bias represents a serious threat to the conclusions we want to make from our statistical analyses. Numbers and rates can be easily computed from any data source, but the substantive inferences that derive from them are directly tied to the nature and magnitude of sampling bias. In short, the major point is again GIGO.

FAULTY CAUSAL INFERENCES

Another type of validity problem in criminological research involves the accuracy of our causal inferences. This notion of **causal validity** is a major concern whenever we are attempting to test or assert causal relationships among a set or sets of variables. This basic causal inference is symbolized as **X ➔ Y**, where X is the **independent variable** (i.e., the cause) and Y is the **dependent variable** (i.e., the effect).

All introductory books in research methods will identify three necessary conditions that must be present when making any causal inference of the form **X ➔ Y**. First, X must precede Y in time. This is called the **temporal ordering** assumption. Second, X and Y must be statistically related in that changes in X (i.e., decreases or increases) are linked to changes in Y (i.e., decreases or increases). This is called an **empirical association**. Third, the empirical association between X and Y must not be caused by some other variable that is related to and precedes in time both X and Y. This is called the assumption of non**spuriousness**. If each of these three conditions can be demonstrated, we can legitimately claim that X is a cause of Y.

To make this stuff about X causing Y less abstract, consider the following two examples of causal inferences:

- **Smoking Marijuana (*x*) Causes More Serious Drug Use and Abuse (*y*):** If marijuana is the "gateway drug" (i.e., cause) for more serious drug abuse (i.e., effect), it must be shown that (1) marijuana use occurs before other drug use, (2) people who have smoked pot have also used other drugs, and (3) there are no other variables that cause both types of drug use and, if there are such common variables, their influence has been taken into account. While the conditions of temporal ordering and empirical association are strongly supported in previous research, most studies of the "gateway drug" hypothesis conclude that this relationship is largely spurious (i.e., due to factors like low self-control and peer influences that affect all types of drug use).

- **Broken Homes (*x*) Cause Juvenile Delinquency (*y*):** Although an empirical association has been found between these two variables, the conditions of temporal ordering and nonspuriousness are not strongly supported in the available research. In particular, family disruption (i.e., "broken" homes) does precede the onset of juvenile delinquency in some cases, but family disruption is also a consequence of delinquency (e.g., parents separate and divorce over arguments about their child's delinquency). In terms of the possible spuriousness of this relationship, previous studies have identified several variables (e.g., differences in family income, parental monitoring, and quality of parenting) that are associated with both family disruption and delinquency. When statistical adjustments are made for these other factors, the magnitude of the empirical association between broken homes and delinquency decreases dramatically. Rather than the family structure per se, the quality of parenting appears to be the more important factor in understanding delinquency. However, even for this variable, the direction of the causal ordering is often unclear.

When more than two variables are considered, there may be both causal and noncausal relationships among them. The nature of these interrelationships is important because it helps us interpret and explain the statistical results that are obtained in any particular study. The ideas of spurious association, **developmental chain**, and different types of causes (e.g., proximate causes and distal causes) are graphically displayed in Figure 2.1.

As illustrated by the broken arrow (— — ➤) in the first panel of Figure 2.1, statistical evidence of a spurious association is found when the basic relationship between X and Y disappears after we take into account another variable (Z) that is determinant of both X and Y. The basic relationship between X and Y also may disappear in a developmental or causal chain, but in this general case, variable X is causally related to Z, which, in turn, is causally related to Y. Good theory and a solid understanding of the research literature on the particular substantive topic are the best ways to evaluate whether basic relationships are causal or spurious.

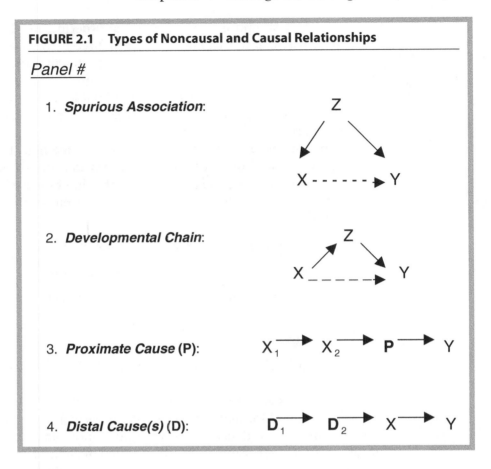

FIGURE 2.1   Types of Noncausal and Causal Relationships

Within the context of causal chains, there are both proximate and distal causes. **Proximate causes** are those factors that are temporally closest or most directly related to the outcome variable (i.e., the "effect"). **Distal causes** are those factors that influence the outcome variable in an indirect route through some other intervening variable. As is true of spurious association, when a variable is a distal cause, its influence on the outcome variable is eliminated or, at least, diminished dramatically when these other variables are taken into account (see Figure 2.1, Panel 4).

The best types of research studies for making sound causal inferences use **experimental designs** with **random assignment** to different groups. The experimental group in these designs consists of people who get the "treatment" (e.g., a new drug), while the comparison or control group involves people who get something else (e.g., another drug, a placebo [sugar tablet], or nothing). Using this type of experimental design, the causality assumptions about temporal ordering and the presence of an empirical association can be established directly by monitoring the behavior of both groups after they get the experimental treatment or placebo. When random assignment to various groups is conducted, other factors that may influence the dependent variable should become equally dispersed across groups, thereby allowing clearer inferences about the causal importance of the treatment.

Experiments are the preferred research method for evaluating causal relationships, but there are various practical constraints (e.g., ethical issues, time, money, and accessibility) that limit their widespread use. For example, the best way to determine whether physical castration is an effective treatment for sex offenders is to

1. select a representative sample of sex offenders,

2. randomly castrate half of them and do nothing to the others,

3. release all of them in both groups from custody, and

4. monitor the number of post-release sexual assaults for each group.

Obviously, there are numerous ethical and legal problems with this research design that prohibit us from actually doing this. Instead, researchers in this area are forced to use alternative research protocols that are far less sound for making causal inferences (e.g., using volunteers for human subjects, and using less valid and more indirect measures of future sexual aggression like self-reported feelings and physiological arousal to sexually explicit pictures). Similar problems plague researchers who try to use experimental designs in other substantive areas. When experimental designs are not used and causal inferences are made, GIGO raises its ugly head again.

A final type of problem with faulty causal inferences arises when data analysts and public consumers of statistical information commit what is called the **ecological fallacy**. Improper causal inferences occur in these situations when data is collected or reported at some particular aggregate or ecological level (e.g., neighborhoods, cities, or states) and inferences are then made about the behavior of individuals. For example, cities with a higher concentration of black residents have higher rates of violent crime than cities with lower proportions of black residents. The ecological fallacy in this case would be to conclude that black people are more likely to commit violent crimes than white people. However, it is possible that it is white people in predominantly black communities who are actually the violent offenders, but because we didn't collect information on individual people, we really can't evaluate the accuracy of these causal assertions about individuals. Making these inferences in this case is committing an ecological fallacy.

POLITICAL INFLUENCES

It is a simple fact of modern life that social statistics have become increasingly important to consumers and interest groups in contemporary American society. We are saturated daily with statistical information, and this data has become a major source of social and political power. Politicians use statistical data to hammer their opponents and to applaud their own efforts. Large companies and their CEOs use statistical data to assess their market performance and to generate more business. Sheriffs and police chiefs use crime statistics for targeting particular areas for crime prevention activities, to increase monetary resources, and to get re-elected as effective crime fighters.

Given the widespread use of statistical information in numerous contexts, it should not be surprising to learn that social statistics are grossly abused for a wide variety of nefarious and/or political reasons. The phrases *cooking the numbers*, *data fudging*, and *data fraud* are just a few ways to describe the political influences that sometimes creep into statistical analyses. In these cases, the "garbage in" is politically motivated and not necessarily the result of bad measurement, bad sample, or faulty casual inferences.

There are several classic examples of "cooking the numbers" for political purposes. This list of classics in criminology and criminal justice would include the following:

- U.S. Justice Department officials in the mid-1980s claimed that as many as 4,000 people were murdered by serial killers in the United States each year. This number was derived by taking cases of unsolved homicides and attributing all of them to the actions of serial killers. Philip Jenkins (1994) contends that justice officials grossly inflated these annual estimates to justify the creation of a new Violent Crime Apprehension Program (VICAP) and to deflect attention away from negative publicity surrounding the FBI during this time period.

- Based on police reports compiled and submitted under the FBI's *Uniform Crime Reports,* Philadelphia has one of the lowest rates of serious crime among the largest cities in the United States.

However, federal audits and independent inquiries into their crime-reporting practices reveal that the Philadelphia Police Department has been grossly underreporting the number of serious crimes for decades in order to maintain the image of the United States' "safest big city." As a way of circumventing the primary FBI reporting categories, many rapes in Philadelphia are deliberately misclassified and downgraded as "investigations" and "trespasses"—these reclassified offenses do not have to be recorded in the monthly reports sent to the FBI (see, for details, Mosher, Miethe, and Phillips 2001).

A different type of political influence on statistical analysis involves the ability to control what type of statistical information is being funded for research and/or disseminated for public consumption. This type of political power is especially insidious because it affects our very conceptions of social reality.

There are many examples of political influence through information control. Studies of the medical benefits of marijuana smoking, for example, were rarely funded prior to the last decade because the possibility of its beneficial effects conflicted with the dominant political ideology that marijuana is a dangerous drug. The current mass attack on tobacco is reflective of similar political and social influences. It is now politically and socially correct to trash tobacco as an evil and addictive drug, and anti-tobacco statistics have replaced pro-tobacco numbers in various media outlets.

Social and political issues like gun control, abortion, capital punishment, and welfare reform are fertile grounds for statistical abuse, distortion, and fabrication because they are emotionally charged and divisive issues. The extreme zeal and passion of a small group of advocates for each position greatly contribute to the likelihood of statistical fraud.

Given the social and political power associated with statistical profiles, it is important for informed consumers to be a bit suspicious of the various statistical claims made in everyday life. Some social statistics clearly serve political agendas, and some don't. Although you don't have to be a card-carrying conspiracy theorist to be a good consumer and user of statistics, a healthy dose of critical thought is essential when collecting, analyzing, and interpreting criminological data. It is also healthy for purposes of enhancing the accountability of claim makers and deterring their further acts of statistical deception and distortion.

HUMAN FALLIBILITY

A final source of fallibility in statistical analyses includes basic human errors in the collection, coding, and analysis of social data. These errors involve acts of omission and commission that are linked to various aspects of human behavior. The most common sources of error within this general category include mistakes in information processing, response errors, and problems with "hired help."

Errors in information processing derive primarily from the inadequacies of the human senses. People get easily distracted, hungry, tired, and bored. These basic aspects of human fallibility translate into errors when recording observational data (e.g., when doing field research and taking field notes), transcribing verbal accounts, typing data into spreadsheets or other data files, and transferring numbers from computer output and calculators to final project reports. While most of these errors may be inconsequential, a misplaced decimal point or being a column off when entering data into a spreadsheet may dramatically distort substantive findings if they are not detected and corrected.

Another source of human fallibility involves response error. Similar to the notion of reliability, response error refers to the variability in human responses over repeated observations.

Previous research on questionnaire construction indicates that certain types of information elicited in social surveys have higher response error than others. Survey questions about behaviors (e.g., do you smoke cigarettes?) and attributes (e.g., what is your age, sex, and race?) have low response error, meaning that people will respond essentially the same way to these questions over time. Questions about human values (e.g., do you believe in capital punishment?) also have low response error. However, vague attitudinal questions (e.g., do you strongly agree, agree, disagree, or strongly disagree that Styrofoam is a good product?) have extremely high response errors. The high response errors associated with questions about attitudes are one of the primary reasons why the U.S. Census Bureau does not usually include attitude questions in their surveys.

The idea that you "get what you pay for" explains errors in research that derive from hiring other people to collect, code, and analyze your data. Although there are clear exceptions to this trend, hired help is often underpaid, and they usually don't have the same commitment to a research project as the primary investigators. Under these conditions, some errors in information processing are likely to occur in nearly all research projects. These errors from hired help may be reduced considerably by (1) using multiple data coders to minimize burnout, (2) cross-checking data entry and coding by having at least two people code and enter the same information, and (3) performing extensive preliminary data analyses to uncover numerical values that fall outside the range of legitimate values for particular variables.

SUMMARY OF MAJOR POINTS

- Substantive conclusions from statistical analyses are essentially worthless when you have bad measurement and bad sampling, make faulty causal inferences, fail to consider the social and political influences that lead to "cooking the numbers," and do not identify and correct the errors that arise from human fallibility in data collection, coding, and statistical analysis.

- Measurement invalidity occurs when you are not measuring what you think you are measuring. This problem can be reduced by sound logical thinking, knowing the previous research literature on this topic, and using multiple indicators of the major concepts to investigate whether similar substantive conclusions are reached across these alternative measures.

- Sampling bias is a major threat to the generalizability of substantive conclusions from statistical analyses. When sampling bias exists, sample statistics will provide poor estimates of population values. Nonprobability sampling techniques (e.g., samples drawn on the basis of convenience or availability) are especially problematic because of sampling bias and the inability to estimate the magnitude of sampling error within them.

- Proper causal inferences require the presence of three basic conditions: (1) temporal ordering (i.e., X precedes Y in time), (2) empirical association (i.e., X and Y are related), and (3) nonspuriousness (i.e., the basic relationship between X and Y is not due to the influence of other variables that are related to and precede both X and Y). Experimental designs with random assignment are the best research procedures for evaluating causal relations between variables.

- Substantive conclusions from statistical analysis are susceptible to both social and political influences. Political agendas affect both the nature of research findings and their dissemination for public consumption.

• Human fallibilities contribute to errors in information processing and response errors. Errors in data collection, coding, and analysis that are committed by "hired help" can be minimized through extensive cross-checking of the data's quality.

• Informed public users and consumers of statistical data must be critical thinkers and always be aware of the notion of "garbage in, garbage out."

KEY TERMS

Causal Validity	Measurement Validity
Dependent Variable	Nonprobability Sampling
Developmental Chain	Operationalization
Distal Causes	Probability Sampling
Ecological Fallacy	Proximate Causes
Empirical Association	Random Assignment
Experimental Designs	Sampling Bias
Garbage In, Garbage Out (GIGO)	Sampling Error
Generalizability	Spuriousness
Independent Variable	Temporal Ordering

APPLYING WHAT YOU HAVE LEARNED

1. Most criminologists believe that police data has high measurement validity as an accurate measure of the actual extent of crime in American society.

   a. True

   b. False

2. If a measure of police honesty is said to have high measurement validity, which of the following outcomes would you expect?

   a. Police who say they are dishonest should have higher complaints and reprimands for bribery than other officers.

   b. Police who say they are honest should have lower complaints and reprimands for bribery than other officers.

   c. Police who say they are "on the take" should make more money outside of their salary than other officers.

   d. All of the above would be true if these measures of police honesty have high measurement validity.

3. The most common type of sampling used in criminological research is

   a. Nonprobability sampling.

   b. Probability sampling.

4. Which of the following is a potential source of sampling bias in criminological research?

   a. Outdated sampling frames (i.e., lists from which the sample is drawn).

   b. Nonresponse by particular groups of people who are in your study.

   c. The use of volunteers for research subjects who may be quite different from nonvolunteers.

   d. All of the above are potential sources of sampling bias.

5. Large random samples based on probability sampling are widely preferred over small, nonprobability samples because

   a. the magnitude of sampling error can be assessed in probability-based samples.

   b. these samples are often more representative of the wider population than is true of small, nonprobability samples.

   c. all people are included in any large random sample.

   d. all of the above are true.

   e. only a and b are true.

6. To claim that X is a cause of Y, what conditions must be present?

   a. X must precede Y in time.

   b. X and Y must be associated.

   c. The relationship between X and Y must be nonspurious.

    d. All of the above are necessary for causal statements.

    e. Only a and b are true.

7. In the causal chain A ➔ B, what is the independent variable and what is the dependent variable?

    a. *A* is the dependent variable, and *B* is the independent variable.

    b. *A* is the independent variable, and *B* is the dependent variable.

    c. Both *A* and *B* are independent variables.

    d. Both *A* and *B* are dependent variables.

8. Here is a casual chain: A ➔ B ➔ C ➔ D ➔ E. What is (or are) the proximate cause(s) of E?

    a. A

    b. B

    c. C

    d. D

    e. A, B, C, and D

9. Many U.S. cities (e.g., Honolulu, Las Vegas, Orlando, and San Diego) rely extensively on tourism as their major industry. Given what you read in this chapter about GIGO and the politics of crime data, what would you expect to find about the crime rates in these cities?

    a. Their actual crime rates may be far lower than reported by the police.

    b. Their actual crime rates may be far higher than reported by the police.

    c. Their crime rates are an accurate representation of their true level of crime.

10. A source of human fallibility in collecting and analyzing data is

    a. hunger.

    b. boredom.

    c. using low-paid help.

    d. all of the above are true.

Here are some more detailed questions to show what you have learned. Make sure to think about the major sources of GIGO when you answer them. Be an informed and critical consumer of this information by approaching each of these questions from a "Yes, but . . ." orientation. My answers to these questions are included in the back of the book (Appendix E). Use the concepts and terminology talked about in this chapter.

11. The amount of ice cream consumed in a city and its crime rates are highly related. Cities with higher rates of ice cream consumption have higher crime rates. Can we conclude from this that eating a lot of ice cream causes people to be criminal? Why or why not?

12. Rates of sex offending and recidivism for sex crimes are often lower in Scandinavian countries (such as Norway, Sweden, and Denmark) than the United States. These other countries use both chemical and physical castration as treatment for sex offenders, whereas these methods are not used extensively in the United States. Based on these findings, can we conclude that castration reduces the likelihood of sex offending and the risks of repeating these offenses? Why or why not?

13. Data summarized by the National Drug Court Clearinghouse suggests that drug offenders in drug courts have lower rates of repeat offending (i.e., recidivism) than drug offenders who are processed through the regular criminal courts. Does this mean that drug courts are more effective than other courts in dealing with substance abuse? Why or why not?

14. States with capital punishment have higher murder rates than states without capital punishment. Based on this finding, can you conclude that the threat of capital punishment is not a general deterrent for homicide? Why or why not?

15. Criminological research (see Zatz, Mann, and Rodriguez 2006) consistently shows minority overrepresentation in arrests (i.e., the proportion of all arrests involving blacks relative to the proportion of the population that is black) and imprisonment decisions. Does this mean that police and other criminal justice officials are engaging in racial profiling and other racist practices? Why or why not? ✦

3

Issues in Data Preparation

Statisticians and master chefs have many things in common. They tend to be perfectionists and try to minimize errors in what they do. Preparation and presentation are essential for each occupation. They seek out the highest quality of ingredients (e.g., the freshest vegetables or large random samples), but they often manage their craft with less optimal alternatives (e.g., by substitution of ingredients or using nonprobability samples). For both groups, errors in measurement (e.g., adding too much cayenne pepper or wasabi sauce or using bad indicators of concepts) can also ruin the final product. During the process of preparation, however, both statisticians and chefs have the ability to "cook" their product in a slightly different way to improve its flavor and/or deceive its consumer.

This chapter explores some of the basic issues in the preparation of social data for statistical analysis. It covers why and how we develop numerical codes and categories to represent concepts, the types and levels of measurement of attributes and variables, the coding and recoding of data, and the use of computer software programs for data entry. This probably doesn't sound very interesting, right? Well, let's see if I can convince you to read onward by enticing you with titillating examples of data preparation in studies of sex, drugs, rock-and-roll, and murder! I'll start with the "why" question and coding murder cases.

WHY IS DATA PREPARATION IMPORTANT?

Criminological data is rarely, if ever, in a form that is immediately ready for statistical analysis. Instead, the data often needs to be initially collected through various research methods (like telephone or mail surveys, personal interviews, **naturalistic observations**, and experiments). In these cases, there is a lot of preparatory activity in collecting data before you can even get to the fun part of analyzing data.

Among researchers who examine archival records and conduct other types of **secondary data analysis**, there are no headaches from data collection (because someone else has already done this for you), but the existing data still must be rearranged, coded and recoded, and otherwise modified to fit your particular needs. No matter how large or small the research project, some type of data preparation is a necessary first step in statistical analysis.

The necessity of data preparation can be easily illustrated. For example, suppose you want to study the type of weapons used in murders. Further assume that you already have access to police descriptions of individual homicide cases. An example of a narrative summary of one murder is shown in Table 3.1.

TABLE 3.1   A Narrative Account of a Homicide

"The 39-year old husband (the offender) claims that, during an argument, his 34 year old wife (the victim) beat him with a phone. The wife is much larger than the husband. The husband states that the wife went for a handgun kept in a closet, the two struggled over it. In the struggle, the gun fires once, killing the wife. The husband then calls the police."

Source: Langan and Dawson (1995).

If you were solely interested in the weapon used in this particular case, no data preparation is really necessary. You simply read the account and conclude, "This case involved a handgun." Period. End of story. Wow, isn't doing research easy?

Unfortunately, most research is far more complex and comprehensive in both its number of cases (i.e., sample size) and the number of variables. When these additional variables and cases are added, a **content analysis** of homicide narratives requires extensive data preparation by

1. establishing multiple coding categories and counting rules for each variable (e.g., if the victim is described as "shot," it is classified as a *gun* homicide even when the words *firearm/gun* are not included in the description);

2. deciding how to define and handle **missing data**; and

3. typing data codes into a spreadsheet or other software to provide multiple-variable analyses.

How to do this coding will be shown later in this chapter. However, the major point is that some type of data preparation needs to be done in any meaningful statistical analysis.

Another example of basic preparatory actions in the context of secondary data analysis involves the recoding of the original variables. Take, for example, the coding of the age of homicide offenders in Chicago (see Table 3.2).

TABLE 3.2 Homicide Offender's Age	
Offender's Age	**Number of Cases**
10 and under	1
11–20	260
21–30	191
31–40	66
41–50	22
51–60	3
61–70	6
71–80	1
Total	550

Data Source: Block and Block (1998).

As depicted in Table 3.2, assume that a newspaper story on Chicago homicides displays the age of offenders in 10-year increments. If you wanted to look at 20-year increments instead, you would have to "prepare" this data differently by (1) merging the adjacent categories (e.g., the age intervals 11–20 and 21–30 become the age interval 11–30), and (2) adding the number of homicides in this combined category. This minor preparatory step would then allow you to crunch the numbers to discover, for example, the percent of offenders in this sample that were between 11 and 30 years old. By the way, the statistical answer to this question is 82% (451 / 550). Check your math!

However, suppose you also want to make other age group comparisons (e.g., the percent of offenders who are senior citizens [defined as 65 or older], middle-aged [35 to 65], or juveniles [i.e., < 18 years old]). Now you've got a major problem because these age categories span only parts of some of the original intervals (e.g., 35–65 covers only part of the years in the original 31–40 and 61–70 intervals). The only way to fix this mess is to (1) try to get access to the original "raw" data that hopefully expressed age in 1-year intervals, and (2) prepare it differently for statistical analysis by recoding it into your preferred age categories. Unfortunately, this additional preparatory work may be very labor intensive and/or an exercise in futility when the original raw form of the data is not available or accessible.

To be totally convinced of the importance of data preparation in criminological research, you should consider the following three facts:

- First, any research involving data collection requires the completion of various preparatory steps before any type of data analysis is undertaken. You simply can't do this type of research without it. Period. This initial preparatory activity includes the very act of collecting data, coming up with definitions of the major concepts, establishing rules for coding and classifying observations, and entering the information into computer software or calculators capable of performing the data analysis.

- Second, data preparation is even necessary in most types of secondary data analysis. Within this research tradition, there are fewer preparatory issues in the data collection process (because data collection has already been done by someone else), but coding and recoding are still central aspects in the use of this type of research method.

- Third, cavalier treatment and/or ignorance of the fundamental issues in data preparation are a major cause of the "Garbage In, Garbage Out" syndrome that plagues social science research. To be informed consumers and users of social statistics, good analysts must pay close attention to the basic issues surrounding the collection and early preparation of statistical data before "crunching" the numbers.

These are the primary reasons *why* data preparation is so important in sound statistical analyses. The question about *how* data is prepared for subsequent analysis is the topic for the remainder of this chapter.

OPERATIONALIZATION AND MEASUREMENT

A fundamental aspect of all research involves the ideas of **operationalization** and **measurement**. These terms are closely related. Specifically, operationalization is the process by which particular meaning is attached to abstract concepts for purposes of developing observable indicators and measures of these concepts. Measurement is the outcome of this process. When we have poor operationalization of our major concepts, we also have the dastardly problem of measurement invalidity, a primary contributor to the GIGO syndrome.

These fundamental ideas can be easily illustrated by how criminologists measure the concept of *crime*. The prevalence and nature of "crime" are measured by three different methods in criminological research: (1) official police reports, (2) victimization surveys, and (3) self-reported offending surveys (see, for review, Mosher et al. 2001). Police data is most commonly used as the measure of the prevalence and social profile of crime. However, both victim and offender surveys indicate that police data dramatically undercounts the prevalence of crime and provides a somewhat biased image of the profile of offenders (e.g., blacks are far more overrepresented in police arrest reports than is found in self-report studies of offending). Under these conditions, the uncritical use of police data in criminological research would raise serious questions about the measurement validity underlying any substantive conclusions from this research.

Another example of this process of operationalization involves how we define a *sex offender*. While most people would agree that rapists and child molesters are sex offenders, how would you classify prostitutes, "johns," exhibitionists, voyeurs (i.e., "peeping toms"), pornography readers, and/or adulterers? Depending on what is operationally defined as a *sex offender*, you will get substantively different results about their prevalence and distribution.

Regardless of what basic concept is the focus of the research, my basic point is that the establishment of clear and unambiguous operational definitions is a crucial preparatory step for both data collection and analysis. Another component of this process, however, involves decisions about the type and levels of measurement of the selected indicators of these abstract concepts.

Indicators of concepts may be measured in qualitative or quantitative terms. These indicators of concepts are measured qualitatively when we talk about them in terms of differences in the type or kind of attributes. Indicators are measured quantitatively when they reflect differences in order, magnitude, duration, and/or intensity. Within the field of statistics, the term *variable* may refer to things that differ in either quality or quantity. Accordingly, statistical analysis involves both **qualitative variables** and **quantitative variables**.

Related to the distinction between qualitative and quantitative variables is the level of their measurement. There are four distinct levels of measurement of social variables: **nominal**, **ordinal**, **interval**, and **ratio measurement**. As will be shown later, particular statistical procedures are only appropriate for variables that are coded at particular levels of measurement. In short, this is why we have to discuss this stuff.

Nominal Measurement of Qualitative Variables

Nominal measures involve the measurement of attributes (i.e., things that vary in type or kind). When preparing data to be measured at this level, it is required that the categories be **mutually exclusive** and **collectively exhaustive**. Various examples of nominal measures that have these properties are summarized in Table 3.3.

TABLE 3.3 Examples of Nominal Measures	
Demographic Attributes	
Gender:	Male Female
Race:	Black White Other
Occupation:	1 = Bailiff, 2 = Defense Attorney, 3 = Judge, 4 = Police Officer, 5 = Prosecutor, 6 = Stenographer, 7 = Warden, 8 = Other
State of Birth:	1 = Alabama, 2 = Alaska . . . 50 = Wyoming
Attitudes/Behaviors	
Crime Committed:	1 = Violent, 2 = Property, 3 = Drug, 4 = Other
Last Drug Used:	Alcohol Caffeine Heroin Marijuana Other
Death Penalty Attitude:	1 = Favor, 2 = Oppose, 3 = Undecided
Fear Statistics?	1 = No, 2 = Yes, 8 = Don't Know

You will notice in some of these examples of nominal measures that numbers are used in the response categories (e.g., 1 = Alabama, 2 = Alaska . . . 50 = Wyoming). However, these numbers just designate that the categories are different in type or kind, not that one category (e.g., Wyoming) is 49 units bigger than another (i.e., Alabama). The ideas of distance, order, and/or magnitude are not relevant in nominal measures of attributes. In short, don't think *quantity* when talkin' *quality*, even when you see numbers.

Measurement of Quantitative Variables

Ordinal measures are the most basic form of quantitative measurement. As the name implies, the categories underlying variables at this level can be arranged in order of magnitude from "high-to-low" (descending) or "low-to-high" (ascending) order. The distance between these ordered categories, however, is either unequal or unknown. Common ordinal response categories are summarized in Table 3.4.

TABLE 3.4 Common Response Categories for Ordinal-Level Measures

- none < some < a lot
- never < rarely < sometimes < always
- lower < middle < upper
- daily > weekly > monthly > yearly
- 100–90% > 89–80%, > 79–70% > 69–60% > less than 60%

As the highest level of measurement of quantitative variables, both interval and ratio measures are distinct from ordinal scales because the distance between the ordered response categories is equal. Ratio measures are further unique because of the presence of a nonarbitrary zero point that permits the formation of ratio comparisons (e.g., we can say someone who is 40 is twice as old as someone who is 20 because an age of 0 is possible). For most practical problems, however, the distinction between interval and ratio measures is trivial and largely ignored.

Issues in Levels of Measurement

During the process of operationalization, decisions have to be made about what level of measurement to employ for different variables. In some cases, this decision is determined solely by the nature of the variable itself (e.g., sex and race are inherently nominal variables). However, for most other variables (like legal punishments or criminal behavior), it is possible to ask questions about "what type . . ." and "how much or many . . ." For example, you could measure "criminality" by a nominal measure (e.g., "Have you ever murdered anyone—yes or no?"), ordinally (e.g., "How many people have you killed—none, some, a lot?"), or by an interval or ratio scale (e.g., "How many people have you murdered—0, 1, 2, 3, 4, 5, . . . etc.?").

When in doubt about what level of measurement to use during data collection, conventional wisdom suggests using the highest level of measurement (e.g., interval or ratio). This is recommended because there is a hierarchy among these measures in which ratio or interval variables (the highest level of measurement) can also be recoded later to represent either ordinal or nominal variables. However, this situation does not work in reverse—that is, if you start with nominal measurement, it cannot be later changed to any other level of measurement. So, if you have no idea what you are doing when deciding how to measure a variable, the safest course of action is to employ interval or ratio categories for this variable.

CODING AND INPUTTING STATISTICAL DATA

An important, but surprisingly neglected, aspect of the research process is the physical activity of **coding** and inputting statistical data into a format that can be analyzed numerically. This step is already done for people who perform secondary analysis of existing data files (i.e., **"canned" data sets**). However, people who collect their own data must ultimately get it in this "canned" form. What are the tools necessary to put data in a big can? A codebook, a computerized spreadsheet, and a lot of strong coffee to keep you awake, or access to really good students you can entice to perform the often mind-numbing task of coding data files.

A **codebook** is nothing more than a set of rules that gives standard guidance for coding and recording information. For each variable in a data set, a codebook usually includes the following items:

- A short name or acronym that provides immediate recognition of a variable's content (e.g., in a study of crime, the letters *ORACE* to denote the offender's race). Most computer programs call this the *variable name*.

- A slightly longer label to further help identify the particular variable. This is called the *variable labels*.

- A list of specific letters or numbers that will represent the response categories for each coded variable. This is often called the *value labels*.

- Special remarks or comments to help further achieve uniform coding practices.

Table 3.5 provides a short example to illustrate these properties of a codebook. Look at this codebook carefully because it will be used soon to demonstrate the actual coding and entry of information into a data file or spreadsheet.

TABLE 3.5	**Codebook for Studying Lethal Weapons and Other Factors in Homicides**	
Variable Name	**Variable Label**	**Value Codes for Response Categories (special instructions)**
IDNUM	Case ID Number	001 to 999 (use consecutive numbering)
OSEX	Offender's Sex	1 = Male 2 = Female 9 = Missing/Don't Know (DK) (code primary offender's sex in multiple-offender cases)
OAGE	Offender's Age	Code Actual Age in Years; 98 = 98 or older, 99 = Missing/DK (code primary offender's age in multiple-offender cases)
ORACE	Offender's Race	1 = Black 2 = White 3 = Other 9 = Missing/DK
VETHNIC	Victim's Ethnicity	1 = Hispanic 2 = Non-Hispanic 9 = Missing/DK
WEAPON	Lethal Weapon Used	1 = Gun (all types) 2 = Knife/Sharp Objects 3 = Hands/Feet 4 = Blunt Object (bricks/clubs/bats/rocks) 5 = Other Method
LOCAT	Location of Crime	1 = In/Near Home 2 = Street/Park 3 = Business Establishment 4 = Other Public Place 5 = Other Private Place 9 = Missing/DK
MOTIVE	Offense Motive	1 = Argument/Dispute 2 = Robbery/Burglary 3 = Drug Related 4 = Gang Related 5 = Other Motive 8 = Multiple Motive 9 = Missing/DK (code only 1 primary motive in multiple-motive cases—if unclear primary motive in these cases, code = 8)

Now that you have a general idea of how to set up a codebook, let's see what happens when we use these coding rules to actually develop a numerical data file. Consider the following two narrative summaries of murders. Watch how we use the codebook to magically turn these words into numerical codes (see Table 3.6).

As the sample size increases, the time and effort required to code such narrative data also increase dramatically, but the logic of these three basic steps remains the same. Once you've completed Step 3 in Table 3.6, you are ready for the final stage of preliminary data preparation: inputting the data into a software package that has the capacity to visually display and analyze it. The most common data input and analysis programs are described below.

TABLE 3.6   How Words Become Coded Into Numbers for Data Analysis

Step 1: Narrative Summaries of Two Homicide Cases

"The 39-year old husband (the offender) claims that, during an argument, his 34 year old wife (the victim) beat him with a phone. The wife is much larger than the husband. The husband states that the wife went for a handgun kept in a closet, the two struggled over it. In the struggle, the gun fires once, killing the wife. The husband then calls the police." Case # 001. (Source: Langan and Dawson 1995)

"19 year old, Latin male victim was in a car with 3 other Latin males. They stopped to purchase drugs (marijuana). Two Black males approached the car and gave them an envelope containing drugs. The Latin males attempted to flee without paying. The victim was shot by one of the Black males. Only the 23-year old shooter was charged." Case # 002. (Source: Wilbanks 1984)

Step 2: Word-Based Coding of the Two Cases Using Codebook Categories

IDNUM	OSEX	OAGE	ORACE	VETHNIC	WEAPON	LOCAT	MOTIVE
001	Male	39	Missing	Missing	Handgun	Home	Argument
002	Male	23	Black	Hispanic	Gun	Street	Drugs

Step 3: Number-Based Coding of the Two Cases Using Codebook Categories

IDNUM	OSEX	OAGE	ORACE	VETHNIC	WEAPON	LOCAT	MOTIVE
001	1	39	9	9	1	1	1
002	1	23	1	1	1	2	3

AVAILABLE COMPUTER SOFTWARE FOR BASIC DATA ANALYSIS

There are virtually an unlimited number of statistical packages and **computer software** programs that are available for data input and statistical analysis. Most of them have funny names or acronyms: BMDP, Micro-

Crunch, MicroCase, Microsoft Excel, MiniTab, SAS, Shazam, SPSS, Stata. Most universities have site licenses that permit student access to many of these software packages in computer labs across their campuses. If you are bored and have nothing better to do, call your local university IT (instructional technology) person or any serious computer tech person to find out what's available for free.

By far, the most commonly used software for data input and basic statistical analysis in the social sciences is **SPSS** (Statistical Package for the Social Sciences). It includes all the basic statistical procedures known to humans. It is widely available on most college campuses, most of your research-minded professors know how to do SPSS, and it comes in a low-carb, low-fat version for both graduate and undergraduate students. The undergraduate version of SPSS is limited in the number of variables (50) and cases (1,500).

Another option for statistical analysis is through **Microsoft Excel**. An Excel **spreadsheet** is also a common platform for imputing raw data and then transferring it to some other statistical program like SPSS. However, Excel has been used increasingly to perform the types of basic statistical analysis covered in this book (e.g. computing means, standard deviations, and correlations). For large data sets and the simultaneous analysis of multiple variables (i.e., multivariate analysis), Excel is more difficult to use and less flexible than SPSS.

Due to my desire to minimize the financial costs to students and the wide availability of this software to college students in university computer labs, you will not have to purchase any computer equipment to do the problems described in this book. Most computations will be done by hand (see also Chapter 1). However, as a pedagogical tool for the stimulated statistical consumer, many of the remaining chapters will include a brief section on SPSS and/or Excel procedures to highlight how the statistical techniques are actually done in these software packages.

SUMMARY OF MAJOR POINTS

- Insufficient attention to issues surrounding data preparation and coding is a major cause of the "garbage in, garbage out" syndrome in statistical analyses.

- Attention to issues of data preparation is especially important for researchers who conduct their own data collection. However, even among analysts who use secondary data, issues of data coding and recoding are relevant.

- The process of operationalization involves how we go about attaching specific meaning to abstract concepts. Through operationalization and measurement, we are able to develop specific indicators of these concepts, and establish qualitative and quantitative variables.

- The primary levels of measurement are nominal, ordinal, and interval or ratio measures. Nominal measures correspond to qualitative variables and the measurement of attributes. Ordinal measurement is the most elementary measure of quantity, duration, and intensity. Interval and ratio measures have ordinal properties of relative magnitude, but they also have equal distance between the categories.

- Codebooks are important to establish in the process of operationalization and measurement because they provide the basic rules for how words and numbers are actually translated into numerical data.

- Numerous computer software packages are available for data inputting and statistical analysis. SPSS and Microsoft Excel spreadsheets are the most prevalent statistical packages available today for criminological research.

KEY TERMS

"Canned" Data Set
Codebook
Coding
Collectively Exhaustive
Computer Software
Content Analysis
Interval Measurement
Measurement
Microsoft Excel
Missing Data
Mutually Exclusive

Naturalistic Observation
Nominal Measurement
Operationalization
Ordinal Measurement
Qualitative Variables
Quantitative Variables
Ratio Measurement
Secondary Data Analysis
SPSS
Spreadsheets

APPLYING WHAT YOU HAVE LEARNED

1. Specific meaning is attached to abstract concepts through a process called

    a. operationalization.

    b. data analysis.

    c. sampling.

    d. natural observation.

2. Official police data, victimization surveys, and self-report offending surveys yield the same results about the prevalence of crime and the social profile of offenders.

    a. True

    b. False

3. Which of the following is an example of a quantitative variable?

    a. The crime rate in U.S. cities.

    b. The length of prison sentences given to convicted felons.

    c. The type of criminal offense that leads to a prison sentence.

    d. All of the above are quantitative variables.

    e. Only a and b are quantitative variables.

4. Attaching numbers to qualitative variables (e.g., coding Male = 1 and Female = 2) makes them quantitative variables.

    a. True

    b. False

    c. It depends on the type of qualitative variable.

5. Categories of a variable are mutually exclusive when they

    a. overlap.

    b. don't overlap.

    c. include all possible categories of a variable.

Provide a nominal, ordinal, and interval or ratio measure of each of the following concepts:

6. Anger? Nominal: _____ Ordinal: _____ Interval/Ratio: _____

7. Employment? Nominal: _____ Ordinal: _____ Interval/Ratio: _____

8. Income? Nominal: _____ Ordinal: _____ Interval/Ratio: _____

9. Drug use? Nominal: _____ Ordinal: _____ Interval/Ratio: _____

10. What is wrong with the following measurement of age?

    Age: < 20, 20–45, 40–60, 70 and older? _____ ✦

4

Displaying Data in Tables and Graphic Forms

Here are two alternative ways of presenting the same information. What do they tell you about drug arrests over time, and which one is easier to interpret, Table 4.1 or Figure 4.1?

TABLE 4.1	Drug Arrests
Year	**Number**
1980	580,900
1985	811,400
1990	1,089,500
1995	1,476,100
2000	1,579,600
2004	1,745,700

Data Source: FBI (2005).

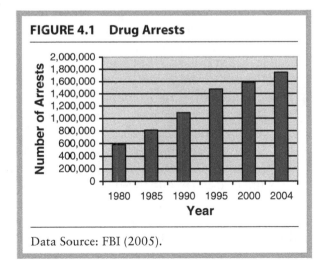

FIGURE 4.1 Drug Arrests

Data Source: FBI (2005).

Statistical information is displayed in a variety of forms in everyday life. It is summarized in tables, charts, graphs, and arrays of numbers. Sometimes it is not summarized at all, and the analysts must figure out how to best present this material. Regardless of its particular visual or numerical form, good research practice involves the construction of statistical tables and graphs that summarize this information without distorting the actual patterns within the data.

The process of constructing data tables and graphs is not rocket science. All you have to do is group together common values into the same category, display these common categories in a table or graph, and then describe the pattern. It is often true that "a picture is worth a 1,000 words," and good tables and graphs provide concise and unambiguous pictures of criminological data.

The current chapter describes the basic ways in which data is grouped and presented in tables, charts, graphs, and maps. It focuses on the methods for constructing frequency distributions, converting them into more standardized percentage distributions, and displaying them in visual ways that may be more persuasive and appealing to consumers. Tabular and visual displays are described for both qualitative and quantitative variables. Let's begin with the basic question of why presentation matters in life and statistics.

THE IMPORTANCE OF DATA TABLES AND GRAPHS

Given people's basic aversion to numbers, one definite way to annoy them is to throw out a lot of numbers in a haphazard manner. To illustrate this point, let's suppose you wanted to know the prevalence of illegal steroid use among prison guards. Further assume that someone collected data from 20 prison guards and asked them, "Have you ever used illegal steroids to enhance muscle growth?" Responses include "No" (coded 0), "Yes" (coded 1), and "None of your business" (coded 9). Hypothetical raw data for these 20 guards and a tabular display of this information are presented in Table 4.2.

For most normal consumers of statistical information, a raw data file of binary codes (i.e., 0's and 1's) is not very interesting. Instead, most consumers don't want the details; they just want the bottom line. The "bottom line" in this hypothetical case is the summary numbers presented in the lower part of Table 4.2—especially the stat that 55% of these folks said they had used illegal steroids.

TABLE 4.2 Hypothetical Data on the Steroid Use of 20 Prison Guards

1	0	1	9	0
1	0	0	0	9
0	1	1	1	1
1	0	1	1	1

Steroid Use	Tally	Frequency	Percent
0 = No	iiiii ii	7	35
1 = Yes	iiiii iiiii i	11	55
9 = Refused Answer	ii	2	10
Totals	20	20	100

So, why is it important to use summary displays of data like tables, charts, and graphs? How about these basic interrelated reasons: Consumers are lazy, want just the "bottom line," don't care about the details, and prefer looking at pictures and tables rather than a lot of numbers. Good analysts of criminological data can capitalize on these basic human preferences by displaying summary data in a clear, concise, and substantively meaningful manner. If you want people to pay attention to your statistical claims, the form and nature of its presentation matter. Different ways of presenting meaningful displays of criminological and criminal justice data are described below.

TYPES OF TABULAR AND VISUAL PRESENTATIONS

There are several basic ways of presenting data in summary form. These include frequency and percentage tables, conversions to ratios and rates, bar and pie charts, and other graphic images (e.g., line graphs, and maps). Because these data presentations vary in some cases by the level of measurement, we describe these summary displays separately for qualitative variables and quantitative variables. However, in either case, the analyst must make a series of decisions about the response categories and the style of presentation that provide the most accurate and useful summary of the data.

Tables and Graphs for Qualitative Variables

Qualitative variables are those that vary in type or kind. The actual number of response categories for qualitative variables depends upon the particular substantive question and the coding scheme utilized. For example, consider the different types of response categories that may be used in the following two contexts:

- Studies of racial profiling in police arrest practices often use only two racial categories (e.g., *black* or *white*) because of the presumed inability of officers to make finer distinctions in routine traffic stops. However, the U.S. Census Bureau includes 63 distinct categories for classifying the race of U.S. residents. Researchers conducting secondary analyses of Census data have the flexibility to reclassify race in a variety of alternative ways. Such flexibility is impossible when race is coded as *black* or *white*.

- Studies of global trends in the retention and abolition of capital punishment may have qualitative codes of geographical units that represent countries (190–200 different countries), major world regions (8–10 regions), or level of economic development (coded as *developed countries* or *developing countries*).

When making these coding decisions, it is important to consider the basic requirements of any classification scheme. These requirements are that the response categories are **mutually exclusive** (e.g. categories don't overlap) and **collectively exhaustive** (e.g., all people and/or objects are classified), and that the groupings within categories are culturally meaningful and relatively homogeneous (e.g., the same kinds of things are included within the same categories: The category *violent crime* includes murders and rapes, but not shoplifting). Once these basic coding decisions are made and the data collected, the analyst is now ready to decide how to best present this information in summary form.

The most common way of displaying qualitative data involves a frequency distribution. A **frequency distribution** is a tabular display of response categories and the number of people or objects within each category. Several examples of the proper forms of frequency tables for qualitative variables are shown in Tables 4.3a and 4.3b.

These tables illustrate several of the basic structural features of appropriate summary tables of frequency and **percentage distributions**. These properties include the following:

- A descriptive title that indicates the nature of the information in the table. For example, the title "Distribution of Countries

TABLE 4.3a Example of Frequency and Percentage Distributions for Qualitative Variables: Distribution of Countries Within World Regions

World Regions	Frequency (f)	Percent (%)
Asia	29	16
Africa	53	29
Caribbean	13	7
Central America	7	4
Europe	44	24
Middle East	13	7
North America	3	2
Oceania	11	6
South America	12	6
Total	185 (*N*)	100%

Data Source: *CIA Fact Book* (2003).

TABLE 4.3b Example of Frequency and Percentage Distributions for Qualitative Variables: Legal Status of Capital Punishment in 185 Countries

Death Penalty	Frequency (f)	Percent (%)
Legally Abolished	87	47
Legally Retained	98	53
Total	185 (*N*)	100%

Data Source: Amnesty International (2005).

Within World Regions" (Example 1) immediately conveys to the reader that the table is going to show information about countries and world regions.

- A short heading (e.g., "World Regions" or "Death Penalty") that provides a general name of the major variable in which information is compiled and categorized.

- A list of all response categories for the variable (e.g., the categories *Asia*, *Africa*, and *South America*, and the categories *legally abolished* and *legally retained*). The response categories may be ordered alphabetically or according to their relative frequency (i.e., arranged from highest to lowest prevalence). The first three response categories would be *Africa*, *Europe*, and then *Asia* if they are arranged in terms of their relative number of countries within them (i.e., 53, 44, and 29, respectively).

- A column of frequencies, or counts of the number of units within each of these response categories. The letter *f* is often used to symbolize this column of frequency counts.

- A column of percentages that is found by taking the frequency in a given category (e.g., 29 Asian countries) and dividing it by the total number of units in the study (e.g., 185 total countries). The percentage "scores" are the most commonly interpreted pieces of information in a table because they are **standardized scores**. When the percentage distributions are shown in a table, it is not necessary to include the frequency distributions within each category. The actual number of people or objects for each response category can be derived from the percentage scores if the total number of cases is included in the table. For example, the number of European countries ($n = 44$) can be found by multiplying the proportion of countries in this category (.24) by the total number of countries in the world (185) to get the value of 44 (.24 × 185 ≈ 44).

- A listing of the total number of observations in this study (called **N** for number) at the bottom of the frequency column. A similar listing with the label **100%** is placed at the bottom of the percentage column to further convey to the reader that this column contains percentage scores and that all response categories are included (because they sum to 100%).

- A reference to the data source or author of the report from which the table is reproduced or constructed. In these examples, the sources are the *CIA World Factbook* (2003) and Amnesty International (2005). By providing this source information, other researchers and consumers can verify the accuracy of the data presentation and explore the methodological limitations of the original data.

An informed consumer of statistical data will look closely at how the data in tables are organized and presented. They will also explore the coding decisions that result in particular observations being classified in one response category rather than another. For example, in this classification of countries within world regions, where do you put a country like Turkey? As a member of the Council of Europe, it is usually classified as an European country. However, its physical proximity to the Middle East and West Central Asia may lead to its classification in other world regions. Similarly, if countries have a temporary moratorium on capital punishment or haven't executed anyone for over 10 years, are they classified as *abolitionist* or *retentionist* countries? As these comments suggest, the statistical presentation of data patterns is only as good as the data used in their construction. Remember the idea of "garbage in, garbage out" (GIGO)? If you don't, go back one major step and reread Chapter 2.

Given sound measurement and nothing else weird in the data collection, what are the major substantive conclusions that derive from the summary data in Table 4.3? You tell me first. Come on, look back again at Table 4.3 and come up with the "bottom line" answer. Here is what I think this table tells us:

1. Africa and Europe are the world regions with the most countries, and

2. most countries have legally retained capital punishment

Simple, yes? Did you notice the sources of these data (i.e., the U.S. Central Intelligence Agency [CIA] and Amnesty International [AI])? Do you think the strong political agendas surrounding both organizations have anything to do with these findings? Are there any conspiracy theorists among you?

For those data consumers who prefer pictures over numbers, two basic ways to present qualitative data in visual form are pie charts and bar charts. A **pie chart** is simply a pie shape in which the size of its pieces represents the relative frequency of observations within each response category. These same ideas are conveyed in a **bar chart**, except the size of the pieces is represented by the length of its bars. These visual methods are illustrated in Figure 4.2a and Figure 4.2b using the same data on the number of countries in each world region. You should immediately notice that your substantive conclusions are identical across tabular and visual methods (e.g., Africa is the world region with the most countries—it has the largest numbers, the biggest pie piece, and the longest bar).

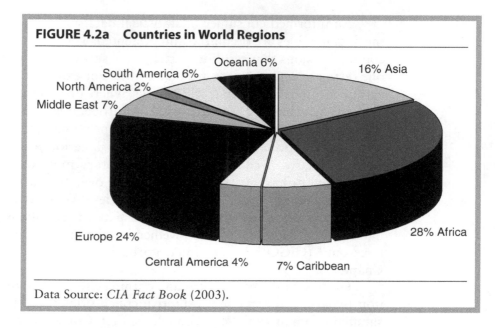

FIGURE 4.2a   Countries in World Regions

Data Source: *CIA Fact Book* (2003).

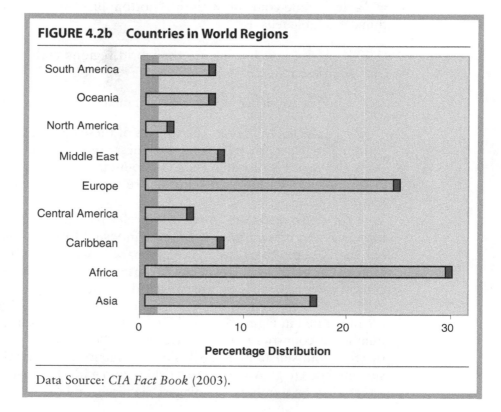

FIGURE 4.2b   Countries in World Regions

Data Source: *CIA Fact Book* (2003).

Tables and Graphs for Quantitative Variables

Many of the issues and rules for constructing tables and graphs for qualitative variables also apply to quantitative variables. For example, the analyst must avoid garbage in data collection and measurement, decide on how many response categories of the variable(s) to include, and maintain the properties of mutually exclusive, exhaustive, and culturally sensitive categories. For both types of variables, summary presentations may also include tables, charts, and graphs. Pie charts in both cases become less useful when trying to represent more than 10 response categories. Why? Because many of the slices of the pie become too small to be uniquely recognized.

The primary difference between tables and graphs for qualitative and quantitative variables involves differences in what they represent (i.e., qualities versus quantities). Accordingly, quantitative variables that have continuous values (like time, which may be broken down into smaller and smaller units like seconds, tenths of seconds, hundreds of seconds, etc.) must be rounded when presented in table form.[1] Rounding these variables will affect how many people and/or objects fall in a given category. In addition, successive response categories for quantitative variables can be combined to develop cumulative frequency and percent distributions that represent the relative proportion of cases above or below a particular category. How to construct cumulative distributions that are unique to summary displays of quantitative variables are described below.

Suppose you were interested in the age distribution of homicide offenders. A summary display of the age of offenders in 10-year intervals is shown in Table 4.4. The data represents all U.S. homicides in 2004 in which the offender's age was known (see the note at the bottom of Table 4.4).

One of the first things you should notice in Table 4.4 is that there are a lot of numbers and columns in this table. In fact, there are far too many for conveying any simple summary pattern. Don't worry. I have only put in all of these columns because I want to use this table to demonstrate various types of computations. Good quantitative summary

---

1. Quantitative variables are either continuous or discrete in their distributions of possible values. A continuous quantitative variable can be subdivided into smaller and small units (like the time example given above). Discrete quantitative variables, in contrast, cannot be divided into smaller units. For example, the number of felony arrests of a serial killer cannot take on a value of 1.5 or any other fraction. It is a discrete variable. Numbers are rounded for continuous variables to make them easier to summarize and place in tabular form.

TABLE 4.4	Age Distribution of U.S. Homicide Offenders in 2004			
Age Group	Frequency	Cumulative Frequency < Than	Percent	Cumulative Percent < Than
≤ 19	2,053	2,053	19.9	19.9
20–29	4,395	6,448	42.6	62.5
30–39	1,829	8,277	17.7	80.2
40–49	1,245	9,522	12.1	92.3
50–59	495	10,017	4.8	97.1
60–69	184	10,201	1.8	98.9
≥ 70	120	10,321	1.1	100.0
Total *N*	10,321		100.0%	

Data Source: FBI (2005).

Note: A total of 15,935 homicides were known to the police in 2004. 5,614 of these homicides were missing information on the offender's age. The current analysis is based on the 10,321 homicides without missing data on the offender's age.

tables have only a couple columns of data (e.g., a percentage and cumulative percentage column).

The computation methods for the columns marked *Frequency* and *Percent* in Table 4.4 are identical to the computations for tables of qualitative variables. For example, the value of 42.6% for the category *20–29* means that about 43% of the offenders were in their 20s. This percentage is found by dividing the number of offenders in this age group by the total number of offenders in the data set (i.e., 4395 / 10321 = .426 = 42.6%). Nothing new here, okay?

As its name implies, **cumulative distributions** are accumulations of numbers or percents above or below a particular value(s). Once you have put together a frequency or percent distribution, all you have to do to establish a cumulative distribution is a little addition and division. Let me illustrate these simple computations for cumulative distributions by asking you the following question: What percent of homicide offenders in Table 4.4 are younger than 30 years old?

The easiest way to compute the percent of offenders younger than 30 years old is to simply add the number of people from the two categories that fit this group. Follow these steps:

- Add 2,053 (offenders who are 19 or younger) and 4,395 (offenders 20 to 29 years old), and you have the cumulative value of 6,448.

- Divide this value (6,448) by the total number of observations in the data (10,321), multiply this value by 100, and you get 62.5%—the same value that is shown under the *Cumulative % < Than* column for the row of information for the 20–29 age group.

If you use the percentage scores, you basically get the same value, except for some occasional small rounding error. In this example, if you add 19.9% and 42.6%, you get the same value of 62.5%.

What is the percentage of offenders under 60 years old in Table 4.4? The answer is 97.1%, and it is found by

1. dividing 10,017 by 10,321 and multiplying by 100, or

2. adding the percents up to and including the category 50–59 (19.9% + 42.6% + 17.7% + 12.1% + 4.8% = 97.1%).

This also tells you that very few (i.e., only about 3%) homicide offenders are 60 or older (100 − 97.1 = 2.9 ≅ 3.0%).

A **histogram** for quantitative variables is similar to a bar chart for qualitative variables. The only real difference is that quantitative variables are often continuous variables; therefore, the bars in this visual representation need to be connected to illustrate this continuous distribution. A histogram of this national data on the age of homicide offenders is shown in Figure 4.3.

The interpretation of the results portrayed in this histogram is similar to those illustrated in the tabular distribution (see Table 4.4). In particular, both methods show that the most common age group for homicide offenders involves people in their 20s. They also indicate that senior citizens in their 70s or older are rarely homicide offenders.

Another way of visual presentation of quantitative data is through a **line graph** that simply plots the frequency of outcomes on a graph of X and Y coordinates. When the response categories are grouped together (e.g., like in 10-year intervals), a line graph often just connects points that represent the middle or midpoint of each category (e.g., the interval 20–29 would reduce to the point of 24.5—24.5 is halfway between 20 and 29). By connecting these points with a line, we can see the relative frequency among the categories. A good example of a line graph is presented later in this chapter (see Figure 4.5).

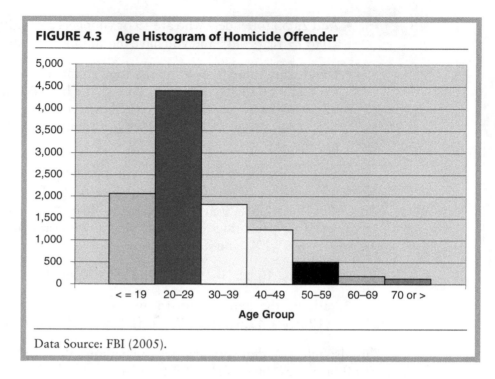

FIGURE 4.3   Age Histogram of Homicide Offender

Age Group

Data Source: FBI (2005).

Ratios and Rates

Another basic way to display or organize qualitative and quantitative data in criminological research is to convert it into ratios and rates. A **ratio** is simply a measure of the relative frequency of one category of a variable compared to another. A **rate** is a particular type of ratio that is conveyed as a number per given standard units. It is computed as the proportion of possible cases in a given category that is then standardized by some population base (e.g., per 100 arrests, per 1,000 households, per 100,000 population, or per million U.S. dollars). The basic formulas for converting frequency in the subcategories of a variable into ratios and rates include the following:

$$\text{Ratio} = \frac{Number\ in\ Subcategory\ 1}{Number\ in\ Subcategory\ 2}$$

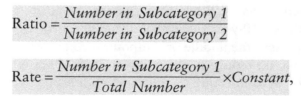

$$\text{Rate} = \frac{Number\ in\ Subcategory\ 1}{Total\ Number} \times Constant,$$

where the constant is in 100s, 1,000s, or other standard units.

Examples of ratio comparisons are widely found in studies of gender and racial differences in crime and criminal justice practices. For example, when the numbers of arrests of males (subcategory 1) are compared to female arrests (subcategory 2), the following gender arrest ratios are derived for specific offenses from national police data (FBI 2004):

- Murder and Non-Negligent Manslaughter Arrests:
  - → Male Arrests = 8,460; Female Arrests = 1,094
  - → *Male-to-Female Arrest Ratio = (8,460 / 1,094) = 7.7*

- Aggravated Assaults Arrests:
  - → Male Arrests = 248,482; Female Arrests = 65,097
  - → *Male-to-Female Arrest Ratio = (248,482 / 65,097) = 3.8*

- Embezzlement Arrests:
  - → Male Arrests = 6,236; Female Arrests = 6,327
  - → *Male-to-Female Arrest Ratio = (6,236 / 6,327) = .99*

- Prostitution and Commercialized Vice Arrests:
  - → Male Arrests = 19,297; Female Arrests = 43,145
  - → *Male-to-Female Arrest Ratio = (19,297 / 43,145) = .45*
  - → *Female-to-Male Arrest Ratio = (43,145 / 19,297) = 2.2*

The interpretation of these gender arrest ratios is straightforward. Males are nearly eight times (7.7) more likely to be arrested for murder than females, and about four times (3.8) more prone to arrest than females for aggravated assault. In contrast, the arrest ratio is about 1.0 for embezzlement, indicating that men and women are about equally likely to be arrested for this crime. The arrest ratio is far below 1.0 (.45) for prostitution, indicating that women are far more prone than men to be arrested for this particular offense. When expressed as a ratio of female-to-male arrestees, women are arrested for prostitution at a ratio of 2.2 times higher than their male counterparts.[2]

The use of rates is widespread in criminological research. In fact, most published reports using crime and criminal justice data will convey

---

2. You will get the same results if you compute ratios on the basis of the percent distributions within categories. For example, 69.1% of the persons arrested for prostitution in 2004 were female and 30.9% were male, so the female-to-male arrest ratio is 2.2 (69.1 / 30.9). This is the same ratio value achieved on the basis of the frequency or number of arrests in each category. This example illustrates that ratios can be computed from tables of either frequency or percentage distributions. Use whichever distribution is convenient or available.

this information as a rate per standard unit. For example, the U.S. crime rate is expressed per 100,000 inhabitants, police expenditures are reported in dollars per capita, and treatment services within correctional budgets are often calculated per inmate. The National Crime Victimization Survey (NCVS) estimates the rate of personal victimization per 1,000 residents aged 12 or older and property crime victimization rates per 1,000 households (see Catalano 2005). Several examples of these NCVS rate calculations for 2004 include the following:

- **Robbery rate of 2.1 per 1,000 persons aged 12 or older.** Computed as: (number of robbery victimizations in 2004 / U.S. population aged 12 or older in 2004) × 1,000 = (501,820 robbery victimizations / 241,703,710 people) × 1,000 = *2.1 per 1,000*).

- **Simple assault rate of 14.2 per 1,000 persons aged 12 or older.** Computed as: (number of simple assault victimizations in 2004 / U.S. population aged 12 or older in 2004) × 1,000 = (3,440,880 assaults / 241,703,710 people) × 1,000 = *14.2 per 1,000*).

- **Household burglary rate of 29.6 per 1,000 households.** Computed as: (number of household burglary victimizations in 2004 / number of U.S. households in 2004) × 1,000 = (3,427,690 burglaries / 115,775,570 U.S. households) × 1,000 = *29.6 per 1,000*).

As summary displays of criminological data, ratios and rates are important because they provide standardized measures from which comparisons can be made. Similar to percentages (which are the same as rates per 100 units), both ratios and rates make it easier for us to compare their relative size across groups or subcategories. For example, the U.S. murder rate in 2004 was 5.5 per 100,000 inhabitants and 10.2 in 1980. These rates and the ratios that can be derived directly from them (10.2 / 5.5 = 1.9) provide us immediate knowledge that the relative risks of murder in 1980 were nearly double the risks in 2004.

Although ratios and rates are extremely useful for comparative purposes, these summary statistics are susceptible to various problems of measurement and sampling. When small numbers of cases are involved, both rates and ratios can be misleading. For example, a particular state may have a black-to-white execution ratio of 5.0, suggesting that blacks are far more prone than whites to be given a death sentence. However, if this ratio is based on data from only six executions (five involving blacks, one involving whites), we would not place as much importance on this finding as we would if it was based on a larger sample of cases.

Maps of Qualitative and Quantitative Variables

Criminologists and crime analysts have increasingly used maps as a method for visually displaying the distribution of a variable across geographical units. Similar to pie charts, various colors and shading are used in maps to convey both qualitative and quantitative distinctions across these geographical units. The key elements of this type of visual display are illustrated in the map of state differences in capital punishment laws and practice (see Figure 4.4).

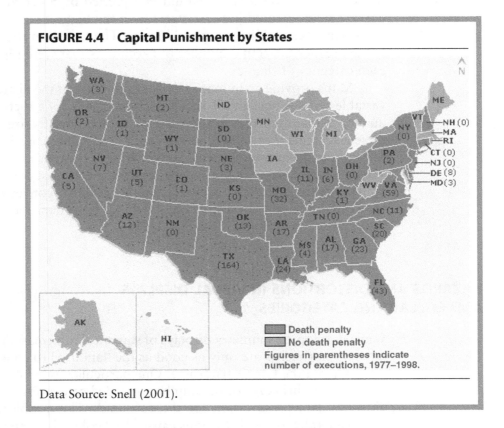

FIGURE 4.4   Capital Punishment by States

Data Source: Snell (2001).

As shown in the legend for the map, the different shading of the states represents whether or not they have retained or abolished the death penalty. The state's abbreviations within the map help the reader easily identify the geographical locations. Rather than distorting the size of particular states, the map is also properly scaled according to the state's relative land mass.

As a visual tool for conveying statistical information, the map in Figure 4.4 clearly shows that (1) most states retain the death penalty and

(2) abolitionist states are more commonly located in the upper Midwestern region of the country. By comparing the numbers in parentheses, it is also evident from this map that Texas far exceeds other states in its number of executions from 1977 to 1998. Astute analysts of this map will also notice that several death penalty states have not conducted any executions over this time period.

Another way of representing this information about state differences in capital punishment would focus on the number of executions. In this case, abolitionist states would be signified by no shading, and the darkest shades would indicate states with the highest number of executions (e.g., Texas, Virginia, and Florida). The legend in the map would tell the reader the actual number of executions that were represented by each category of shading.

Maps provide an immediate visual summary of the distribution of a variable over geographical space. However, the construction of high-quality maps often requires the use of computer software to generate these visual images and to superimpose data within the particular boundaries of the geographical areas. Similar to other graphs and tables, measurement error, sampling problems, and other errors of commission and omission also affect the accuracy of the findings conveyed in maps. Other major sources of distortion of data patterns depicted in maps and other visual methods are described below.

HAZARDS AND DISTORTIONS IN VISUAL DISPLAYS AND COLLAPSING CATEGORIES

When developing summary displays of statistical information, visual and tabular approaches are only as good as the data used to construct them. This is again the GIGO syndrome. One particular form of this problem involves the shrinkage of the number of coded categories to overly simplify the data presentation for the consumer. This problem is known more generally as the distortions caused by "collapsing categories."

To illustrate how collapsing categories affects substantive results in a tabular display, let's consider what happens when we change the coding of crime data categories. Table 4.5 illustrates this idea by showing the frequency and percentage distributions of serious crime offenses (i.e., the FBI Index Crimes) in the United States in 2004 using two coding schemes: (1) the representation of each index crime separately, and (2) the grouping and reclassification of these index crimes into the general categories *violent offenses* and *property offenses*.

TABLE 4.5 Why Coding Decisions Matter in Tabular Presentations

Specific Index Crimes	Frequency	Percent	General Index Crimes	Frequency	Percent
Murder	16,109	.1	Violent Crime	1,367,009	11.7
Forcible Rape	94,635	.8			
Robbery	401,326	3.4			
Aggravated Assault	854,911	7.3			
Burglary	2,143,456	18.3	Property Crime	10,328,255	88.3
Larceny/Theft	6,947,685	59.4			
Motor Vehicle Theft	1,237,114	10.6			
Arson	68,245	.6			
Total N	11,695,264	100%		11,685,264	100%

Data Source: FBI (2004).

The summary display in Table 4.5 is hard to read for most normal people. However, what is important to understand is what would happen in terms of one's substantive conclusions if you looked only at one of these two possible ways of coding and classifying criminal offenses. For example, looking at the specific index crimes, the dominant conclusion is that *larceny/theft* is by far the most common serious crime known to the police, accounting for nearly 60% of all serious crimes. You would conclude that murders are essentially trivial relative to the distribution of other specific offenses. In contrast, looking at the general offense categories, you readily conclude that property crimes account for nearly 90% of the serious offenses known to the police. However, focusing solely on the "general categories" would lead analysts and consumers to ignore the substantively important findings that (1) most serious property crimes are larcenies and thefts, and (2) most serious violent crimes are aggravated assaults.

The obvious solution to the problem of distortions due to having too many or not enough response categories is to present both tables. Unfortunately, this obvious solution is not a feasible one for most situations because typical consumers do not want to view multiple or complicated tables—they want one simple table and preferably a picture! Under these conditions, the informed analyst must provide the simplest yet most accurate summary of the findings. In the case of the summary data in Table 4.5, I would include only the information about the *specific index crimes* in a tabular form, but make sure that the consumer knows that most known offenses fall in the general index category of *property crimes*.

The distortion of substantive findings through the manipulation or adjustment of coding categories can also affect visual representations of social data. This idea is illustrated in Figure 4.5 by showing the changing shape of the line graph depiction of the homicide rate in the United States over time by simply changing how the time period is coded. Notice here that (1) the wide yearly variability in U.S. homicide rates is eliminated and (2) the general trends over time are changed dramatically by altering the grouping of the yearly series into successive 10-, 25-, and 50-year intervals.

So, has the U.S. homicide rate changed over time? The line graphs in Figure 4.5 suggest that this answer in part depends on the particular time series used to illustrate this pattern. Based on yearly data patterns, you would probably conclude the U.S. homicide rate has vacillated greatly

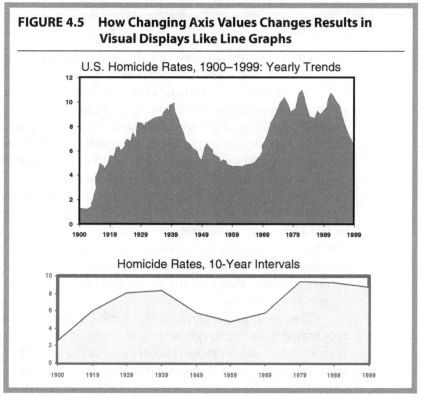

FIGURE 4.5   How Changing Axis Values Changes Results in Visual Displays Like Line Graphs

U.S. Homicide Rates, 1900–1999: Yearly Trends

Homicide Rates, 10-Year Intervals

(continued)

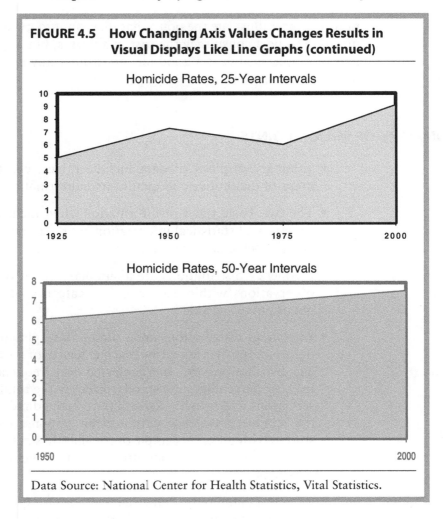

FIGURE 4.5   How Changing Axis Values Changes Results in Visual Displays Like Line Graphs (continued)

Data Source: National Center for Health Statistics, Vital Statistics.

over the twentieth century. However, it has changed far less when it is represented by 25- and 50-year intervals.

The final way in which visual displays of summary data can be misleading or distort the basic distribution is by changing the range of values on the axis. In particular, good practices within social statistics involve making sure that the scores on the y-axis and x-axis each begin at 0 (i.e., the coordinate [0,0]). However, you often see graphs and charts that begin at other points or have squiggly break marks on the axis (like this symbol: ≈) to indicate a disruption in the numbering sequence on the graph. Although this is often done for harmless, practical reasons (e.g., to save space on a page), there are evil people who use these graph distortions to better illustrate the point that they want to make. Again, you do not have to be a conspiracy theorist in all cases, but a quick look at the axis of graphs is always a good idea to identify any possible weird data manipulations.

SUMMARY OF MAJOR POINTS

- Summary displays of data include tables, charts, graphs, and maps of qualitative and quantitative information.

- The two basic types of information often included in a tabular summary of statistical information are the frequency distribution and the percentage distribution.

- Frequency distributions are a summary count of the number of observations within each response category of a qualitative or quantitative variable.

- Percentage distributions are a summary display of the percent of observations that fall within each category of a variable. Percentage distributions are often preferred over frequency distributions because percentages are standardized by the total number of observations and provide the ability to make direct comparisons of the relative prevalence within given response categories across studies with different sample or population sizes. The same is true of rates and ratios, which are alternative types of standardized measures.

- The most commonly used visual methods for qualitative variables include bar charts and pie charts. The most widely used visual methods for quantitative variables involve pie charts (when there are a limited number of categories), histograms, and line graphs. Maps of geographical areas may be used for both qualitative and quantitative variables.

- Statistical consumers often prefer visual displays of summary data over tabular presentations because of the general distaste for numbers and the ease in which visual information may be interpreted.

- Cumulative distributions are unique summary displays for quantitative variables to indicate the proportion or number of observations that are above or below a particular point on a quantitative scale.

- The categories of variables used in tabular and visual summaries must be mutually exclusive, collectively exhaustive of all possible responses, and culturally sensitive.

- Summary displays of statistical information can be easily distorted by the recoding and collapsing of response categories and by changing the scale used in the axis of graphic representations.

- The idea of "garbage in, garbage out" applies to the data collection, measurement, and coding decisions that occur prior to the presentation and analysis of summary displays of statistical information.

- "Good practices" in the construction of tables and visual displays of summary data include proper labeling of the descriptive title, the response categories used, the number of observations, the source of the data, and a sufficient number of categories that summarizes the distributions without distorting them.

KEY TERMS

Bar Chart	N (number of observations)
Cumulative Distribution	Percentage Distribution
Frequency Distribution	Pie Chart
Histograms	Rate
Line Graphs	Ratio

USING COMPUTER SOFTWARE TO CREATE TABLES AND GRAPHS

The tables and graphs displayed in this chapter can be produced by different types of computer software programs. Various types of Microsoft Office products (e.g., *PowerPoint*, *Excel*, and *Word*) were used to generate the tables, charts, and graphs. With just a little practice, anyone can use these products and create nice-looking charts and graphs.

The SPSS statistical package also provides the options for creating various types of tables, bar charts, and pie charts. SPSS also will provide the user with cumulative frequency and cumulative percentage distributions. For the other software packages, the calculations are impossible or incredibly cumbersome with large data sets. However, both Excel and PowerPoint may be preferred over SPSS in creating graphs and charts that can be quickly constructed and are visually appealing.

SPSS Applications (*Optional Section*)

The basic way of doing tabular and visual displays in SPSS is through the analytic procedure called *frequency.* To access this procedure in an SPSS data file, do the following: (1) Click on the **Analysis** tab in SPSS; (2) scroll down until you find the **Frequency** option, and click on that option; (3) a list of variables will be shown on the menu, and click on the particular variable(s) you are interested in; (4) click on the **Option** tab and select the particular procedures you want (e.g., *chart* or *graph*); and (5) click **OK** afterwards and then **Run** to get SPSS to group together common observations in a frequency distribution. The cumulative percentage will be provided automatically in this SPSS output even if it is not appropriate for your given problem.

APPLYING WHAT YOU HAVE LEARNED

1. Here is an arrangement of the race of 20 individuals, where 1 = Black, 2 = White, and 3 = Other: Use this data to answer the following questions:

   2 1 3 1 2 2 2 1 2 1
   3 2 1 2 2 2 2 1 1 2

   a. Construct a frequency distribution. Make sure all information is properly labeled.

   b. Construct a percentage distribution. Make sure all information is properly labeled.

   c. Summarize the major finding from this table.

2. Here is some hypothetical data on the number of traffic tickets received by 30 teenage drivers. Use this data to answer the following questions.

   4 0 0 2 1 5 1 1 0 0
   0 1 1 0 0 1 0 2 2 1
   0 0 0 15 0 1 1 0 0 0

   a. Construct a frequency distribution. Make sure that all information is properly labeled and that you develop categories that make sense.

   b. Construct a percentage distribution. Make sure all information is properly labeled.

   c. Summarize the major finding from this table.

3. Provide a mutually exclusive, collectively exhaustive, and culturally sensitive classification for the variable *educational attainment*.

4. When do you use a cumulative distribution?

5. Fill in the cumulative percentage distribution for the following variable.

City Size	%	Cumulative % < Than
< 10,000	10	_____
10,001–20,000	5	_____
20,001–50,000	15	_____
50,001–100,000	25	_____
100,001–1 million	22	_____
Over 1 million	23	_____

a. Briefly summarize the major findings based on the percentage distribution for the variable *city size*.

b. What percent of these cities have a population of 50,000 or less?

c. What percent of these cities have a population of 1 million or less?

d. What percent of these cities have a size of < 10,000 *or* greater than 1 million?

6. What is wrong with the following frequency and percentage distributions, and how would you fix these problems?

Victim's Age	f	cf ≤	%	c% ≤	c% >
10 and under	17	17	2.4	2.4	100.0
11–20	202	219	28.8	31.2	68.8
21–30	270	489	38.5	69.7	30.3
31–40	106	595	15.1	84.8	15.2
41–50	62	657	8.8	93.6	6.4
51–60	20	677	2.9	96.5	3.5
61–70	11	688	1.6	98.1	1.9
71–80	9	697	1.3	99.4	.6
Over 80	4	701	.6	100.0	0.0
Total	701				

7. What does the following bar chart tell us about the number of gang members reported in Las Vegas newspapers over time?

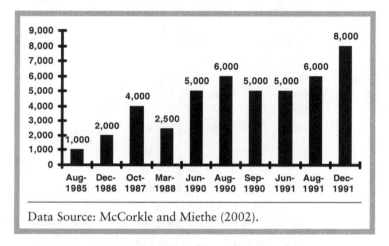

Data Source: McCorkle and Miethe (2002).

What does this bar chart tell you about the number of gang members in Las Vegas, Nevada, in the mid-1980s to the early 1990s? (*Hint:* Think about measurement validity and sampling issues.)

8. What does the table below tell you about the most dominant weapon used in homicides in Washington, DC?

Lethal Weapon in Homicide			Revised Table*		
Weapon Used	**f**	**%**	**Weapon**	**f**	**%**
Firearm	187	77.6	Firearm	187	80
Knife	27	12.0	Knife	27	12
Hands, Fist, Feet	3	1.2	Other Weapon	19	8
Blunt Objects	2	.8	Total N	233	100
Other Weapon	14	5.8			
Unknown	9	3.7			
Total N	242	100			

*Excludes missing data ($n = 9$ cases).

Data Source: Washington, DC, Metropolitan Police Department (1999)

9. What table provides a better representation of this data on lethal weapons in homicide data, the original table or the revised table? Why?

10. What is wrong with the following table about drivers stopped by police, and how would you fix these problems?

Drivers Stopped by Police by Sex, Race, Ethnicity, and Age, 1999

Characteristics of Driver	Drivers Stopped at Least Once	
	Number	Percent of All Drivers
All Drivers Total	19,277	10.3
Male	11,722	12.5
Female	7,555	8.2
White	14,846	10.4
Black	2,232	12.3
Hispanic	1,615	8.8
Other	584	8.9
16 to 19 years old	2,032	18.2
20 to 29 years old	5,560	16.8
30 to 39 years old	4,526	11.3
40 to 49 years old	3,764	9.4
50 to 59 years old	2,094	7.7
60 years old and over	1,302	3.8

Data Source: Schmitt, Langan, and Durose (2002).

11. What do the following line graphs illustrate about the prevalence of death sentences over time and racial differences in them?

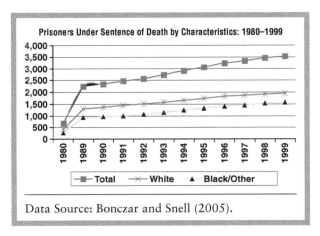

Data Source: Bonczar and Snell (2005).

12. China had an estimated population of 1.3 billion people in 2004 and performed an estimated 3,400 executions that year. The U.S. population in 2004 was estimated at 294 million, and 58 executions were committed.

   a. Compute the execution rate per 100,000 residents for both China and the United States.

   b. Using their execution rates per 100,000 residents, what is the China-to-U.S. execution ratio? Interpret what this value means.

13. A small city of 500 people had 30 robberies in the last year.

   a. What is the city's robbery rate per 1,000 residents?

   b. What is the city's robbery rate per 100,000 residents? ✦

5

Modes, Medians, Means, and More

The single most common situation in which homicides occur in the United States involves an intraracial argument among adult black male acquaintances or family members in which one offender kills the victim with a gun in an urban area. However, this most frequent (modal) profile represents less than 5 percent of all U.S. homicides (see Miethe and Regoeczi 2004).

Given that this most typical homicide situation accounts for only a very small minority of homicides, is it meaningful to highlight this particular profile for future criminological research and public policy on crime control? For social statisticians, this question centers on whether the mode is a useful measure of typicality when it does not represent either a majority or large minority of cases in a study.

Instead of fancy graphs and frequency tables, the typical consumer of statistical information wants even greater simplicity. In short, these consumers want one single number to represent the entire galaxy of statistical information for particular variables of interest. That single number is the "bottom line" for the consumer and a fundamental basis for social comparisons. Equipped with this magic number, we proceed to evaluate whether we are average, typical of most people, or deviants who fall far above or below this standard.

For statisticians and others who perform data analysis, the technical terms for these magic numbers are *measures of central tendency, location*, and *typicality*. You will recognize them by their more common "street" names or monikers: means, medians, and modes. Regardless of their particular names, they are indeed magic numbers because we enshrine them with a kind of mystical aura and/or truth. Just think: one simple number to represent the totality of scores on some variable? Wow—this is both amazing and frightening.

This chapter describes the basic principles involved in the use and computation of summary measures of typicality (e.g., modes), central tendency (e.g., means), and location (e.g., medians and percentile ranks).

The math involved in these computations is very simple. For potential analysts and informed consumers, the most important lesson is learning when these particular measures should be applied in a given problem and their relative strengths and limitations as a single magic number to represent a wider distribution of scores.

MODES AND MODAL CATEGORIES

For the most math-phobic students on the planet, the **mode** is your best friend in statistics. It requires no mathematical computations and can be readily identified in a frequency distribution. The mode is simply the most commonly occurring number or category in a frequency distribution. When categories for a quantitative variable are grouped together, the **modal interval** involves the response category that is most prevalent.

While the mode is the most commonly occurring outcome in a frequency distribution, it does not necessarily represent the majority of cases in this distribution. Our initial example in this chapter provided the modal homicide profile, but this profile represented less than 5 percent of all U.S. homicides. Similarly, George W. Bush was first elected as the "modal but minority" president because he received the most votes but not the majority of them. Other examples of modes and modal categories include the following:

- The modal serious crime known to the police in 2004 is a larceny/theft. There were 6.9 million larcenies reported by the police. The next most common crime was burglary, with about 2.1 million offenses (FBI 2004).

- The vast majority of American households did not have a criminal victimization in the last year (i.e., the modal household is crime-free) (Klaus 2006).

- The modal family income in the United States is between $50,000 and $75,000, and the modal educational attainment for Americans is "high school graduate" (U.S. Census 2004).

- The most common punishment for felony defendants convicted in state courts was a prison sentence (Durose and Langan 2004).

- The modal student reading these examples has already gotten the point that the mode is the most frequently occurring category.

TABLE 5.1 How to Change the Modal Interval by Changing the Interval's Size (example: age group of drivers stopped by the police)

Age Groups	Frequency of Stops	Age Groups	Frequency of Stops	Age Groups	Frequency of Stops
≤ 19	2,032	≤ 19	2,032	≤ 19	2,032
20–29	5,560	20–29	5,560	20–29	5,560
30–39	4,526	30–49	8,290	30–39	4,526
40–49	3,764	50–59	2,094	≥ 40	7,160
50–59	2,094	≥ 60	1,302		
≥ 60	1,302				
Total N	19,278		19,278		19,278

Note: The modal category for each way of constructing age intervals is highlighted.

Data Source: Schmitt, Langan, and Durose (2002).

As is true of everything else discussed in this book, substantive conclusions about the modal score or modal interval depend upon how we have measured the particular variables and the particular response categories. Table 5.1 illustrates how the modal category may be changed dramatically by simply collapsing and rearranging the categories or the width of their intervals. You should notice immediately how the modal age category for drivers stopped by the police changes based on the different ways of coding these age groups.

So, what age group is at the highest risk of being stopped by the police (i.e., what is the modal age?)? The correct answer is "it depends" on how age is categorized. If you want to show that the police are picking on "old" people (i.e., those over 40 years old), you would select the third coding scheme listed in Table 5.1. However, if you wanted to show police bias against drivers in their 20s, you would use the first coding system for age in this table. For those of you with hidden political agendas, this is how you can legitimately lie and cheat with summary statistics like the mode—that is, changing the category grouping so that your favorite group becomes the mode.

As a "magic number" that is used to represent the entire distribution of scores, the utility of the mode depends on its typicality and the substantive context. For all elected officials, the mode is the bottom-line summary statistic because it tells you which candidate got the most votes. It is also a valuable statistic when it represents the vast majority of cases in a distribution. For example, the mode is a meaningful statistic to convey that (1) the modal American (i.e., > 95% of them) is not a victim of violent crime in any given year, (2) the modal weapon in about 75% of homicides is a firearm, and/or (3) the "modal majority" of U.S. citizens support capital punishment for convicted murderers.

When the mode is less typical (i.e., doesn't represent the majority) and plurality is not a direct path to entitlements (e.g., getting elected, awards, or jobs), however, it is a less useful summary statistic. For example, California is the modal state based on its population size, but only 12% of Americans live there. Although Californians may take pride in their modal status, do international scholars who look at national trends and the vast majority of people living elsewhere really care that it is the most populated state? Under these conditions of low typicality, the mode has less profound significance as a descriptive statistic.

There are several additional points that you should consider about the mode as a summary measure. These points include the following:

- When two or more response categories are almost equal in their relative frequency (e.g., they differ by only 1 count), the mode gives exclusive priority to the most frequently occurring category. Close doesn't count here, because the mode is always the most frequent score or value.

- The term *bimodal distribution* is used to describe variables that have two categories of equal or near equal frequency. Many attitudes about emotionally charged social issues (e.g., capital punishment and gun control) have bimodal distributions—that is, people either "strongly agree" or "strongly disagree" with these issues and very few people are neutral or have "mild" attitudes on them. Technically, a bimodal distribution must have two categories with equal frequencies, but we often use this term in situations in which two categories clearly dominate in the distribution of the scores. So, close *does* count in defining *bimodal* in actual statistical applications, but the mode is still the single most common value(s) in the distribution.

- The mode is an appropriate descriptive statistic for both qualitative and quantitative variables. Other statistical measures of typicality, central tendency, and/or location (e.g., means and medians) require at least ordinal and preferably interval or ratio measurement of quantitative variables.

THE MEDIAN AND OTHER MEASURES OF LOCATION

Another summary measure used by statisticians to describe a set of observations focuses on its position or location within this distribution. The most popular measures of location involve the median (i.e., the 50th percentile score), quartile ranks, and other percentage points.

The **median** is the midpoint score of a distribution. It is equivalent to the 50th percentile ranked score. Similar to the median on the highway, it is the point that divides the distribution in half—one-half of the scores are above this point, and one-half of the scores are below this point. Whenever you find this midpoint of a distribution, you have found the median.

The computational methods for figuring out the median scores are not very complicated in most cases. As shown in Table 5.2, the basic steps involve the following:

1. Arrange scores from low to high; and

2. find the middle score defined by the formula $(N + 1) / 2$, where N = the number of scores.

When there is an even number of scores, this middle score will fall between two numbers. In this case, the median is found by taking the average of these two scores.

TABLE 5.2   How to Find the Median Score (examples)

Odd Number of Raw Scores		4	6	2	5	7
1. Arrange scores from low to high ⟶		2	4	5	6	7
2. Find $(n + 1) / 2$ score: $(5 + 1) / 2$ = 3rd rank score ⟶		2	4	5	6	7
3. The median is that ranked score: median = 5.						

Even Number of Raw Scores	4	6	2	5	9	7
1. Arrange scores from low to high ⟶	2	4	5	6	7	9
2. Find $(n + 1) / 2$ score: $(6 + 1) / 2$ = 3.5th rank score ⟶	2	4	5	6	7	9
3. The median is the average of the two scores: median = $(5 + 6) / 2 = 5.5$.						

Criminologists and informed consumers are often presented with data in summary form. When quantitative data is organized within intervals of a frequency distribution, it is possible to estimate the median score from this distribution. To show how a median is estimated from grouped data, consider the age distribution of U.S. homicide offenders in Table 5.3.

TABLE 5.3   How to Compute a Median from Grouped Data (example: age distribution of U.S. homicide offenders in 2004)

Rounded Age Interval	True Age Interval	Frequency	Cumulative Frequency < Than	Percent	Cumulative % < Than
≤ 19	0–19.5	2,053	2,053	19.9	19.9
20–29	19.5–29.5	4,395	6,448	42.6	62.5
30–39	29.5–39.5	1,829	8,277	17.7	80.2
40–49	39.5–49.5	1,245	9,522	12.1	92.3
50–59	49.5–59.5	495	10,017	4.8	97.1
60–69	59.5–69.5	184	10,201	1.8	98.9
≥ 70	≥ 69.5	120	10,321	1.1	100.0
Total N		10,321		100.0%	

$$\text{Median} = md = L + \frac{(n/2) - F}{f} \times w = 19.5 + \frac{5,160.5 - 2,053}{4,395} \times 10 = 26.6$$

$$\text{Median} = md = L + \frac{(50) - P}{p} \times w = 19.5 + \frac{50 - 19.9}{42.6} \times 10 = 26.6$$

Data Source: FBI (2005).

The first step in the estimation of a median from grouped data is to find the interval that contains this case. Given that there are 10,321 homicide cases in Table 5.3, the midpoint case is the 5,161st case ([N + 1] / 2 = 5,161). Looking at either the cumulative frequency or percentage distributions, you will notice that the median age will fall somewhere in the interval between 20 and 29 years old. The age interval actually runs from 19.5 to 29.5—this is the true limits or range of the interval, and the rounded limits are 20 to 29. So, the median age is somewhere in this range.

Once the interval that contains the median case is identified, the next step involves the extrapolation (i.e., estimation) of the median value within this interval. This median from grouped data is called the **refined median**.

When using the frequency distribution, the computing formula for the refined median is the following:

$$\text{Median} = md = L + \frac{(n/2) - F}{f} \times w,$$

where L = the true lower limit of the interval that contains the median case,

n = number of observations,

F = the cumulative frequency up to but not including the interval that contains the median case,

f = the frequency in the interval that contains the median case, and

w = the width of the interval that contains the median case.

When using the percentage distribution, the computing formula for the refined median is the following:

$$\text{Median} = md = L + \frac{(50) - P}{p} \times w,$$

where L = the true lower limit of the interval that contains the median case,

50 = the 50th percentile,

P = the cumulative percentage up to but not including the interval that contains the median case,

p = the percent of cases in the interval that contains the median, and

w = the width of the interval that contains the median case.

As shown in the examples in Table 5.3, it does not matter if the refined median is computed using the frequency distributions or the percentage distributions. In both cases, the median age is estimated to be 26.6. This means that one-half of the homicides in the United States involve offenders who are under 26.6 years old and one-half of the homicide offenders are over 26.6 years old.

The formulas for the refined median can be easily modified to establish other position points in a distribution. These include any quartile or percentile rank. For example, if you wanted to find the age associated with the 75th percentile (or, equivalently, the 3rd quartile), the computing formula using the percentage distribution is the following:

$$\text{75th Percentile} = L + \frac{(75) - P}{p} \times w,$$

where L = the true lower limit of the interval that contains the 75th percentile case,

75 = the 75th percentile,

P = the cumulative percentage up to but not including the interval that contains the 75th percentile case,

p = the percent of cases in the interval that contains the 75th percentile case, and

w = the width of the interval that contains the 75th percentile case.

In the national data on age of homicide offenders (Table 5.3), and applying the formula above, the 75th percentile case is 36.6 years old (29.5 + ([75 − 62.5] / 17.7) × 10 = 36.6). This means that three-fourths of U.S. homicide offenders are younger than 36.6 years old.

For computing any other percentile rank or quartile, the logic is virtually identical. The only difference is the particular point that you use for your calculations. For example, to find the 90th percentile score for the age of homicide offenders in Table 5.3, just do the following:

- Insert 90 as the percentile score (i.e., $L + \dfrac{(90) - P}{p} \times w$).

- Find the true lower limit of the interval that contains the 90th percentile case (L)—this true lower limit is 39.5.

- Find the cumulative percentage up to but not including the interval that contains the 90th percentile case (P)—this cumulative percentage is 80.2.

- Find the percent of cases in the interval that contains the 90th percentile case (p)—this percent value is 12.1.

- Determine the width of the interval that contains the 90th percentile case (w)—this interval's width is 10.

- Plug the values in the formula, and find the 90th percentile case:
$$\text{90th Percentile} = L + \frac{(90) - P}{p} \times w = 39.5 + \frac{(90) - 80.2}{12.1} \times 10 = 47.6.$$

- Thus, 90% of homicide offenders are 47.6 years old or younger.

The importance of selecting a particular measure of location depends on the substantive question in the research. When one is concerned about the midpoint of a distribution of scores, the median is the measure of location to use. However, if someone wants to know what score represents the top 25% or bottom 25%, then these particular percentile ranks are the best summary measure.

THE MEAN AND ITS MEANING

By all authoritative accounts, the most popular "magic number" used in statistics and life is the mean. The **mean** (technically, the arithmetic mean) is synonymous with the idea of the "statistical average" and our use of the word *average* in everyday life. For most of us, being "average" in various domains of life is okay. We call people weird and/or bizarre because they deviate from our notion of average.

To relieve your math anxiety, seek comfort in the fact that you don't have to be a mathematician to "crunch" out a mean score for a distribution. In fact, to compute a mean in most cases, all you have to do is follow two simple steps:

1. Add up all the numbers (symbolized as Σx), and

2. divide this sum by the number of observations (symbolized as N).

You have just mastered the math for computing the mean. The most important part to understand about the mean is knowing when it is *meaningful* to use. You will get plenty of examples of this point in the next few pages.

It is easy to demonstrate the extent to which the mean is the central statistical concept used in social life. "Mean" thinking is ubiquitous. Just take a quick look at the following everyday stats about human behavior that are based on statistical means:

- The average life expectancy for males in the United States is 74.5 years. It is 79.9 years for females (National Vital Statistics Reports 2004).

- The average homicide rate in the United States over the twentieth century was 6.9 per 100,000 population (Archer and Gardner 1987; FBI 1950–2000).

- A murder occurs in the United States every 32.6 minutes, a rape every 5.6 minutes, a car theft every 25.5 seconds, and a burglary every 14.7 seconds (FBI 2004).

- The average travel time to work is 24.7 minutes (U.S. Census 2004).

- The average household income is $60,070 (U.S. Census 2004).

- The per capita income in the United States is $24,020 (U.S. Census 2004).

Although mean ratings are widely used in all aspects of life, these magic numbers are largely meaningless as a measure of typicality or central tendency in many of these applications. This is the case because these statistical averages are highly affected by extreme scores or values. These influential points (also called **outliers**) have the adverse consequence of overly inflating or overly deflating the average score.

To understand how the mean is affected by extreme scores, consider what happens to the average score on an exam when you have just one or two "curve busters" in a criminology class. Table 5.4 provides some hypothetical data on several possible distributions of scores on these exams.

TABLE 5.4   The Consequences of Extreme Scores on Means

Student	Exam 1 Scores	Exam 2 Scores	Exam 3 Scores	Exam 4 Scores	Exam 5 Scores
Bob	100	90	80	65	70
Carol	60	50	60	75	70
Ted	60	50	60	65	70
Alice	60	90	80	75	70
$\Sigma X =$	280	280	280	280	280
$N =$	4	4	4	4	4
$\overline{X} = \Sigma X / N =$	70	70	70	70	70

Let's describe some symbolic notation in Table 5.4 before we talk about what this table reveals about the adverse effects of extreme scores on the mean. Here's the meaning of some of these terms and concepts:

- The value X refers to the scores of the individual students for the particular exam. Later in this book, we will use subscripted numbers like X_1, X_2, X_3, X_4, and X_5 to designate different variables (e.g., each of the five separate exams).

- The sum of the individual scores on each exam is symbolized by Σ. In the case of Exam 1, the value of Σ is 280 (i.e., 100 + 60 + 60 + 60 = 280).

- The sample size is symbolized by N (i.e., the Number of cases).

- The mean ($\overline{X}$) represents the sum of the X scores divided by the number of cases—or algebraically, Mean = $\overline{X} = \Sigma X / N$.

- In this particular example, the means are identical for all exams—that is, $\overline{X} = 280 / 4 = 70$ for each exam.

Although the means are identical for all five exams in Table 5.4, their typicality and/or representativeness of all four individuals who took them varies across each exam. Within these examples, the mean is the most representative of scores for Exam 5 (because all students got the mean score of 70). It is less typical of the scores for Exam 1 (because the perfect score of 100 for Bob inflates the mean above the typical score of 60 received by the other three students). The influence of extreme scores is also shown on Exam 2, where one-half of the students got low A's (scores of 90) and one-half got F's (scores of 50), yielding an unrepresentative mean score of 70.

Because of the influence of extreme values on average ratings, it is very important that informed analysts actually look at the distribution of scores before interpreting the mean as a substantively meaningful summary statistic. In the examples in Table 5.4, this initial review of the distribution of scores would lead to the acceptance of the mean as the infamous "single magic number" to represent the typical scores for Exam 3, Exam 4, and especially Exam 5. However, by looking at the distribution of scores, most researchers would question the utility of the mean as an accurate descriptive statistic for Exam 1 because of Bob's exceptional score.

When an outlier(s) is found in a distribution of scores, the informed analyst must answer two questions: (1) What caused it? And (2) what should be done about it? If odd scores are due to human errors in information processing (e.g., coding errors by hired help), those values are treated as "missing information" and deleted from the analysis. In other cases, we may recode the extreme value(s) to some lower category to minimize their adverse affect. For example, when computing an average number of criminal offenses committed by sex offenders, the offenses of a highly prolific super-predator may be recoded to fall into the top category of 100 or more crimes. Such a recoding of the top category would minimize the impact of this influential point on substantive conclusions about the average amount of criminal activity among sex offenders.

Weighted Means

For most situations of social data analysis, the mean is easily computed by summing up all scores and dividing by the number of scores. However, there are other situations in which the data is already grouped together in categories and differential importance should be given to each of them. In these situations, the same basic formula is used to compute the mean (i.e., $\overline{X} = \Sigma X / N$), but we "tweak" it a little to give more weight to some of the X scores in this calculation. Let's show an example of how this works.

All of you are familiar with your grade point average (GPA), correct? Well, when school administrators compute your GPA, they do not just convert your letter grade into points and then divide by your total credits. Instead, they compute a **weighted mean** that gives more importance (i.e., weight) to courses that are worth more credits. The computing formula for a weighed mean is $\overline{X}_{wt} = \Sigma wX / N_w$, where w = the weight factor and N_w = the weighted number of observations. Table 5.5 provides an example of computing GPA using the formulas for unweighted and weighted means.

TABLE 5.5 Computing Means and Weighted Means

Course	Credits (w)	Grade	Points (X)	Credits × Points (wX)
Math	5	A	4.0	5 × 4.0 = 20
Dance	1	F	0.0	1 × 0.0 = 0
Phys. Ed.	1	F	0.0	1 × 0.0 = 0
Chemistry	5	A	4.0	5 × 4.0 = 20
$N = 4$	$N_w = 12$		$\Sigma X = 8$	$\Sigma wX = 40$

Mean: $\overline{X} = \Sigma X / N = 8 / 4 = 2.0$

Weighted Mean $= \overline{X}_{wt} = \Sigma wX / N_w = 40 / 12 = 3.3$

As shown in Table 5.5, substantive conclusions about your GPA are dramatically different depending on whether you use the weighted or unweighted mean. In this particular case, you want school administrators to use the weighted mean because you will have a 3.3 GPA per credit (i.e., a mid-B average) rather than a 2.0 GPA per class (i.e., a low C average).

The choice of using weighted versus unweighted means really depends on the appropriate *unit of analysis* for a particular study. In the GPA example, school officials assume that one's GPA *per credit* is the preferred unit for measuring one's academic record. Similarly, average statistics on various topics (like number of defense attorneys, incarcerations, executions, or unlicensed firearms) may be presented on a per capita, per household, per city, per county, and/or per state basis. However, if criminological data is only available on a state-level basis (i.e., average arrests per state), a weighted mean for arrests can be computed by (1) multiplying each state's average by its population size, and (2) dividing this sum by the total U.S. population across all 50 states.

As was true of the GPA example, substantive results about average crime trends will often vary across units of analysis and types of mean ratings. Depending on the particular research question, the computation of weighted means may or may not be the proper measure of the statistical average. Both theory and previous research will often serve as good guides to help you decide on using a weighted or unweighted mean.

Strengths and Limitations of Mean Ratings

The mean is what most people are really talking about when they mention the notion of average. This statistical average uses all scores in its computation and serves as the "balancing point" in a distribution of scores—that is, the mean is that point on a distribution where the sum of all the scores above the mean and all the sum of all the scores below the mean are identical.[1]

The major limitation of the mean as a summary measure of a distribution of scores is that its numerical value is strongly affected by very low or very high scores. While these outliers may be excluded once they are determined to be due to extremely weird individuals or to errors in data collection, the mean may still not best represent the typical score even when outliers are excluded. The mean is also not the best measure of central tendency when the distribution of scores is skewed (i.e., when scores concentrate on one side of the distribution).

CHOICE OF MEASURE OF CENTRAL TENDENCY AND POSITION

Whether or not the mean, median, or mode is used as the magic number to summarize a distribution of scores depends on the underlying distribution of scores and the particular research question. For politicians who

---

1. In the next chapter, we will talk about the deviations of an individual score from the mean scores. If you calculate the mean correctly, the sum of all of these deviation scores from the mean will be equal to zero. This property of deviation scores around the mean is another way of saying that the mean is the balancing point in a distribution—that is, it balances out positive and negative deviation scores above and below the mean. Don't worry if this sounds weird to you now because it will become clearer in the next chapter.

seek election or reelection, the "bottom line" is the modal vote. However, for comparisons across different groups (e.g., do males have more prior arrests than females?), both the mean and median are often preferred because they may better represent the entire distribution of scores.

When a variable is normally distributed, the choice of measure of central tendency is largely irrelevant because the mean, median, and mode are the same value under these conditions. However, when a variable is not normally distributed and concentrated within one tail of the entire distribution of scores, the median is the preferred measure of typicality. The relative position of the mean, median, and mode under different shaped distributions is shown in Figure 5.1.

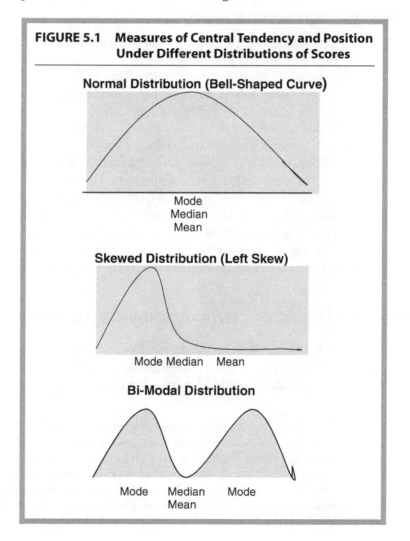

FIGURE 5.1   Measures of Central Tendency and Position Under Different Distributions of Scores

Normal Distribution (Bell-Shaped Curve)

Mode
Median
Mean

Skewed Distribution (Left Skew)

Mode   Median   Mean

Bi-Modal Distribution

Mode   Median   Mode
Mean

The important point is that these "magic numbers" are only as useful as their underlying distributions. When scores are equally likely across their entire range of values, none of the measures of central tendency, location, or typicality provide an unambiguous descriptive summary of the scores. When there is a **skewed distribution** (i.e., scores concentrate more on one half of the distribution than the other), the median is the preferred measure of central tendency. So, before you decide on what measure to use in a research study, remember that an informed analyst will first look at the entire distribution of scores.

SUMMARY OF MAJOR POINTS

- Summary descriptive statistics are often treated as "magic numbers" by uninformed readers and data analysts. Using only one particular statistical measure to capture the entire distribution of scores is hazardous in most cases.

- The most commonly applied summary measures in social research involve the mode, means, and medians.

- The mode is the most frequently occurring number or category in a distribution. It is the most frequent score and may or may not represent the majority of cases.

- The median represents the middle score in an ordered array of numbers. It can be estimated when scores are grouped into categories and intervals by using a formula for the refined median.

- Aside from the median, other summary measures of position include quartiles and percentiles. The general formula for the refined median can be easily modified to figure out the score on a quantitative variable that corresponds to any percentile rank.

- The mean is the arithmetic average. It is what people often think about when they use the word *average*. This statistical average is computed by summing up all scores and dividing this sum by the number of observations.

- The mean is strongly influenced by extreme scores called outliers or influential points.

- The choice of the appropriate measure of typicality and location depends on the particular research question and the nature of the distribution of scores. Means and medians are only appropriate for variables measured on some quantitative scale.

• When scores on some variable are normally distributed (i.e., the bell-shaped curve), the mode, median, and mean are all represented by the same value. For skewed distributions (i.e., when scores concentrate in one half of the distribution and taper off abruptly in the other half), the median is preferred over the mean as a measure of typicality.

KEY TERMS

Mean	Refined Median
Median	Skewed Distributions
Mode	Weighted Mean
Outliers	

MAJOR FORMULAS

Mean: $\overline{X} = \Sigma X / N$

Weighted mean: $\overline{X}_{wt} = \Sigma \mathbf{w}X / N_w$

Refined median (from frequency distributions):
$$\text{Median} = md = L + \frac{(n/2) - F}{f} \times w$$

Refined median (from percent distributions):
$$\text{Median} = md = L + \frac{(50) - P}{p} \times w$$

Percentile rank (example = 75th percentile):
$$\text{75th Percentile} = L + \frac{(75) - P}{p} \times w$$

SPSS and Excel Applications (*Optional Section*)

Each of the measures of central tendency and location is easily produced by computer software programs. How to do these procedures in **SPSS** and **Microsoft Excel** is described below.

SPSS will compute these measures through its procedure called *descriptives*. To access this procedure in SPSS, simply follow these steps: (1) Click on **Analyze**, (2) click on **Descriptive Statistics**, (3) pull down the menu and click on **Frequencies**, (4) select the variables for your analysis, (5) click on the **Statistics** button, and (6) select the particular measures of central tendency (e.g., mean, median, or mode) and percentiles (e.g., quartiles or particular percentile scores).

Many of these basic summary statistics are also available through Microsoft Excel. For example, to derive an average (i.e., mean) in Excel, do the following: (1) Highlight the scores to be averaged, (2) click on the icon marked with the Greek symbol for summation (Σ), and (3) click on the word **Average**. The arithmetic mean will be immediately displayed after performing these steps.

APPLYING WHAT YOU HAVE LEARNED

1. Which of the following is a measure of central tendency, typicality, and/or location in criminological research?

   a. Mode.

   b. Median.

   c. Mean.

   d. All of the above.

   e. Only a and b are true.

2. Our use of the word *average* in ordinary language is best represented by the statistical concept of the

   a. mode.

   b. median.

   c. mean.

3. The most frequently occurring score in a distribution is called the

   a. mode.

   b. median.

   c. mean.

4. Under what conditions is the mode an important statistical measure?

    a. When plurality matters in the particular substantive question.

    b. When it represents either a large minority or a majority of observations.

    c. When extreme scores are excluded.

    d. All of the above.

    e. Only a and b are true.

5. A mode can be found for both qualitative and quantitative variables.

    a. True

    b. False

6. There is one and only one mode for each distribution of scores.

    a. True

    b. False

7. As a measure of typicality and location, the median

    a. represents the middle score of a distribution.

    b. can have more than one numerical value.

    c. can be computed on both qualitative and quantitative variables.

    d. all of the above are true.

8. When is the best time to use the median as a statistical measure?

    a. When you have quantitative variables with skewed distributions.

    b. When you have qualitative variables with skewed distributions.

    c. When a qualitative variable is normally distributed.

    d. None of the above are true.

9. Outliers are extreme scores that have the most severe impact on

    a. the mode.

    b. the median.

    c. the mean.

    d. all of the above are affected by outliers.

10. An informed consumer should use a weighted mean rather than standard mean when summarizing the distribution of scores.

    a. True

    b. False

    c. It depends on the particular research question that is being examined.

11. Why are the mean, median, and mode considered "magic numbers" by your book's author?

12. Explain how George W. Bush can be considered the "modal minority" president in the 2000 election against Al Gore.

13. What is the mode for the following scores: 2, 1, 7, 8, 9, 2, 5?

14. What is the modal robbery target in the example below?

Robbery Target	%
Street/Highway Mugging	48
Commercial House	14
Gas or Service Station	2
Convenience Store	6
Residence	12
Bank	2
Miscellaneous	16
Total	100

Data Source: FBI (1999).

15. What is the median score in this distribution: 2, 5, 7, 4, 9?

16. What is the median score in this distribution: 2, 5, 7, 4, 9, 11?

17. Compute the median age from the following data:

Age of Offenders	Frequency
10 and under	1
11–20	260

(continued)

Age of Offenders	Frequency
21–30	191
31–40	66
41–50	22
51–60	3
61–70	6
71–80	1
Over 80	0
Total	550

18. Why does the U.S. Census Bureau place primary importance on the *median* family income rather than the *mean* family income as the best measure of family income?

19. Compute the mean on the basis of the following scores: 2, 4, 3, 5, 1.

20. The percentage of residents in three cities who were victimized by a violent crime is summarized in the following table:

City	Percentage of Violent Victims	Population Size
City A	4.0	100,000
City B	2.0	10,000
City C	9.0	1,000,000

   a. What is the average percent victimized per city?

   b. What is the average percent victimized per population?

21. If you were told that the average American household consumes and/or smokes one pound of marijuana per year, what else would you have to know to trust this average number as being representative of typical marijuana consumption? ✦

6 Measures of Variation and Dispersion

About 1 in 3 black males, 1 in 6 Hispanic males, and 1 in 17 white males are expected to go to prison in their lifetime (Bonczar 2003). Criminal justice research for decades has tried to document and explain this racial variability in imprisonment risks.

One of the central concepts in statistical thinking involves the idea of variation. *Variation* simply means that people, objects, and events vary in their type, kind, degree, magnitude, and/or intensity.

Statisticians want to develop measures that better represent the nature and magnitude of variation, whereas criminologists and other social scientists want to explain variation. For example, why are the lifetime risks of imprisonment higher for black males than other social groups? What is the nature and magnitude of variation in illegal drug use by gender, class, residency patterns, and any other sociodemographic characteristic? How much variation in the use of capital punishment across countries is explained by variability in their social, political, and/or economic conditions? The basic issue in all these cases involves trying to account for the variation in some particular variable.

In a world of clones, the notion of diversity or variation does not exist. However, in all other contexts, variation is an essential feature of all aspects of human existence. As was true of measuring typicality and central tendency, there are also different ways to measure the nature and magnitude of variation and/or dispersion in a set of scores.

This chapter summarizes and describes several types of measures of dispersion used in criminological research. The primary descriptive measures include the range, the variance, and the standard deviation. Subsequent chapters will use this information about dispersion and variation to define entire distributions of scores and to perform particular statistical analyses of this variation and its components. However, this brief chapter will focus exclusively on how we measure variation in criminological data.

THE RANGE OF SCORES

The most elementary and basic measure of dispersion of scores on a quantitative variable is the range. The **range** is simply defined as the difference between the smallest and largest scores in a distribution. Whether this range is a useful summary statistic depends in large part on the particular substantive application. For example, if I told you that scores on the next stats exam will range from 0% to 100%, this information may be a bit troubling to some students (e.g., those who fear getting the 0 score), but it is really not that informative for most of you. However, if I told you scores will range from 90% to 100%, that is useful stuff.

To further illustrate the relative utility of the range as a summary measure of dispersion, consider the range of annual salaries for five hypothetical job offers you just got. These salary ranges are shown in Table 6.1. Given these salary ranges, what job would you select?

TABLE 6.1	Selecting a Job Based on Salary Ranges	
Job	**Salary Range**	**Low to High Salaries**
Job A	0	$50,000 to $50,000
Job B	10,000	$45,000 to $55,000
Job C	30,000	$35,000 to $65,000
Job D	50,000	$25,000 to $75,000
Job E	100,000	$0 to $100,000

For those of you focusing on guaranteed income for the here and now, the best salary would be Job A. In this case, the range of 0 indicates that everyone gets $50,000 per year. Period. No salary raises for seniority or wheeling and dealing by hiring a "head hunter." In sharp contrast, the extremely confident (overconfident?) person would probably select Job E because of the possibility of getting $100,000. The large salary range for Job E would be largely irrelevant to this person because he or she would never consider getting the low-end salary. The compromise between these two extreme positions would be the other three jobs.

Although knowledge of the mean, median, and modal salaries would definitely help you make your decision, the salary ranges in Table 6.1 provide a preliminary basis for job selection. This is especially true in the case of Job A, where there would be no ambiguity about your expected salary. Thus, when the range of scores is extremely limited, the range provides a decent summary measure of the full dispersion of scores.

As a measure of dispersion, however, the primary limitation of the range is that the extreme values that comprise the "low" and "high" scores are often the exceptional ones. For example, it is entirely possible that everyone except two people got a salary of $60,000 for Job E—the two exceptions being the employee who didn't get paid at all and the one who made $100,000. In this case, the range is not representative of the distribution of scores and the concentration of them at $60,000. This low representativeness of extreme scores is the primary reason why the range is a somewhat limited measure of dispersion.

An alternative measure of dispersion involves the **interquartile range**. This range of scores represents the distance between the 25th percentile case (i.e., the 1st quartile) and the 75th percentile case (i.e., the 3rd quartile). This interquartile range covers the middle 50% of the cases in the distribution. Because it doesn't involve the most extreme scores, it is often assumed that the interquartile range provides a more stable and representative measure of the dispersion of scores. However, its major limitation is similar to that of the full range in that it is based solely on the location of two scores.

THE VARIANCE AND STANDARD DEVIATION

Two measures of dispersion that derive from the analysis of all observations in a distribution are the variance and the standard deviation. These related measures are based on the notion of dispersion and/or variation around the mean. They are the most common measures of dispersion for quantitative variables.

The **variance** represents the average sum of the squared deviations from the mean. This somewhat odd description will make more sense when we break down each of these components and show the computational details. The steps involved in the computation of the variance are illustrated in Table 6.2 and summarized below. The basic formula for the variance is

$$\text{Variance} = \frac{\Sigma(X - \overline{X})^2}{N},$$

where $\Sigma(X - \overline{X})^2$ = the sum of the squared deviations from the mean and N = the number of observations.

The basic steps to compute the variance involve the following:

- Compute the mean ($\bar{x}$).
- Compute the deviation of each score from the mean ($x - \bar{x}$).
- Square each deviation score $(x - \bar{x})^2$.
- Sum up all of these squared deviations $(\Sigma (x - \bar{x})^2)$.
- Divide this sum of the squared deviations by the number of observations $(\Sigma (x - \bar{x})^2 / N)$.
- The resulting average sum of squared deviations from the mean is the variance.

TABLE 6.2   Example of Computing the Variance

x	$x - \bar{x}$	$(x - \bar{x})^2$
3	$3 - 4 = -1$	$(-1)(-1) = 1$
5	$5 - 4 = +1$	$(+1)(+1) = 1$
2	$2 - 4 = -2$	$(-2)(-2) = 4$
8	$8 - 4 = +4$	$(+4)(+4) = 16$
2	$2 - 4 = -2$	$(-2)(-2) = 4$
$\Sigma = 20$	0	26

Mean $= \Sigma X / N = 20 / 5 = 4$

Variance $= \dfrac{\Sigma (X - \bar{X})^2}{N} = 26 / 5 = 5.2$

The variance does not have an intuitive interpretation because it is representative of squared units. What you can say about the variance is that the greater the variance, the wider the variability within the distribution of scores. However, a related measure of dispersion that is expressed in the same units as the original variable is the standard deviation.

The **standard deviation** of scores can be easily derived from the variance by simply taking the square root of the variance (i.e., standard deviation = $\sqrt{\text{variance}}$). As is true of the variance, the larger the standard deviation, the greater the dispersion of scores in the distribution.

Because they are based on the entire distribution of scores, both the variance and the standard deviation are affected by outliers and other extreme scores. An examination of Table 6.2 illustrates this point. Notice that the X score of 8 not only increases the mean but also contributes to the greatest squared deviation from the mean (i.e., a value of 16 versus a value of 4 for the next most influential point). As a result of these properties, an informed analyst will examine the nature of the distribution of scores before deciding to compute and interpret either the variance or standard deviation.

Variances and Standard Deviations for Binary Variables

Although most applicable as measures of dispersion for quantitative variables, both variances and standard deviations may be computed in the special case of the measurement of attributes that are binary coded. These binary codes represent the presence (coded 1) and absence (coded 0) of particular qualitative attributes. For example, the binary coding of race could be represented by the codes 0 = *non-white*, and 1 = *white*. Similarly, binary coding of gender could be coded with males as the higher value (0 = *female*, 1 = *male*) or with females as the higher value (1 = *female*, 0 = *male*). Which categories are coded as 0 or 1 is not important. Instead, the crucial element is that a qualitative variable is expressed as a binary variable.

When dealing with binary variables, the variance is simply the product of the proportion of cases in each category. This is symbolized as $p * q$, where p = the proportion of cases in the category marked as 1 and q = the proportion of cases in the category marked as 0. The standard deviation for a binary variable is found by just taking the square root of the variance (i.e., $\sqrt{pq}$). So, if 75% of people are bored with this stuff and 25% are not bored, the variance of boredom in this example is .1875 (i.e., .75 × .25). This special case of the variance and standard deviation for binary variables will become important when we discuss confidence intervals and hypothesis testing about population proportions in later chapters (see Chapters 8, 9, and 10).

Population Versus Sample Variances and Standard Deviations

The material presented thus far on measures of central tendency and dispersion has not made a distinction between population and sample statistics. I have not yet included this distinction in computing formulas because I wanted to present this material in the least complicated way possible. However, now is the time to briefly describe this fundamental distinction and its implications for computing formulas.

The basic idea about population parameters and sample statistics is that the former are unknown and are estimated from the latter. In more basic English, this means that we use sample statistics from random samples to estimate these unknown population parameters. In this process of statistical inference about population parameters, a slight adjustment is made to provide a better (i.e., what statisticians call an "unbiased" estimate) guess of these population values. In the case of the variance and standard deviations, we simply use *N-1* rather than *N* in the denominators when computing sample estimates of these population parameters.

Using Latin characters for sample statistics and Greek symbols for population parameters, the respective sample and population variances and standard deviations are given by the following formulas:[1]

$$\text{Sample Variance} = s^2 = \frac{\Sigma(X - \overline{X})^2}{N-1}$$

$$\text{Population Variance} = \sigma^2 = \frac{\Sigma(X - \mu)^2}{N}$$

$$\text{Sample Standard Deviation} = sd = s = \sqrt{\frac{\Sigma(X - \overline{X})^2}{N-1}}$$

$$\text{Population Standard Deviation} = \sigma = \sqrt{\frac{\Sigma(X - \mu)^2}{N}}$$

When dealing with large samples (i.e., $N > 50$), this correction to provide unbiased estimates of population parameters has a minimal effect on substantive conclusions. However, the distinction between sample and population values is crucial, and we will make this *N–1* adjustment whenever sample data are used in our subsequent discussions of estimating confidence intervals around population values and of hypothesis testing about population values based on sample results.

SUMMARY OF MAJOR POINTS

- A major concept in statistical analysis involves the notions of variation and dispersion. The goal of much criminological research is to explain variation in qualitative and quantitative variables.

---

1. In these formulas for the population variances and standard deviations, the mean of a variable in the population is symbolized as μ. In actual statistical analyses, we use the sample mean $(\overline{x})$ as our best estimate of this population mean (μ).

- The most elementary measure of dispersion is the range of scores. It represents the difference in the value of the lowest and highest scores in a distribution. Because these extreme scores may be exceptional cases, the range is of limited utility in most studies.

- The interquartile range covers the middle 50% of cases in a distribution. It is often considered more stable and a better representation of the distribution of scores than the full range.

- The variance and standard deviation are the most commonly used measures of dispersion for quantitative variables. They measure the magnitude of squared deviations from the mean. Larger variances and standard deviations are indicative of larger variability in scores.

- Variances and standard deviations may be computed in the special cases of qualitative variables that are binary coded. Binary variables have only two values (i.e., 0 and 1) and represent either the presence or absence of the particular attribute.

- When using sample data to estimate population values, an adjustment must be made to provide unbiased estimates of these population parameters. In the case of the computation of sample standard deviations and variances, the adjustment is to divide the sum of squared deviations by the quantity *N–1* rather than N.

KEY TERMS

Interquartile Range	Standard Deviation
Range	Variance

MAJOR FORMULAS

$$\text{Sample Variance} = s^2 = \frac{\Sigma(X - \overline{X})^2}{N-1}$$

$$\text{Population Variance} = \sigma^2 = \frac{\Sigma(X - \mu)^2}{N}$$

$$\text{Sample Standard Deviation} = sd = s = \sqrt{\frac{\Sigma(X - \overline{X})^2}{N-1}}$$

$$\text{Population Standard Deviation} = \sigma = \sqrt{\frac{\Sigma(X - \mu)^2}{N}}$$

$$\text{Variance for a Binary Variable} = \sigma_B^2 = p \times q \equiv pq$$

$$\text{Standard Deviation for a Binary Variable} = \sigma_B = \sqrt{p \times q} \equiv \sqrt{pq}$$

APPLYING WHAT YOU HAVE LEARNED

1. Necessary information to compute the range includes

    a. a quantitative measurement of the variable (i.e., a quantitative variable).

    b. knowledge of the lowest and highest values on the variable.

    c. the mean of the variable.

    d. all of the above are necessary to compute a range.

    e. only a and b are true.

2. Assume that in a sample of 10 cities, the mean number of car thefts in the last month was 200 and the standard deviation was 15. If you included another city in your sample and it had 200 car thefts in the last month, what effect would adding this city to your sample have on the standard deviation?

    a. The standard deviation will become greater than 15.

    b. The standard deviation will become less than 15.

    c. The standard deviation will remain the same.

3. In general, the larger the variance of scores,

    a. the larger the standard deviation.

    b. the greater that dispersion of scores away from the mean.

    c. the smaller the modal score.

    d. all of the above are true.

    e. only a and b are true.

4. Is it possible to have a negative value for the variance or standard deviation?

a. No, because both measures are based on squared deviations from the mean, and by squaring these deviations all values become positive.

b. Yes, because both measures involve deviations from the mean that may be either positive or negative and can sum up to a negative value.

5. Extreme scores affect which of the following measures of dispersion?

a. Variance.

b. Standard deviation.

c. Range.

d. All of the above are true.

e. Only a and b are true.

6. The population variance is often estimated from the sample variance.

a. True

b. False

7. Interquartile ranges will always be narrower in width than the range.

a. True

b. False

8. Assume that you were interested in the proportion of parolees who recidivate by committing a new offense upon prison release. Recidivism is measured as *yes* or *no*. In this example, what measure of dispersion would you use?

a. The variance for a binary variable

b. The standard deviation for a binary variable

c. The variance or standard deviation for a quantitative variable

d. Only a and b

Here are some questions requiring written responses and/or calculations.

9. Why is the range a fairly unstable measure of the dispersion of scores in a distribution?

10. What is the range for the following scores?   4, 3, 9, 2, 1, 7

11. The interquartile range represents the differences between the first and third quartile scores in a distribution. This is identical to the difference between the 25th percentile and the 75th percentile scores. Using the formula in Chapter 5 for computing percentile ranks from grouped data, calculate the interquartile range for the following distribution of scores. Provide both the lower and upper limits of the interquartile range. *Hint:* You need to figure out the true limits that underlie each rounded score (e.g., the score of 1's true limit really ranges from .5 to 1.5). You also need to construct a cumulative percentage distribution to figure out the intervals that contain 25th and 75th percentile scores.

X	f	%
1	10	12.5
2	20	25.0
3–5	10	12.5
6–8	15	18.8
7–9	25	31.2
	N = 80	100.0

12. What effect, if any, do extreme scores have on the value of the standard deviation and variance?

13. Compute the sample variance and sample standard deviation for the following scores: 2, 4, 6, 10, 8, 5, 7

14. Compute the population variance and population standard deviation for the following scores: 2, 4, 6, 10, 8, 5, 7

15. Two jobs in the field of criminal justice have the same average salary of $40,000, but the standard deviation is $10,000 in one case and the standard deviation is $100 in the other. What job would you select, and why?

16. What is the numerical value of the standard deviation and the variance for the following distribution of scores? 5, 5, 5, 5, 5, 5, 5

17. When is the standard deviation preferred over the variance as a measure of dispersion?

18. If 80% of prison inmates are drug dealers and 20% are not drug dealers, what are the numerical values of the variance and standard deviation? ✦

7

The Normal Curve and Sampling Distributions

If we know a variable is normally distributed and know its mean and standard deviation, we can determine what proportion of cases or observations fall between any two scores.

For example, if the length of prison sentences for major drug offenders is normally distributed with a mean of 8 years and a standard deviation of 1.5 years, we know that (1) 50% of drug offenders got 8 years or longer, (2) about 95% got between 5 and 11 years, (3) the top 5% of them got 10.5 years or longer, and (4) less than 1% got less than 4.5 years.

You will learn how to derive these values from a normal distribution in this chapter.

As noted in the first chapter, statistics are used for the purposes of description and inference. Frequency tables, graphs and charts, measures of central tendency (e.g., means, medians, and modes), and measures of dispersion (e.g., ranges, standard deviations, and variances) are the basic tools used by statisticians to provide descriptive summaries of variables. The process of **statistical inference** involves using these descriptive summaries as the basis for making estimates of unknown population values and testing hypotheses about them.

To understand the logic of statistical inference, it is important to know the particular properties of various distributions and how they are used for comparative purposes to reach conclusions about likely population values from sample data. Accordingly, this chapter focuses on the properties of the **normal probability distribution** (i.e., the bell-shaped curve) and other basic sampling distributions (e.g., the binomial, t-, chi-square (χ^2), and F-distributions). Each of these distributions will be discussed again in subsequent chapters to demonstrate their importance for statistical inference.

THE NORMAL CURVE

The most widely used and assumed distribution in social statistics is represented by the bell-shaped curve. It is called the standard **normal distribution** or just the *normal curve* for short. While some people question the use of the word *normal* to describe this distribution (e.g., because it may perpetuate a fallacy that all probability distributions have this shape), the normal curve is nonetheless a good approximation of the distribution of scores for many variables. In fact, a widely known statistical theorem (the **Central Limit Theorem**) states that, regardless of the original shape of the distribution, the sampling distribution of all possible outcomes of a particular test statistic (like a mean) will increasingly approximate a normal distribution as we increase our sample size. It is this basic theorem and the prevalence of distributions of scores that approach a normal distribution that contribute to the widespread use of the normal curve in statistical thinking.

The standard normal distribution has many basic properties by definition. These interrelated properties include the following:

- Unimodal (i.e., it has only one mode).

- Symmetrical around its mean (e.g., each half of the distribution is a mirror image of the other).

- A normal distribution is a continuous theoretical distribution that ranges from negative to positive infinity ($\pm \infty$). An increasingly smaller area is covered as scores move out from either side of the mean.

- As a symmetrical distribution, one-half of the area underlying a normal distribution is above the mean (i.e., what is called the *positive tail* of the distribution) and one-half of the area is below the mean (called the *negative tail* of the distribution).

- The mean, median, and mode are represented by the same value.

- The standard normal distribution is standardized so that its mean is 0 and its standard deviation is 1.

- A fixed proportion of observations will always fall within given intervals of standard deviations from the mean. For example, for a normal distribution, 34.13% of the cases will always fall between the mean and 1 standard deviation above the mean.

- If a variable is normally distributed and you know its mean and standard deviation, you can define the proportion of cases that are (1) greater than some point on this distribution, (2) less than some point on this distribution, and/or (3) between any two points in this distribution.

These well-defined properties of a normal distribution make it an ideal basis for the standardization and comparison of scores with different means and different standard deviations. As described below, these standard comparisons are possible by converting the original or raw scores into *normal deviates*. These standard scores are more commonly referred to as *z-scores*.

Z-SCORES AS STANDARD SCORES

A widely used standard score involves the computation of z-scores. A **z-score** reflects the number of standard deviations from the mean. Large positive z-scores indicate that a score is substantially higher than the mean, whereas large negative z-scores indicate that a score is substantially lower than the mean. Z-scores close to 0 reflect raw scores that are close to their respective mean scores. Regardless of the particular mean or standard deviation, any raw score can be converted to a z-score by using the following formula:

$$z = \frac{X - \overline{X}}{SD},$$

where X = any raw score, $\overline{X}$ = the mean, and SD = the standard deviation.

To illustrate how z-scores are standardized scores, consider the situation in which you want to know whether or not you are average, above average, or below average on various social indicators in American society. Further assume that you make $50,000 per year, have 16 years of education, have an IQ of 120, and drive a car that gets 30 miles per gallon. How do you compare to the rest of Americans on each of these measures?

Unfortunately, your relative social standing on these variables cannot be determined unless you also know the mean for all Americans and the standard deviation of these scores. However, with this information and your own raw scores, you can easily convert your scores to z-scores to find out the number of standard deviations above or below average you fall on each measure. These calculations are shown in Table 7.1.

TABLE 7.1   Converting Raw Scores to Standardized Z-Scores*

Variable	Your Score (X)	Mean ($\overline{X}$)	Standard Deviation (SD)	Z-Score
Income	$50,000	$30,000	$10,000	+ 2.00
Education	16 years	12 years	2 years	+ 2.00
IQ Score	120	100	10	+ 2.00
Miles per Gallon	30 mpg	24 mpg	3 mpg	+ 2.00

*Conversion Formula: $z = \dfrac{X - \overline{X}}{SD}$

The idea that z-scores are standardized scores is clearly revealed by the identical numbers in the last column of Table 7.1. Specifically, regardless of the particular variable or its mean or standard deviation, your standard score is an identical score of z = +2.00 across all variables. In each of these cases, you are +2.00 standard deviations above the mean. For persons who like money and like being judged as more intelligent and environmentally friendly than average, being two standard deviations above "normal" should be a source of pride and accomplishment. Way to go. You are a multidimensional success!

You should also notice in Table 7.1, and in general, that if your raw score on each of these variables was identical to the mean for that particular variable (e.g., you made $30,000 and the mean is $30,000), your z-score would be 0 (30,000 – 30,000 / 10,000 = 0). This also shows how z-scores represent standard scores by adjusting for the particular unit measurements used in the original data. That is why z-scores are so neat. It doesn't matter if you're talking about miles per gallon, dollars, yen, years, or nanoseconds—z-scores place all these units on a level playing field for comparative purposes.

When coupled with the knowledge that a variable is normally distributed, the conversion of raw scores to standardized z-scores achieves added importance because it allows us to make definitive statements about relative prevalence of particular outcomes. For example, if all variables in Table 7.1 are normally distributed, a z-score of +2.00 would place you in the top 2.28% of all people on each variable. How we derive this percentile rank from z-scores is the direct result of knowing the properties of the normal curve. You will learn how to do this shortly.

As mentioned earlier, one of the primary properties of any normal distribution is that a constant proportion of cases fall within given standard deviations (i.e., z-scores) from the mean. Table 7.2 shows the proportion of cases in a normal distribution that occur within 1, 2, and 3 standard deviations from the mean. Appendix A provides a more complete listing of the area under a normal curve that (1) falls between the mean and a particular z-score (Column B of Appendix A), and (2) is more extreme than this particular z-score (Column C of Appendix A). The understanding of the logic of statistical inference requires knowledge of the derivation of these numbers and the area under a normal distribution covered by them.

For any normally distributed variable, Table 7.2 and Appendix A indicate that a fixed area or percent of cases fall within given standard deviations from the mean. For example, the interval between the mean and 1 standard deviation (*sd*) above the mean represents an area of .3413 (i.e., 34.13%), the interval between the mean and 2 *sd*'s above the mean covers an area of .4772 (i.e., 47.72% of cases), and 49.87% of the cases in a normal distribution fall between the mean and 3 *sd*'s above the mean. Each of these values is obtained by

1. finding the z-scores of 1.00, 2.00, and 3.00 in Column A of these tables; and

2. reading over to Column B to find the area that falls between the mean and these particular z-scores.

READING A NORMAL CURVE TABLE

Given the widespread use of the normal distribution in various applications of social statistics, it is very important to understand how to read a normal curve table and derive information from it. I will illustrate these ideas with the z-scores of +1.0 and +2.0, but the same logic applies to any positive or negative value. When I am done with this illustration, you will know how to convert a raw score to a z-score, a z-score to an area, an area to a percentage, and a percentage to a percentile rank (i.e., Raw Score → z-score → Area → Percentage → Percentile Rank).

Let's start with IQ as an example. Suppose that IQ is normally distributed in the United States with a mean of 100 and a standard deviation of 10. Your IQ is 110. Converting this raw score into a standard score

TABLE 7.2   Areas of the Normal Curve Represented by Select Z-Scores

Column A Z-Score	Column B Area From Mean to Z-Score	Column C Area > Z-Score
1.00	.3413	.1587
2.00	.4772	.0228
3.00	.4987	.0013

Graphic Representation of Areas Within +/− 1 sd, +/− 2 sd, and +/− 3 sd

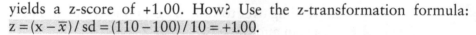

yields a z-score of +1.00. How? Use the z-transformation formula: $z = (x - \bar{x}) / sd = (110 - 100) / 10 = +1.00$.

Now, here is what we can learn about your IQ when it is transformed to a z-score of +1.00 and we know that IQ is normally distributed.

- First, the positive z-score of 1.00 indicates you are above the mean (i.e., you did better than the average person on this IQ test). Technically, the z-score tells you that you are 1 standard deviation above the mean (100 [mean] + 10 [1 sd] = 110 [your score]).

- Second, you can figure out what percentage of people have an IQ between the mean (i.e., 100) and 110 by doing the following:

  1. Look at Column A of a normal curve table for the z-score of 1.00 (see Table 7.2 or, more generally, Appendix A).

  2. Read across this row until you get in Column B.

  3. Take this area listed in Column B (.3413), and multiply it by 100 to convert it into a percentage (34.13%).

Thus, for a normally distributed variable, 34.13% of the cases will fall within the interval between the mean and +1.00 z-scores above the mean. In this IQ example, 34.13% have an IQ between 100 and 110.

- Third, you can figure out what percent of the people did better than you (i.e, have an IQ of 110 or greater) by doing the following:

  1. Look at Column A for your z-score of 1.00.

  2. Read across this row until you get to Column C.

  3. Take this area value in Column C (.1587), and multiply it by 100 to convert it into a percentage (15.87%).

Thus, 15.87% of the scores on a normally distributed variable are greater than +1.00 z-scores above the mean. In this example, only 15.87% of the people did better on the IQ test than you did. In other words, you're in the top 15.87% of the U.S. population on this IQ test.

Now, what if your actual IQ score was 90? What can converting this score to a z-score tell you about your IQ relative to others? By converting this raw score to a z-score and looking at a normal curve table (see Appendix A), you can easily answer the same basic three questions about your IQ by following the similar logical steps:

- First, your raw score converts to a z-score of −1.00 [$z = (x - \bar{x}) / sd$ $= (90 - 100) / 10 = -1.00$]. Your IQ is below average this time, one standard deviation or z-score below the mean to be precise. Not good. You don't want to be below the average person who took this type of test.

- Second, 34.13% of people will have an IQ between the mean and −1.00 z-scores below the mean. This is graphically illustrated in Table 7.2 and is derived from the normal curve table in Appendix A by doing the following:

  1. Find your z-score of −1.00 (just forget the sign and look for z = 1.00 because normal curves are perfectly symmetrical, so the area between the mean and +1 sd above the mean is identical to the area between the mean and −1 sd below the mean),

  2. go across to Column B and find the area of .3413, and

  3. multiply this area by 100 to convert it into a percentage (i.e., .3413 × 100 = 34.13%).

- Third, only 15.87% of the people did worse than you did (i.e., had a z-score of –1.00 or less). This was found by

    1. looking in Column A of the normal curve table for a z-score of 1.00 (see comment above about forgetting the negative sign here),

    2. moving across until you enter Column C, and

    3. converting the number in Column C (.1587) into a percentage by multiplying it by 100 to get 15.87%.

Thus, 15.87% of a normally distributed variable will have a z-score of –1.00 or more negative. In this IQ example, you can brag that you did better than 15.87% of all IQ test takers. However, your enemies will "spin" this by saying that you are in the lowest 15.87% or, more cruelly, that 84.13% of people on the planet did better than you. This 84.13% number is found by adding together the percent of people who have a score between the mean and 1 sd below the mean (i.e., 34.13%) and the percent that will be above the mean (i.e., 50% of scores on a normally distributed variable are above the mean). Thus, 34.13% + 50% = 84.13%. Having a score of 84% in this particular case is not good at all!

Before we move on to another example, notice what happens when we add the percent of cases in a normal distribution that are within 1 standard deviation above the mean (34.13%) and within 1 standard deviation below the mean (34.13%). This sum is 68.26%, and it indicates the proportion of cases within ±1.00 z-scores from the mean. In this IQ example, it tells you that about 68% of the IQ's are between 90 and 110. When we later discuss statistical inference and confidence intervals (Chapter 8), we will use this information about the normal curve to say that we are 68% confident that the true value falls within ±1 standard deviation from the sample mean. Stay tuned for more on this in the next chapter.

Now it's your turn. Let us say you have an IQ of 120, the mean is again 100, and the standard deviation is 10. Answer the following questions using what you just learned about reading the normal curve table in Appendix A and deriving information from it:

1. What z-score corresponds to your raw score of 120?

2. What percentage of people will have an IQ between 100 and 120?

3. What percentage of people will have an IQ of 120 or greater?

4. What percentage of people will have an IQ between 80 and 120?

Here are the answers and how you should have derived them:

1. $z = +2.00$ (i.e., $z = (x - \bar{x}) / sd$ ➜ $120 - 100 / 10 = 2.00$)

2. 47.72% of IQs are between 100 and 120 (i.e., convert 120 to a $z = +2.00$ ➜ go to Column A of the normal curve table and find the value of 2.00 ➜ go across to Column B of that table to find the value of .4772 ➜ multiply by 100 to get the value of 47.72%). Notice that this question just translates into what percent of the cases of a normal distribution fall between the mean and +2.00 z-scores from the mean because 100 is the mean.

3. 2.28% of IQs are at 120 or higher (i.e., $z = 2.00$ ➜ column C value = .0228 ➜ multiply by 100 = 2.28%).

4. 95.44% of IQs are between 80 and 120 (i.e., convert both 80 and 120 to z-scores, then look at Column B of the normal curve table to find area between the mean and that z-score of 2.00 [47.72% for both $z = 2.00$ and $z = -2.00$], and then add these percentages together [47.72% + 47.72 = 95.44).

Now, let's mix this up a little bit to show the versatility in using z-scores and the normal curve. Again, assume that we are interested in IQ and it is normally distributed with a mean = 100 and sd = 10. However, this time we don't know our raw IQ score, but the Princeton University Testing Center tells us our percentile rank is in the top 5%. With this information, we can still derive our raw IQ score by doing the following steps:

•   Take the percentile rank of 5% and convert it to decimal form (.05).

•   Go to Column C of the normal curve table and read down this column until you find the value closest to .05. In this example, there are two possible choices (i.e., .0495 and .0505) that are both equal distance from .05. Here you have three options: (1) Pick the first number you run into going down the list (in this case, you'd pick .0505), (2) pick the second number that occurs (in this case, .0495), or (3) use both numbers and read across to column A and take the average of the two z-scores that correspond to these two areas. You will get roughly the same results regardless of which approach you use here to pick the z-score when the area is perfectly between two points.

•   After you pick the decimal number in Column C, read across to Column A to find the corresponding z-score. In this case, if we picked .0505 in Column C to represent the top 5%, we will select the z-score of 1.64 in Column A. This z-score is a positive value (i.e., Z = +1.64) because we are talking about the top 5%. If we were asking about the bottom 5%, this z-score would be –1.64.

- Plug this z-score into the formula for the z-transformation, and solve for X (i.e., your raw score). The basic z-formula is $z = (x - \bar{x}) / sd$. In this case, we have +1.64 = (x – 100) / 10 ➔ 1.64 (10) = x – 100 ➔ x = 116.4. Thus, to be in the top 5% for IQ, you would need to have a score of 116.4 or higher. *Note:* I just did a little algebra here by solving for X by isolating x on one side of the equal sign by (1) multiplying both sides of the equation by 10, and then (2) adding +100 to the left side of the equation to isolate the value of x.

- In a similar vein, if you want to know what IQ you need to be in the lowest 5%, you would follow the same logic until the final stage of solving for X. At this point, you would plug in –1.64 for z (instead of +1.64, because you are looking at points below the mean). So, the computing formula would be –1.64 = (x – 100) / 10 ➔ –1.64 (10) = x – 100 ➔ x = 83.6. The end result is that to be in the lowest 5% of IQ, you would have to score 83.6 or lower on the test.

Although it may be hard to convince you of this fact, knowing how to do these z-score transformations is an incredibly powerful skill for being an informed consumer. For example, you will often hear people brag about their social position using percentile ranks (e.g., the top 1% or top 5%) or sometimes even in the language of standard normal deviates (z-scores) from the mean (e.g., +2.5 or +3.0). With knowledge of the means and standard deviations, you can easily derive their raw score (e.g., their yearly income) from their percentile rank or z-score (e.g., the top 10%) even if they refuse to tell you the raw score. Moreover, if someone ever claims they are 3 standard deviations above the mean (i.e, a z-score of 3.00), you should immediately call them either a liar or a very rare or weird person. Why? Because a z-score of +3.00 or larger would place them in the top one-tenth of 1 percent [(z of 3.00 or greater) ➔ area of .0013 (column C of Appendix A) ➔ .13% (.0013 × 100%)]. Since this is such an unlikely occurrence, I would probably conclude they are a liar. So, knowledge of these standard scores and their computational details will help you make informed decisions about the believability of the daily claims that people make about a variety of issues.

To further illustrate the utility of z-scores for normal distributions, let's introduce a little more statistical notation and ascertain the various scores that correspond to particular percentile ranks. The notation for a random variable (X) that is normally distributed (≈ *Norm*) with a given population mean (μ) and population standard deviation (σ) is x ≈ *Norm* (μ, σ). Using this notation and assuming a normal distribution for each variable, you should now be able to figure out how the particular raw scores and percentile ranks were derived in the following examples:

- The top 5% of criminal sentences for convicted murders is 16.92 or more years [x ≈ *Norm* (12, 3)].

- The bottom 10% of educational attainment in the United States involves adults with less than 9.3 years of education [x ≈ *Norm* (12.5, 2.5)].

- The top 1% of the most prolific sex offenders released from prison have 17 prior criminal arrests [x ≈ *Norm* (4.5, 5.4)].

- Being involved in five or more separate incidents of aggressive driving per month represents the top 1.4% of Las Vegas drivers in 1999 [x ≈ *Norm* (1.3, 1.7)].

- When students take a stats exam on the normal curve, the top 5% score 91% or higher, and the bottom 5% get a score of 59% or lower [x ≈ *Norm* (75, 10)].

Although used for illustration purposes, you should know that many of these variables are not normally distributed. In fact, the variables *years in prison, education, prior arrests,* and *aggressive driving incidents* are highly skewed, and their summary statistics (i.e., means and standard deviations) are strongly affected by extreme scores. For these variables, you could still look at their cumulative frequency distribution and determine the percentile rank for particular values. However, you would not be able to derive meaningful raw scores or percentile ranks from only information about the means and standard deviations because you don't have normal distributions. In short, I use these examples only to illustrate how to do these data transformations. Informed consumers and analysts will first make sure the variable approximates a normal distribution before they do any of these z-score conversions and subsequent estimations of percentile rankings from them.

OTHER SAMPLING DISTRIBUTIONS

The normal probability distribution we have called the *normal curve* is just one of many types of sampling distributions. As a class of distributions, **sampling distributions** are theoretical or hypothetical distributions of all possible outcomes of a test statistic (e.g., means and proportions). Their value for statistical reasoning and inference is that they provide a clear comparative standard from which to make informed statistical claims and to test hypotheses about human behavior.

Aside from the standard normal curve, other examples of sampling distributions widely used in social statistics include the binomial distribution, the t-distribution, the chi-square (χ^2) distribution, and the F-distribution. Their properties and their value for comparative purposes are described below.

Binomial Distribution

One of the most basic sampling distributions involves the **binomial distribution**. The binomial is the distribution of the number of r successes on n trials. It is a probability distribution that takes into account the probability of one of two outcomes (e.g., a success or failure) and the different ways in which these outcomes can occur over a particular number of experimental trials.

The formula for the binomial distribution looks a bit intimidating, but it is relatively easy to apply once it is demonstrated in an example. The basic binomial formula for computing the probability of r successes on N trials is symbolized as

$$P\binom{N}{r} = \frac{N!}{r!(N-r)!}\, p^r (1-p)^{N-r},$$

where $P\binom{N}{r}$ = the probability of r successes on N trials,

$N!/r!(N-r)!$ = the number of distinct ways of getting r successes on N trials,

! = the factorial symbol denoting the successive multiplication of decreasing integers (e.g., $5! = 5 \times 4 \times 3 \times 2 \times 1 = 120$), and

$p^r (1-p)^{N-r}$ = the probability of any given sequence of r successes on N trials.

The binomial is applicable to any situation in which you have two possible outcomes on any given trial (e.g., a success or failure, a "head" or "tail" on the flip of a coin, or a guilty or not guilty verdict) and the outcome of each trial (e.g., each coin flip) is not related (i.e., called *independent events*). You can also apply the binomial formula to any number of trials. However, for large trials ($N > 50$), the binomial distribution closely approximates a normal curve, so just use the normal distribution for comparative purposes instead of the binomial.

To illustrate the logic, terminology, and importance of the binomial distribution, let's assume you just flipped a coin five times. There are six possible outcomes from this experimental trial—that is, you can get 0, 1, 2, 3, 4, or 5 heads. These six outcomes represent your sampling distribution of all possible outcomes from flipping five coins. For any given flip of a fair coin, the probability of getting a head is .50 (i.e., half of the time you will get a head when a fair coin is flipped). This probability of success (i.e., getting a head) on one flip is designated as $p = \frac{1}{2}$ and the probability of "failure" (i.e., getting a tail [not a head]) is designated as $1 - p = \frac{1}{2}$. This is not rocket science here. All we are saying is that if you flip a fair coin, half of the time you'll get a head, and the other half of the time you'll get a tail.

Now, it becomes a bit more complicated when we extend this out to five flips of the coin and figure out the probability of the various outcomes. For example, to figure out the probability of getting five heads (i.e., r successes) on five flips (N trials), you have to compute

1. the number of ways you can get five heads on five flips (symbolized by $N!/[r!(N-r)!] = 5!/[5!(5-5)!] = (5 \times 4 \times 3 \times 2 \times 1) / [(5 \times 4 \times 3 \times 2 \times 1)(1)] = 1 / 1 = 1$; and

2. the probability (p) of each of these independent outcomes (i.e., $p(h,h,h,h,h) = (\frac{1}{2})(\frac{1}{2})(\frac{1}{2})(\frac{1}{2})(\frac{1}{2}) = 1/32$).

Thus, there is only one way to get five heads on five flips, and the probability of getting any particular combination of five heads on five flips is 1 / 32. The result is that the overall probability of getting five heads on five flips is .031 (i.e., one way of getting five of five heads × (1 / 32) = 1 / 32 = .031). About three times out of every 100 trials, you would get five out of five heads if you flipped a fair coin. Not a likely outcome.

To figure out the probability of the remaining outcomes on five flips (i.e., 0, 1, 2, 3, or 4 heads), just plug in the particular values for the binomial expansion. For example, the probability of four heads in five flips is:

$$P(4) = P\binom{N}{r} = \frac{N!}{r!(N-r)!} p^r (1-p)^{N-r}$$

$$P(4) = P\binom{5}{4} = \frac{5!}{4!(5-4)!}\left(\frac{1}{2}\right)^4\left(\frac{1}{2}\right)^1 = \left(\frac{5\times4\times3\times2\times1}{4\times3\times2\times1(1)}\right)\left(\frac{1}{16}\right)\left(\frac{1}{2}\right) =$$

$$P(4) = 5/32 = .156$$

Thus, the probability of getting four heads on five flips of a fair coin is .156, an outcome that would occur a little less than one out of every six times you flipped five coins. The remaining probabilities and calculations for this problem are shown in Table 7.3.

TABLE 7.3   Binomial Distribution for Five Flips of a Fair Coin

Number of Heads (R successes)	Combinations × Probability		Overall Probability of R Successes
	N! / r! (N − r)!	$p^r(1-p)^{N-r}$	
5 Heads	5! / 5! 0! = 1	$(\frac{1}{2})^5(\frac{1}{2})^0 = 1/32$	(1) (1 / 32) = 1 / 32 = .031
4 Heads	5! / 4! 1! = 5	$(\frac{1}{2})^4(\frac{1}{2})^1 = 1/32$	(5) (1 / 32) = 5 / 32 = .156
3 Heads	5! / 3! 2! = 10	$(\frac{1}{2})^3(\frac{1}{2})^2 = 1/32$	(10) (1 / 32) = 10 / 32 = .312
2 Heads	5! / 2! 3! = 10	$(\frac{1}{2})^2(\frac{1}{2})^3 = 1/32$	(10) (1 / 32) = 10 / 32 = .312
1 Head	5! / 1! 4! = 5	$(\frac{1}{2})^1(\frac{1}{2})^4 = 1/32$	(5) (1 / 32) = 5 / 32 = .156
0 Head	5! / 0! 5! = 1	$(\frac{1}{2})^0(\frac{1}{2})^5 = 1/32$	(1) (1 / 32) = 1 / 32 = .031

As shown in Table 7.3, the two most probable outcomes if you flip five fair coins are getting two or three heads. In fact, you should get two or three heads about 62% of the time (i.e., .312 + .312 = .624 ≅ 62%). You should also notice that both zero heads and five heads on five flips are relative rare outcomes for a fair coin (e.g., each happening only about 3% of the time).

For many aspiring statisticians, the binomial distribution provides a nice comparative basis for various research applications because it provides a clear and unequivocal representation of the likelihood of any particular outcome or outcomes. These outcomes are what you expect if you took an extremely large or infinite number of trials, each trial or event is independent (i.e., the first "flip" does not affect the next one), and the presumed probability of any single event is true (i.e., p [head] = ½ = .50 for a toss of a fair coin).

Equipped with the information about this theoretical sampling distribution, the informed consumer or analyst can then collect his or her own data and test these presumptions. For example, if you got five heads on five flips of a "fair" coin, you should have some suspicion about this claim because the sampling distribution under these conditions tells you that such an outcome would occur only about 3% of the time if the coin was fair. The basic core of statistical inferences and hypothesis testing rests on this process of comparing expected outcomes derived from a sampling distribution with observed outcomes, and then deciding whether the data and the claims are consistent. This is why the binomial probability distribution and other sampling distributions are so important.

The tendency for a binomial distribution to approach a normal distribution as the number of observations increases can be easily demonstrated. Figure 7.1 shows the sampling distribution of *r* successes over an increasing number of trials. The probability of success in any given trial

FIGURE 7.1   Binomial Distribution

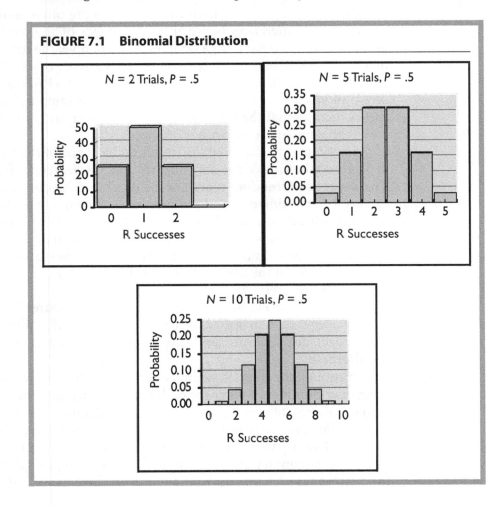

is .5. Even with only two trials (e.g., two flips of a fair coin), the sampling distribution begins to start looking like a normal distribution. The symmetrical and bell-shaped curve is more apparent when the binomial probability distribution is based on repeated trials of $N = 5$ observations and provides a better approximation at $N = 10$ observations. As you might expect based on the progression shown in Figure 7.1, the binomial and normal distributions are virtually indistinguishable at sample sizes of 50 and beyond.

t-Distribution

Closely related to the normal distribution is the **t-distribution**. In fact, the t- and normal distributions converge as the sample size increases. For sample sizes of greater than 50 cases, z-scores are often used instead of t-scores. The differences between the two types of standard scores are minimal when you have large samples. For example, the top 5% of cases in a normal distribution are represented by a z-score of +1.64. The comparable value for a sample size of 50 is a t-score of +1.676 and a t-value of +1.66 when $N = 100$. However, regardless of sample size, statistical theory dictates that the t-distribution is the proper sampling distribution when the population variance is unknown.

In contrast to a normal distribution, the shape of the t-distribution depends on the sample size and, in particular, the degrees of freedom (df). The **degrees of freedom** represent the number of scores that are "free" to vary when estimating a population value. For many of the problems that we will address in subsequent chapters on hypothesis testing and testing the significance of particular parameter estimates, the degrees of freedom will be defined as the number of total observations minus one (i.e., $N - 1$). So, if the sample size is 51, the actual degrees of freedom is equal to 50 (i.e., $51 - 1$).

As shown in Figure 7.2, t-distributions are "flatter" distributions with thicker tails than normal distributions. Within the different t-distributions, the distributions are flatter and thicker-tailed as the sample size (N) decreases.

Although the shape is slightly different, the logic of the idea of sampling distributions is similar for both t- and normal distributions. In particular, t-scores, like z-scores, can be used to identify (1) percentile ranks and (2) the percentage of observations between any two points or more extreme than a particular point. They can also be used to identify extreme and common outcomes within their sampling distribution. Thus, most of what you learned about z-scores fits here as well to explain the purpose and logic of t-scores and their distribution. Specific nuances (e.g., assumptions about equal or unequal variances across groups) with the use of the t-distribution will be described in subsequent chapters.

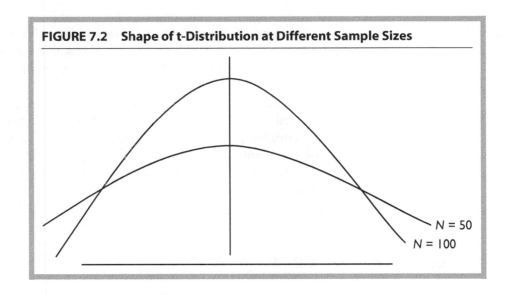

FIGURE 7.2   Shape of t-Distribution at Different Sample Sizes

$N = 50$

$N = 100$

Chi-Square Distribution (χ^2)

Another family of sampling distributions whose shape depends on the degrees of freedom is called the **chi-square distribution** (symbolized χ^2). This distribution is widely used in the case of testing the statistical significance of a relationship between two qualitative variables. Similar to other sampling distributions, chi-square values represent a theoretical and hypothetical distribution of all possible scores under specific assumptions. The particular assumption under the chi-square distribution is that the two variables are not related (i.e., they are independent of each other). These expected values are compared with observed values to make a determination of the feasibility of this claim of independence between the two variables.

The chi-square distribution and properties of this test statistic will be discussed in Chapter 11 within the context of contingency table analyses involving qualitative variables. Similar to t- and z-scores, larger chi-square values represent more extreme values (i.e., exceptional outcomes if the original claim is true).

F-Distributions

The last type of sampling distribution that we will use in this book is the **F-distribution**. This distribution is used in the context of the statistical procedure called *analysis of variance (ANOVA)*. The particular shape of the F-distribution depends on the degrees of freedom in both the numerator and denominator of the ratio of between- and within-group variation. While this may sound strange now, you will discover that the F-distribution is used to compare the relative size of the ratios of between-group and within-group variances.

The F-distribution provides a standard for comparing the components of explained and unexplained variances. Large values of the F-ratio translate into conclusions about statistically significant between-group differences on some outcome variable. I will describe more fully the functions, calculations, and interpretations of the F-distribution in Chapter 12's discussion of the analysis of variance.

SUMMARY OF MAJOR POINTS

- Sampling distributions are theoretical or hypothetical distributions of all possible outcomes of a test statistic (e.g., means or proportions). They are extremely important for purposes of statistical inference and hypothesis testing because they provide a comparative standard from which we can compare expected outcomes and observed outcomes to reach an informed decision about rejecting the claims of others.

- The most widely used and assumed sampling distribution in statistical analysis involves the standard normal probability distribution (i.e., the normal curve).

- The normal curve has many well-known properties. It is a symmetrical, bell-shaped distribution in which a constant proportion of cases fall within given standard deviations from the mean regardless of the particular mean or standard deviation of the variable of primary interest.

- A z-score is a standardized score that adjusts a raw score by its mean and divides it by the standard deviation. Positive z-scores indicate that the observation or person is above the mean, whereas negative z-scores reflect values less than the mean.

- When z-scores are computed for variables that are normally distributed, it is possible to describe the percentile of cases between any two points and the percentile rank for any particular outcome and a more extreme outcome.

- Understanding how to read and interpret the normal curve table in Appendix A is important to be able to convert raw scores to z-scores, z-scores to areas, and areas to percentile ranks.

- The binomial distribution is a sampling distribution of r successes on N trials. It increasingly approximates a normal curve as the sample size (i.e., number of trials) increases. It is a relatively simple sampling distribution to understand, which makes it a good example for illustrating the logic of comparing expected outcomes and observed outcomes to reach conclusions about these expected outcomes.

- Several other sampling distributions (e.g., chi-square, t-distributions, and F-distributions) are also used extensively in statistical analysis. The properties of these sampling distributions and their applications are described in subsequent chapters.

KEY TERMS

Binomial Distribution

Central Limit Theorem

Chi-Square Distribution

Degrees of Freedom

F-Distribution

Normal Probability Distribution

Statistical Inference

t-Distribution

z-Scores

MAJOR FORMULAS AND SYMBOLIC REPRESENTATIONS

Z-Score Transformation: $z = \dfrac{X - \overline{X}}{SD}$

Symbolic Expression of an Approximately Randomly Distributed Variable and Its Mean and Standard Deviation:
$[x \approx Norm\,(\mu, \sigma)]$

Binomial Expansion: $P\dbinom{N}{r} = \dfrac{N!}{r!(N-r)!}\, p^r (1-p)^{N-r}$

APPLYING WHAT YOU HAVE LEARNED

1. Which of the following is a characteristic of a normal curve?

   a. It is unimodal.

   b. It is symmetrical around the mean.

   c. A constant percentage of cases fall within given standard deviations from the mean.

   d. All of the above are true.

2. Z-scores are considered standard scores because they are adjusted to have a mean of 0 and a standard deviation of 1.

   a. True

   b. False

3. If a variable is normally distributed,

   a. 50% of the observations will be less than the mean, and 50% of the observations will be greater than the mean.

   b. about 34.13% of the observations will be between the mean and 1 standard deviation above the mean.

   c. about 34.13% of the observations will be between the mean and 1 standard deviation below the mean.

   d. about 68.26% of the observations will fall within ±1 standard deviation from the mean.

   e. all of the above are true of a normally distributed variable.

4. A negative z-score indicates that

   a. the original raw score on the variable is above its mean.

   b. the original raw score on the variable is below its mean.

   c. an error was made in the calculation of z-scores.

5. The farther away a raw score is from its mean score,

   a. the larger will be its z-score value.

   b. the smaller will be its z-score value.

   c. the closer the z-score will be to 0.

6. The top 5% of cases for a variable that is normally distributed corresponds to a z-score of

   a. +1.96.

   b. +1.64.

   c. −1.96.

   d. −1.64.

   e. We do not know because we do not have enough information.

7. The bottom 5% of cases for a variable that is normally distributed corresponds to a z-score of

   a. +1.96.

   b. +1.64.

   c. −1.96.

   d. −1.64.

   e. We do not know because we do not have enough information.

8. If a variable is normally distributed, 95% of the cases will fall between what two points of this distribution?

   a. $z = \pm 2.33$

   b. $z = \pm 1.96$

   c. $z = \pm 1.64$

   d. $z = \pm 1.28$

9. The shape of the t-distribution

   a. is flatter than the normal distribution.

   b. becomes closer and closer to the shape of a normal distribution when the sample size increases.

   c. depends on the degrees of freedom.

   d. all of the above are true.

   e. only a and b are true.

10. The binomial distribution shows the probability of getting a particular outcome on a given number of trials.

a. True

b. False

11. Why are sampling distributions so important in the process of statistical inference?

12. Assume that the daily arrests for public intoxication in U.S. cities in August are normally distributed with a mean of 108 arrests and a standard deviation of 4 arrests.

   a. What z-score corresponds to a city with 108 arrests?

   b. What z-score corresponds to a city with 112 arrests?

   c. What z-score corresponds to a city with 100 arrests?

   d. What percentage of the cities will have between 108 and 112 arrests?

   e. What percentage of the cities will have between 100 and 108 arrests?

   f. What percentage of the cities will have between 100 and 116 arrests?

   g. What percentage of the cities will have 98 or fewer arrests?

   h. What percentage of the cities will have 118 or more arrests?

   i. How many arrests would represent the top 5% of daily arrests in August?

   j. How many arrests would represent the lowest 5% of daily arrests in August?

   k. How many arrests capture the middle 80% of the daily arrests in August? (*Hint: Middle 80%* implies that 40% of the cases are between the mean and that point below the mean, and 40% of the cases are between the mean and that point above the mean).

13. Given the following information about annual terrorist attacks of U.S. targets [x ≈ *Norm* (31.8, 10.0)], how many attacks would have to occur for a particular year to be in the top 1% of dangerous years?

14. Assume that the success rate for specialized drug courts in the United States is 50% (i.e., one-half of the people in drug court become "drug free," and the other half remain on drugs). Use the

formula for the binomial probability distribution to compute the following probabilities:

a. What is the probability that you would get three rehabilitated drug offenders out of a random sample of five drug court participants?

b. What is the probability that you would get three or more rehabilitated drug offenders out of a random sample of five drug court participants?

c. What is the probability that you would get zero rehabilitated drug offenders out of a random sample of five drug court participants?

d. What is the probability that you would get five rehabilitated drug offenders out of a random sample of five drug court participants?

e. What are the two most unlikely numbers of rehabilitated drug offenders you would get in a random sample of five drug court participants if the success rate is 50%?

15. If the success rate for specialized drug courts was 75% (i.e., $p = 3/4$), what is the probability of getting five successful cases in a random sample of five drug court participants? (*Hint:* Use the expanded binomial formula and insert the value of 3/4 for p and 1/4 for $1 - p$.) ✦

8

Parameter Estimation and Confidence Intervals

According to a survey reported by the Centers for Disease Control and Prevention (CDC 1997), 9% of high school students had carried a weapon to school in the past 30 days.

Can we infer from this finding that about 1 of every 10 high school students in the United States are armed and dangerous while in school?

Given what you have learned in previous chapters, I would hope that most of you would be suspicious about the truth of this statement. By the end of this chapter, you should be able to make an even stronger assertion about the accuracy of this statistical inference.

One of the major goals of **statistical inference** involves the estimation of population parameters. These **population parameters** (symbolized by Greek characters like μ and σ) are unknown values of means, proportions, and standard deviations of some variable in a population (e.g., the percent of U.S. high school students who carry weapons to school). They are really what we want to know in any study. However, because they are unknown, we have to take samples of data to estimate them.

If we have taken totally random samples from a wider population of cases, our sample values will usually provide reasonable estimates of the population values. Under these conditions, we use the **sample statistics** (i.e., $\bar{x}$, p, and s [sd]) as our best guess of their unknown population counterparts (i.e., μ, ρ, and σ) and establish a range of scores around them to increase our confidence in these estimates. This form of statistical inference is called **parameter estimation** and developing **confidence intervals**.

The current chapter describes this process of parameter estimation and developing confidence intervals. It will apply much of what you just learned about theoretical and hypothetical sampling distributions to establish estimates of population values. The logic of parameter estimation and how we develop confidence intervals around estimated population means and population proportions are described below.

SAMPLING DISTRIBUTIONS AND THE LOGIC OF PARAMETER ESTIMATION

To understand the process of parameter estimation, it is crucial that you understand the idea of a **sampling distribution** discussed in the previous chapter. In particular, a sampling distribution is a hypothetical distribution of all possible outcomes of a test statistic. It is derived by taking an infinite number of random samples of a given size, computing the test statistics from each sample (e.g., $\bar{x}$), and repeating this process an infinite number of times.

When these sample statistics from an infinite number of random samples are plotted on a histogram or other frequency-based visual image, the resulting distribution is a sampling distribution. It will cover the entire range of possible outcomes, and this distribution will have a characteristic shape. In particular, the test statistics (e.g., sample means $[\bar{x}]$) will converge around the true mean with some dispersion around this value.

The standard deviation of a sampling distribution is called the *standard error* or, more specifically, the **standard error of the estimate**. It is a measure of sampling error and represents the spread or dispersion of these sample estimates. When applied to the sampling distribution of means, the standard error of these means is given by the following formula:

$$SE_\mu = \sigma / \sqrt{N}$$

You should notice in this formula that the standard error decreases in size as you increase the sample size (N). What this implies is that the sampling distribution of all possible estimates of the population means will be more tightly packed around the true value when the sample size increases. This idea is graphically illustrated in Figure 8.1.

So, what do we know thus far from taking an infinite number of samples of a given size and plotting the means from each sample? Three answers to this question are suggested by the graphic representation of the sampling distributions in Figure 8.1:

- First, the *true* mean (i.e., the actual mean in the population $[\mu]$) may be any value between the lowest and highest value in the distribution (e.g., $\pm\infty$ in hypothetical cases).

- Second, the distribution of sample means converges on this true mean, and they will be normally distributed around it if our sampling distribution involves drawing large random samples of more than 50 observations (i.e. $N > 50$).

- Third, the standard error of the mean reflects the magnitude of dispersion in these sample estimates. Both graphs in Figure 8.1

FIGURE 8.1   Sampling Distributions Based on Sample Size

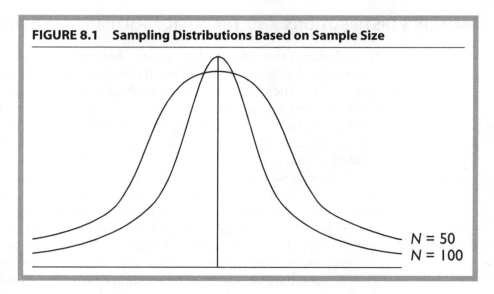

N = 50
N = 100

show the convergence of sample means around the true population mean, but the distribution is more tightly concentrated when
the sample size is larger.

The next step in understanding the logic of statistical inference involves the shape of the sampling distribution and the properties associated with it. In particular, the **Central Limit Theorem** described in the
previous chapter tells us that the sampling distribution of a test statistic
will be normally distributed if we take an infinite number of large random samples. If a variable is normally distributed, we also know that a
fixed proportion of observations will fall within a particular number of
standard deviations above and below the mean. Common intervals of
standard deviations from the mean that are used in statistical inference
include the following:

- About 68% of the observations on a normally distributed variable will fall within ±1 standard deviation from the mean. This is
  symbolized as "$\mu \pm 1\sigma$."

As described in Chapter 7, this value of 68% is found by (1) looking in a normal curve table for a z-score of +1.00; (2) finding the
area that corresponds between the mean and a z-score of +1.00
(in Column B of Appendix A, you will see this area is .3413); (3)
multiplying this area by 100 to express it as a percentage (.3413 ×
100 = 34.13%); (4) remembering that the normal curve is sym-

metrical, so if 34.13% of the observations are between $\mu + 1\sigma$, then 34.13% are between $\mu - 1\sigma$; (5) adding these two percents together (34.13% + 34.13% = 68.26%); and (6) rounding this number to 68%.

- About 90% of the observations on a normally distributed variable will fall within ±1.64 standard deviations from the mean (i.e., $\mu \pm 1.64\sigma$).

- About 95% of the observations on a normally distributed variable will fall within ±1.96 standard deviations from the mean (i.e. $\mu \pm 1.96\sigma$).

- About 98% of the observations on a normally distributed variable will fall within ±2.33 standard deviations from the mean (i.e., $\mu \pm 2.33\sigma$).

- About 99% of the observations on a normally distributed variable will fall within ±2.58 standard deviations from the mean (i.e., $\mu \pm 2.58\sigma$).

The last step in the process of statistical inference involves taking these intervals of standard deviations and using them to develop **confidence intervals**. This step is very easy. For example, if 68% of the cases fall within 1 standard deviation of the mean (i.e., $\mu \pm 1\sigma$), we use this information to make the inference that we are "68% confident that the true value falls somewhere within this interval of $\mu \pm 1\sigma$." Similarly, our 95% **confidence level** corresponds to the interval of $\mu \pm 1.96\sigma$ (i.e., we are 95% confident that the true value falls somewhere within this interval). The same logic applies to developing other confidence levels (e.g., 98% confidence level = $\mu \pm 2.33\sigma$; 99% confidence level = $\mu \pm 2.58\sigma$). In each case, our single best guess of the unknown population value is the sample mean.

INFERENCES FROM SAMPLING DISTRIBUTIONS TO ONE REAL SAMPLE

I don't know what your take has been on the first part of this chapter, but I get the sneaking suspicion that most of you will view everything discussed so far as incredibly obtuse, jargon-ridden, and vague or confusing. Well, I agree. Now, I'm going to try to decode (i.e., "break down") this information into ordinary language. Hopefully, this will demystify this stuff and make more sense.

Everything discussed so far on sampling distributions is hypothetical—it is what would happen if we did this stuff an infinite number of times. Well, we do not take an infinite number of samples and plot these numerous sample values. Instead, we usually just take one sample and compute a couple of summary statistics (e.g., means [$\bar{x}$] and standard deviations [sd]).

The key to statistical inference is to take what we know will happen in the long run (i.e., over an infinite number of trials) and apply this knowledge to our one sample. To make this huge inferential leap from many samples to one sample, however, requires that this one sample be a **random sample** from the wider population. If it is a random sample, we are able to estimate population parameters and develop confidence intervals around them by simply following these basic steps and procedures:

- Draw one random sample from the population.

- Compute the sample means and standard deviations.

- Use the sample mean and standard deviation as the best guess of the population values.

- Figure out the amount of sampling error.

- Bracket the sample value with an interval that shows the likely range of the population value.

It is as easy as that to estimate population values and construct confidence intervals. Unfortunately, this description is a bit too cryptic. Let me just make a few additions and modifications to further specify this process. These clarifications and extensions include the following:

- Draw a *random sample* from the population. If you draw a large random sample ($N > 50$) and the population standard deviation is known, you can use the normal curve for developing a confidence interval. If the population standard deviation is unknown and you have a smaller sample, you will use the t-distribution for these purposes.

- Compute basic *sample statistics* ($\bar{x}$, sd). If you are using the sample standard deviation (sd) to represent the population standard deviation (σ), the formula for the sample sd includes $N - 1$ in the denominator (i.e., $sd = \sqrt{\sum(x-\bar{x})^2 / N-1}$).

- Use your *sample statistics* as your single best estimates of the *population parameters* (i.e., $\bar{x} => \mu$; $sd => \sigma$).

- Compute the *standard error of the estimate*. If the population standard deviation is known, the standard error (SE) is defined by $\sigma / \sqrt{N}$. If the population standard deviation is unknown, estimate the standard error by using the sample standard deviation and sample size (e.g., $SE = sd / \sqrt{N}$).

- Establish a *confidence level* and *confidence interval*. For the normal distribution as the comparative standard, a 95% confidence level corresponds to the interval defined by $\mu \pm 1.96se$ and the 98% confidence level ranges from $\mu \pm 2.33se$. For a t-distribution, the critical values that establish the range of the interval depend on the degrees of freedom. For example, the 95% confidence level for a sample size of 41 (i.e., $N - 1 = 40$ degrees of freedom) is defined by $\mu \pm 2.021se$. The value of ± 2.021 is the t-value for the 95% confidence level at 40 degrees of freedom (see Appendix B for two-tailed test at $\alpha = 0.25$)—these ideas of two-tailed test and α will be discussed fully in Chapter 9).

- Interpret the *confidence interval* by identifying the point estimate (e.g., your single best estimate of the population parameter) and the limits of the interval (i.e., its lowest and highest value) at the specified level of confidence.

It is worth repeating that this whole process of parameter estimation and confidence intervals is predicated on several basic assumptions. First, it assumes that the particular sample used in the analysis is a random sample from the population. If it is not a random sample and/or there is serious sampling bias, this process of statistical inference is basically worthless. Second, sampling error prohibits us from making absolute claims about the likelihood of capturing the true population value. Even though the standard error is an estimate of sampling error, we never know for certain whether our one sample provides statistics that accurately reflect the population values. We can only talk in terms of relative confidence and probabilities in this process of statistical inference.

CONFIDENCE INTERVALS: LARGE SAMPLES, σ KNOWN

The normal curve and z-scores are used in the construction of confidence intervals for a population mean and population proportion when the population standard deviation is known and the sample size is large ($N > 50$). The logic and steps for estimating these different population parameters are summarized below.

Confidence Intervals for Population Means

The basic logic for developing a confidence interval for a population mean has already been described in the last section. Here, I will give several examples to illustrate the computation details, interpretations, and caveats associated with using this particular type of statistical inference.

Executions in U.S. History

As an initial example, let us suppose we are interested in the annual number of executions in American history. Espy and Smylka (1991) have compiled a comprehensive list of 14,634 executions in America from 1608 to 1991.

Rather than analyze data for every year over this long historical period, you decide to select a random sample of 50 years to estimate the average number of U.S. executions per year. Assume that the average annual number of executions in your selected sample was 34.1 ($\overline{x}$ = 34.1). For purposes of this analysis, further assume that we know the population standard deviation, and its value is 47.3 (i.e., σ = 47.3)—this assumption that σ is known will be relaxed when we discuss confidence intervals using t-distribution. Given a large sample (n = 50), we can use the Central Limit Theorem to justify the use of the normal curve to establish the range of the confidence interval. With this information and assumptions, we are ready to develop a confidence interval around the population mean.

The formal statement of the confidence interval for the population mean when you have a large sample and the population standard deviation is known is given by the following formula:

$$\mu \pm Z_{cl}\ SE,$$

where μ = the population mean,
Z_{cl} = the z-scores that correspond to the particular confidence level selected, and
SE = the standard error of the mean, which is calculated as $\sigma / \sqrt{N}$.

The construction of the confidence interval for the population mean for this example of executions involves basically plugging in some numbers and making assumptions. This process includes the following points:

- First, the single best estimate of μ is $\overline{x}$, so the estimated value of the mean annual number of executions is 34.1 ($\overline{x}$ => μ).

- Second, the analyst must decide on what confidence level to use. Let us say we decided on using a 95% confidence level, so our critical z-values that establish the lower and upper limits of the confidence interval are ±1.96.

- Third, an estimate of the standard error of the mean is calculated by using the formula $SE = \sigma / \sqrt{N}$. In this example, the standard error is 6.7 ($47.3 / \sqrt{50} = 6.7$). Plugging in these values results in the following 95% confidence interval:

$$\mu \pm Z_{95\%cl}\ SE = 34.1 \pm 1.96\ (6.7) = 34.1 \pm 13.1 = 21.0\ to\ 47.2$$

It is also possible to use other confidence levels for this problem. For example, the 68% and 80% confidence levels would consist of the following ranges:

$$\mu \pm Z_{68\%cl}\ SE = 34.1 \pm 1\ (6.7) = 34.1 \pm 6.7 = 27.4\ to\ 40.8$$

$$\mu \pm Z_{80\%cl}\ SE = 34.1 \pm 1.28\ (6.7) = 34.1 \pm 8.6 = 25.5\ to\ 42.7$$

So, what does this tell us about U.S. executions? Well, it tells us that our single best guess is that there are an average of 34.1 executions per year. The 95% confidence interval basically says that in 95 out of every 100 random samples, the interval between 21.0 and 47.2 will contain the population mean—that is, we are 95% confident that the population mean, μ, is between 21 and 47.2 executions per year.[1]

When you compare the size of the different confidence intervals, you should notice the relationship between the confidence level and the width of the confidence interval. Specifically, the lowest confidence level (68%) is associated with the narrowest interval, whereas the widest interval is found for the highest confidence level (95%). This choice of how to reach a balance between confidence and precision (i.e., the width of the interval) depends on the particular research question and tradition. For example, the conventional wisdom in many of the social sciences is that a 95% confidence level offers an appropriate balance between these dual concerns of confidence and precision.

Before I leave this example, I want to mention several things about what is called the margin of error. The **margin of error** is what most survey research companies and pollsters refer to as the *fudge factor*. It is also

1. For those of you who are curious about current trends, an average of 64 executions per year were conducted in the United States between the years 2000 and 2005. Our example covers only executions up to 1991, a period of time that on average, appears to have a lower annual volume of executions.

described by Sullivan (2005: 344) as the "give and take" portion of statements like "the mean age of homicide offenders is 24, give or take 3 years." This margin of error (symbolized as E_{marg}) derives from the confidence level and the standard error of the estimate. In the case of large sample confidence intervals for means in which the population standard deviation is known, the margin of error is defined as

$$E_{marg} = Z_{cl} \, (SE) = Z_{cl} \, (\sigma / \sqrt{N})$$

Although the population standard deviation cannot be controlled or minimized (because it is a fixed, given quality), the informed analyst has the ability to minimize the margin of error by altering the other two components in this formula. For example, the error margin may be reduced by (1) decreasing the confidence level (e.g., a 68% confidence level [z = ±1.0] has a smaller error margin than the 95% confidence level [z = ±1.96]) and/or (2) increasing the sample size. The smaller margin of error is one of the primary reasons why it is good practice to select as large of a random sample that is possible in any research project.

Law School Aptitude Test (LSAT)

A primary factor in admission decisions for law school is the student's score on the LSAT. Scores on this test are standardized to range from 120 to 180. Although there are yearly fluctuations in the actual scores, the average LSAT score is around 150 ($\mu = 150$) and the standard deviation is around 10 ($\sigma = 10$).

Suppose you want to estimate the average LSAT score for 2005 by taking a random sample of 200 aspiring law students. You also want to construct a confidence interval that is likely to capture the true mean score on the LSAT for that year.

So, how do you proceed? It is as simple as "painting by the numbers." Just trace the same steps used in the previous example of U.S. executions and do the following:

- Draw a large random sample from the U.S. population. Let us say you selected a random sample of 200 people ($N = 200$) who took the LSAT in 2005.

- Compute the mean LSAT score in this sample ($\bar{x} = 148$) and use this sample mean as your single best guess of the population mean (i.e., $\bar{x} => \mu$).

- Compute the standard error of the estimate by using the formula $SE = \sigma / \sqrt{N}$. In this case, the $SE = 10 / \sqrt{200} = .71$.

- Decide on a confidence level. Let us assume you selected a higher confidence level like 99% to increase the likelihood of capturing the true population value somewhere within your interval. This confidence level translates into a z-score of ±2.58.

- Construct the 99% confidence interval by plugging in the relevant values:

$$\mu \pm Z_{99\%d} \; SE = 148 \pm 2.58 \,(.71) = 148 \pm 1.83 = 146.2 \; to \; 149.8.$$

The last step of this process is to interpret the results. Based on our sample, the single best guess of the average LSAT score in 2005 was 148. We are 99% confident that the true mean score on the LSAT in the population of aspiring law students in 2005 falls roughly between a score of 146 and 150. Got it?

Now, just one quick question: What if you took the LSAT and got a score of 160? What would you conclude? There are at least two possibilities based on the previously computed confidence interval:

- First, you are incredibly bright, a statistical outlier who falls well outside this "normal" range of LSAT takers. This can happen because we are only 99% confident in capturing this true value and you may simply represent that 1% of the time that this does not occur.

- Second, the average LSAT score in 2005 is not 148, but rather something closer to your score of 160.

These two conflicting explanations for your LSAT score of 160 go to the heart of the problem with statistical inference. Specifically, is a rare observation that falls outside of the confidence interval due to (1) random chance alone (i.e., a 99% confidence interval accepts a 1% chance of blowing it—and this is one of these times), or (2) the alleged population mean is wrong based on the sample estimates? If you have drawn a large random sample from this population, statistical theory tells you that 99% of your sample estimates will fall within ±2.58 sd's of the true value—thus giving you this degree of confidence that any weird outcomes would be due to chance alone. Under these conditions, an observed sample estimate that falls outside this interval would lead most analysts to reject the alleged claim about the value of the specific population parameter.

If you ever have serious questions about the accuracy of a sample estimate of a population mean, the best practice is to draw another random sample and see whether you get roughly the same results. However, when it is impractical or impossible to draw another random sample, statistical theory tells you that your sample statistic (e.g., $\bar{x}$) is the best guess of the unknown population parameter (e.g., μ). So, in the absence of any additional information that may question the validity of your sample mean (e.g., it is based on a nonrandom sample, or outliers are included in its computation), the bottom line is that you report the sample mean as your best estimate of the population value and develop a confidence interval that provides some "give and take" around that parameter estimate.

Confidence Intervals for Population Proportions

The logic and procedures to construct a confidence interval around an estimate of a population proportion are identical to the process for confidence intervals around a population mean. The only differences are that we are now talking about proportions or percents (ρ) rather than means (μ), and we use a different computing formula for the standard deviation for a qualitative variable (i.e., $\sigma_\rho = \sqrt{\rho q}$). However, since we are assuming that the population standard deviation is known in this case, the only real practical difference is the symbols ρ's versus μ's. Everything else is the same as before.

One example is sufficient to illustrate how to compute a confidence interval for a population proportion when σ_ρ is known. Let us suppose we want to estimate the proportion of countries in the world that have legally abolished the death penalty. Assume that the population standard deviation of abolitionist countries is known ($\sigma_\rho = .5$). The basic steps involved in estimating the unknown population proportion and developing a confidence interval around this estimate are the same as described in the estimation of confidence intervals for population means. These steps include the following:

- Draw a large random sample of countries. Assume you collected information on the legal status of the death penalty in a sample of 185 countries ($N = 185$).

- Compute the proportion of countries in this sample that have legally abolished capital punishment ($p_{abol} = .47$), and use this sample proportion as your single best guess of the population proportion (i.e. $p_{abol} => \rho_{abol}$).

- Compute the standard error of the estimate by using the formula $SE = \sigma_p / \sqrt{N}$. In this case, the $SE = .5 / \sqrt{185} = .04$.

- Decide on a confidence level. Because you have a large sample and the population variance is known, your confidence level will involve z-scores. You select a 95% confidence level. This confidence level translates into a z-score of ±1.96.

- Construct the 95% confidence interval by plugging in the relevant values:
  $$P_{abol} \pm Z_{95\% ci} \; SE = .47 \pm 1.96\,(.04) = .47 \pm .08 = .39 \; to \; .55$$

- Interpreting this interval reveals that we are 95% confident that the proportion of abolitionist countries ranges somewhere between .39 to .55.

When expressed as percentages, this confidence interval implies that we are 95% certain that the true percentage of countries that have abolished capital punishment is between 39% and 55%. The single best guess is that 47% of the countries have legally abolished the death penalty. The same caveats about the margin of error and making sure you have drawn random samples apply to both confidence intervals for estimating population means and population proportions.

This particular example of capital punishment raises an interesting issue about how the outcomes of estimating population parameters may be selectively interpreted to support one's particular political position. For example, Amnesty International (AI) is a well-known organization that is a strong supporter of the international abolition of the death penalty. If this organization wanted to use the evidence above to support its position, it would focus on the confidence interval because its upper limit implies that a majority of countries (55%) are consistent with AI's political position. This same conclusion would derive from using a 68% confidence level because the upper limit of that interval (i.e., 51%) would still cover the majority of countries. If someone wanted to show that AI's position represents the minority view, they would focus exclusively on the parameter estimate of 47% (i.e., the sample proportion).

Given these different possible conclusions from parameter estimates and confidence intervals, it is important to provide both components in summaries of research findings. In other words, a "fair and unbiased" analyst should present both the single best estimate of the population parameter (i.e., the sample mean or sample proportion) *and* a confidence interval that provides an estimated range around this particular value. This will allow the consumer to make an informed decision about how to interpret this statistical information.

CONFIDENCE INTERVALS: SMALL SAMPLES AND UNKNOWN σ

For most applications in social research, the population standard deviation will be unknown, and constraints of time, energy, access, and money often restrict the size of our samples. Under these conditions, the normal curve and z-scores are not the best basis for establishing the margin of error and confidence intervals around population means or proportions. Instead, the *t-distribution* is used as the comparative standard.

Properties of the t-Distribution

As introduced in Chapter 7, the **t-distribution** is a sampling distribution that increasingly looks like the normal curve as the sample size increases. Its primary difference is that the t-distribution is a flatter distribution with thicker tails, and its actual shape depends on the degrees of freedom (i.e., the number of observations minus one [$N - 1$]). However, it is similar to the normal curve in that raw scores can be converted to standard scores (i.e., t-values). For given degrees of freedom, these standard t-values can also be used to determine the proportion of cases that fall within given standard deviations from its mean. Appendix B shows these boundary scores for the t-distribution that we will ultimately use to develop confidence intervals and test statistical hypotheses.

The t-values in Appendix B are in a different form than the basic normal curve table, but they can be interpreted in a comparable way. Table 8.1 provides an abbreviated version of the t-distribution to show how to interpret this information.

Look at the top row of Table 8.1. The values in this row represent areas of one end (i.e., one-tail) of a t-distribution in which a particular proportion of cases will fall. This is comparable to the information presented in column C of the normal curve table (see Appendix A). In fact, if you find the value of .025 in the first row in Table 8.1 and then read down to the very bottom of this column, you will find the value of 1.96. This value is the same value you get in a normal curve table—it is the value that defines the top 2.5% of the scores (if the z-score or t-score is positive) or the bottom 2.5% (if the z-score or t-score is negative). We will use these different area values in one tail of the distribution in the next several chapters when we test statistical hypotheses. This first row of information is not commonly used when constructing confidence intervals (because most confidence intervals are based on both tails of the distribution of scores, not just one tail of it).

TABLE 8.1   An Abbreviated Table of the t-Distribution

Degrees of Freedom	Selective Areas and Critical Values for t-Distribution					
	One-Tailed Areas:	.10	.05	.025	.01	.005
	Two-Tailed Areas:	.20	.10	.05	.02	.01
10		1.372	1.812	2.228	2.764	3.169
15		1.341	1.753	2.131	2.602	2.947
60		1.296	1.671	2.000	2.390	2.660
120		1.289	1.658	1.980	2.358	2.617
∞		1.282	1.645	1.960	2.326	2.576

For confidence intervals, the crucial information in the t-table begins with the row marked *Two-Tailed Areas*. These areas correspond to what is called the *alpha level* (α). When α is converted to a percent and subtracted from 100, it becomes a confidence level. For example, the two-tailed area of .05 translates into the 95% confidence level (i.e., 100 – % α = 95%). Similarly, a two-tailed area of .02 is equivalent to a 98% confidence level (100 – % α = 98%).

To find the particular t-value that corresponds to a particular confidence level, you need to compute the **degrees of freedom (df)**. For example, if your sample consists of 16 people, you have 15 degrees of freedom ($N - 1 = 16 - 1 = 15df$). If you want a 95% confidence level, the critical values of the t-statistic at 15 df that define this interval are t = ±2.131. If you had a sample size of 121 (i.e., df = 120), the pivotal t-values for constructing the 95% confidence level are t = ±1.98. Note how close these critical t-values are to z-values (z = ±1.96) that define the 95% confidence level when the normal curve is used as the comparative standard. This is why the difference between t- and z-values is largely trivial when you have large samples.

Now that you have a better idea of the t-distribution and its parallels to what we have discussed so far with the normal curve, let's apply this stuff to compute confidence intervals around means and proportions when we have small samples and the population variance is unknown. A couple of examples are described below to illustrate this comparable logic and the interpretation of these estimates of population parameters.

Confidence Intervals for Population Means for Unknown σ

Let us suppose we want to estimate the average gross income of street-level drug dealers. Neither the population mean nor the standard deviation of salaries of these drug dealers is known. Consequently, to estimate these unknown population parameters, we need to draw a random sample from this population and compute sample statistics.

It should come as no surprise to you by now that the logic and procedures that we use to estimate confidence intervals in this case are virtually identical to what we have been doing throughout this chapter. The only differences involve the following:

1. The population standard deviation is unknown, so we have to estimate it from our sample data; and

2. The confidence levels and the subsequent margin of error derive from the t-distribution rather than the normal curve.

The major steps for estimating the average salary of street-level drug dealers and establishing confidence intervals around this parameter estimate are summarized below:

• Draw a random sample of street-level drug dealers in the U.S. population. Obviously, this will not be easy. There is no comprehensive list of drug dealers, and, if you use police records, those who are arrested are probably not representative of all drug dealers. However, for the sake of this example, assume that you could magically draw a random sample and select 61 dealers at random for inclusion in your sample ($N = 61$).

• Compute sample statistics ($\bar{x}$, sd) and use these sample statistics as your single best unbiased estimates of the unknown population parameters ($\bar{x} => \mu$; $sd => \sigma$). Before you compute these sample statistics, make sure that the raw scores (incomes) are approximately normally distributed and that any outliers (e.g., multi-million-dollar street dealers) have been excluded or adjusted for within the sample. Assume that the mean income in the sample is $52,000 ($\bar{x} = \$52,000$) and the standard deviation is $6,000 ($sd = \$6,000$).

• Estimate the standard error of the mean by using the formula $SE = sd / \sqrt{N}$. In this case, the $SE = 6000 / \sqrt{61} = 768.2$. Notice that this formula is different than the one used when the population standard deviation (σ) is known. In the current case, we estimate this population standard deviation by our sample standard deviation (*sd*) and use "*n* – 1" in the denominator for computing *sd* to provide an unbiased estimate of this unknown population parameter.

- Decide on a confidence level. Let us assume you selected a 99% confidence level. At 60 degrees of freedom ($N - 1 = 61 - 1 = 60df$), the critical values to establish the limits of the 99% confidence interval are t = ±2.66. These values are derived from the t-distribution table in Appendix B.

- Construct the 99% confidence interval by plugging in the relevant values:

$$\mu \pm t_{99\%cl, df=60} \quad SE = 52{,}000 \pm 2.66\,(768.2) = 52{,}000 \pm 2043$$
$$= 49{,}957 \; to \; 54{,}043$$

The last step of this process is to interpret the results. Based on our sample, the single best guess of the average income of street-level drug dealers in the United States is $52,000. We are 99% confident that the true average income for these folks falls somewhere between about $50,000 and $54,000.

Before you conclude from this example that drug dealing is a "lucrative job if you can find the work," you should remember the lesson of *GIGO* (garbage in, garbage out). The "garbage in" in this case is that (1) the data is hypothetical, (2) it is basically impossible to get a true random sample of drug dealers even if the data were not hypothetical, and (3) income data is often highly skewed and affected by numerous outliers that make the mean a dubious measure of central tendency. So, do not give up your day job.

The steps described above are basically the process we use to estimate population parameters and construct confidence intervals. If we wanted to use a different confidence level (e.g., 95%, 90%), the only thing you need to do is to find the critical values of the t-statistic that represent these confidence levels. These values are available for your discovery in Appendix B of this book.

Confidence Intervals for Population Proportions for Unknown σ

By now, you are a seasoned veteran on how to do confidence intervals. The last modification of this same basic theme involves the situation in which you are estimating an unknown population proportion and you do not have a clue about its value or its standard deviation. This will be easy now that you have gotten the basic ideas.

As an example, suppose you are a campaign manager for a person running for the job of sheriff. You want to know the approval rating for your candidate. An obvious and common strategy for estimating this approval rating is to draw a random sample of voters and ask them whether they approve or disapprove of your boss. In other words, you are trying to get an estimate of the true proportion of voters who like your candidate.

To place this problem within the context of confidence intervals around an unknown population proportion, let's just follow the same steps that we have been using throughout the chapter. Here are these steps for the last time, with some slight modification because we are dealing with proportions rather than means:

- Draw a random sample of voters in the population. Assume that you have a list of all voters in your jurisdiction and you randomly selected 41 voters for your sample ($N = 41$).

- Compute sample statistics (p_{app}, sd) and use these sample statistics as your single best unbiased estimates of the unknown population parameters ($p_{app} => P_{app}$; $sd => \sigma$). Assume that the proportion of voters in the sample that approved of your candidate was .20 ($p_{app} = .20$) and the sample standard deviation is .4 ($sd = \sqrt{pq} = \sqrt{(.2)(.8)} = .4$).

- Estimate the standard error of a proportion by using the formula $SE = sd / \sqrt{N}$. In this case, the $SE = .4 / \sqrt{41} = .06$.

- Decide on a confidence level. Let's assume you selected a 90% confidence level. At 40 degrees of freedom ($N - 1 = 41 - 1 = 40df$), the critical values to establish the limits of the 90% confidence interval are t = ±1.684. These values are derived from the t-distribution table in Appendix B.

- Construct the 90% confidence interval by plugging in the above values:
  $$p_{app} \pm t_{90\%cl,df=40} \ SE = .20 \pm 1.684\,(.06) = .20 \pm .10 = .10 \ to \ .30$$

The final step of this process is to interpret the results. Based on our sample, the single best guess of the proportion of voters who approve of your candidate is .20 (i.e., 20%). We are 90% confident that the true approval proportion among all voters falls somewhere between .10 and .30 (i.e., 10% to 30%). The bottom line in this case: I personally would start looking for another job—your boss is not being warmly received by voters. Regardless of what confidence level you use, your boss's political career seems to be in the toilet.

SUMMARY OF MAJOR POINTS

- A crucial aspect of statistical inference involves the estimation of population parameters and establishing confidence intervals around these parameter estimates.

- To estimate unknown population parameters, it is necessary to draw a random sample from this population. If you have a random sample from this population, sample statistics can be used to provide reasonable estimates of their corresponding population values.

- Whenever using sample statistics to represent population parameters, there is always a possibility of sampling error. The likelihood of sampling error is reduced by taking large random samples.

- When large samples are used (i.e., $N > 50$) and the population standard deviation is known, confidence intervals for population means and population proportions are computed using z-scores from the normal probability distribution to establish the lower and upper limits of the confidence interval.

- When the population standard deviation is unknown, confidence intervals for population means and proportions are computed using t-scores from the t-distribution to establish the lower and upper limits of the confidence interval.

- The analyst decides on the confidence level to use for a given substantive problem. Commonly used confidence levels in social science research include 68%, 90%, 95%, and 98% confidence levels.

- The margin of error is a measure of the "give and take" surrounding a parameter estimate. It is affected by the (1) standard deviation, (2) sample size, and (3) confidence level. Increasing the sample size and decreasing the confidence level are ways of reducing the margin of error.

- As is true of other statistical computations, the process of statistical inference involving parameter estimation and confidence intervals is also susceptible to the "garbage in, garbage out" syndrome.

KEY TERMS

Central Limit Theorem

Confidence Intervals

Confidence Level

Degrees of Freedom

Margin of Error

Parameter Estimation

Population Parameters

Random Samples

Sample Statistics

Sampling Distribution

Standard Error of the Estimate

Statistical Inference

t-Distributions

MAJOR FORMULAS

Confidence Interval for a Population Mean (population standard deviation is known and large samples):

$$\mu \pm Z_{cl}\ SE$$

Confidence Interval for Population Proportion (population standard deviation is known and large samples):

$$P \pm Z_{cl}\ SE$$

Confidence Interval for a Population Mean (population standard deviation is unknown and small samples):

$$\mu \pm t_{cl,df}\ SE$$

Confidence Interval for Population Proportion (population standard deviation is unknown and small samples):

$$P \pm t_{cl,df}\ SE$$

Margin of Error (large samples):

$$E_{marg} = Z_{cl}\ (\sigma / \sqrt{N})$$

APPLYING WHAT YOU HAVE LEARNED

1. The process of estimating population values from sample statistics is called

    a. operationalization.

    b. measurement.

    c. statistical inference.

    d. neo-populationism.

2. A necessary requirement for statistical inference is that you have drawn a random sample from the population of cases.

    a. True

    b. False

3. Our best guess of unknown population parameters is their corresponding

    a. sample statistics.

    b. sampling distribution.

    c. degrees of freedom.

    d. standard error.

4. The general logic of parameter estimation and developing confidence intervals is similar for

    a. estimating population means and proportions.

    b. situations in which the population standard deviation is known or unknown.

    c. large sample and small sample applications.

    d. all of the above are true.

    e. only a and b are true.

5. When you have a large sample and the population standard deviation (σ) is known, the 95% confidence level is represented by a

    a. z-score of ±1.28.

    b. z-score of ±1.64.

    c. z-score of ±1.96.

    d. t-score of ±1.98.

6. The standard error of an estimate (like a mean or proportion) is a measure of sampling error.

a. True

b. False

7. The margin of error in a confidence interval is affected by

a. the size of the standard deviation.

b. the size of the sample.

c. the confidence level selected.

d. all of the above are true.

8. If a researcher draws a large random sample from a population, the confidence interval will always contain the true population value.

a. True

b. False

9. Assume that police officials in a city claim that only 10% of the residential population have been victims of police harassment. However, you draw a random sample of 300 residents in this city and find that 50% of them say they have been harassed by police. Which of the following factors may account for the discrepancy between the assumed population parameter and your sample statistic?

a. You have drawn a random sample that by chance alone has given you a bad estimate of the population value.

b. You have sampling bias that may have been caused by using outdated lists of residents or only selecting a random sample from people who have registered a complaint against the police department.

c. The alleged claim that only 10% of residents have been harassed by police is not accurate.

d. All of the above are true.

e. Only a and b are true.

10. When figuring out the t-value for a given level of confidence, a sample size of 24 will be associated with how many degrees of freedom?

a. 24

b. 25

c. 23

d. 48

Here are some questions that require written answers and computations.

11. Why is the selection of a random sample from the population so important for making statistical inferences about population parameters and developing confidence intervals?

12. Why do you want large sample sizes for purposes of statistical inference?

13. Assume that you have a random sample of 61 U.S. cities and you know the population standard deviation for homicide rates is 1.2. The mean homicide rate in your sample is 6.8 per 100,000.

   a. What is your single best guess of the average homicide rate in all U.S. cities?

   b. Construct and interpret the 68% confidence interval for the average homicide rate for U.S. cities.

   c. Construct and interpret the 90% confidence interval for the average homicide rate for U.S. cities.

   d. Construct and interpret the 95% confidence interval for the average homicide rate for U.S. cities.

   e. Construct and interpret the 99% confidence interval for the average homicide rate for U.S. cities.

   f. What effect does increasing the confidence level from 68% to 99% have on the width and/or precision of your confidence intervals?

14. Now, assume that you have the same random sample of 61 U.S. cities but you do not know the population standard deviation for homicide rates. The mean homicide rate in your sample is 6.8 per 100,000. The sample standard deviation is 1.2.

   a. What is your single best guess of the average homicide rate in all U.S. cities?

   b. Construct and interpret the 90% confidence interval for the average homicide rate for U.S. cities.

   c. Construct and interpret the 95% confidence interval for the average homicide rate for U.S. cities.

d. Construct and interpret the 99% confidence interval for the average homicide rate for U.S. cities.

15. You draw a small random sample of 15 people to estimate the proportion of adult Americans who report having engaged in drunk driving. The proportion of people in your sample who said they had been a "drunk driver" was .30 (i.e., 30%). The sample standard deviation is .46.

   a. What is your single best guess of the proportion of adult Americans who have driven while drunk?

   b. Construct and interpret the 95% confidence interval for the proportion of drunk drivers among adult Americans.

   c. Construct and interpret the 90% confidence interval for the proportion of drunk drivers among adult Americans.

   d. What are some of the things you need to think about before you reach any substantive conclusion about the level of drunk driving among adult Americans? ✦

9

Introduction to Hypothesis Testing

Criminal trials in the United States are based on the "presumption of innocence" (i.e., the defendant is considered innocent until proven guilty). The prosecutor presents testimony and physical evidence to challenge this presumption. Defense attorneys counter the claims of the prosecution. The judge or jury then reaches a decision to convict or acquit the defendant. Their verdict should be based on the "beyond the reasonable doubt" legal standard or decision rule. When justice is served, guilty people are punished and innocent people go free. However, errors occur in criminal trials because some guilty people are acquitted and some innocent people are found guilty.

The process of reaching a verdict in criminal trials is virtually identical to what researchers do when testing statistical hypotheses. These parallels are summarized below:

- The initial claim (the presumption of innocence) is what statisticians call the **null hypothesis**.

- The assertion of the defendant's guilt made by the prosecution is called the **alternative hypothesis**.

- The "reasonable doubt" decision rule is conceptually similar to the ideas of significance levels, critical values, and zones of rejection in the testing of statistical hypotheses.

- Correct decisions in both criminal trials and statistics involve acquitting the innocent (i.e., accepting true null hypotheses) and convicting guilty people (i.e., rejecting false null hypotheses).

- Errors in verdicts that result in convicting innocent people or acquitting guilty people are what statisticians refer to as making a **Type I** or **Type II error**.

Similar to the criminal trial, the goal of hypothesis testing is to make reasonable inferences about the accuracy of various truth claims. In this type of statistical inference, someone makes a claim about a "fact" of

151

life, and we then collect and analyze a sample of data to evaluate this claim. After setting up some decision rules and analyzing the data, a substantive conclusion is reached about whether to reject or not reject the original claim. This is the essence of the process of hypothesis testing.

This chapter describes the general logic and procedures in testing statistical hypotheses. It begins by noting the common features of hypothesis testing and other types of statistical inference (e.g., parameter estimation and confidence intervals). Basic terminology is presented to provide the general ideas of hypothesis testing. We will start slowly in this chapter by trying to convey the "big picture" rather than the particular computational details. Chapter 10 extends these basic ideas to demonstrate how formal statistical tests of hypotheses about population means and proportions are actually conducted.

CONFIDENCE INTERVALS VERSUS HYPOTHESIS TESTING

Many concepts and ideas you just learned about in confidence intervals apply to hypothesis testing. You compute sample statistics in both cases (e.g., $\bar{x}$, sd, and p), sampling distributions are used to establish critical values and limits (e.g., z-score of $\pm 1.96se$ = 95% confidence level, or 5% error rate), and both procedures assume that you have a random sample(s) from the population.

Although similar in many respects, there is one crucial difference between the two forms of statistical inference. This difference involves assumptions about whether the population parameter(s) are unknown (i.e., something that needs to be estimated from sample data) or presumed to be true. In particular, confidence intervals are formed around unknown population parameters that are estimated with sample data. Hypothesis testing, in contrast, involves an evaluation of claims about population parameters that we basically assume to be true. Under this assumption that the hypothesized value is true, a sampling distribution is theoretically constructed, and then we use sample data to evaluate whether or not this claimed value makes sense.

This difference between confidence intervals and hypothesis testing, however, becomes largely moot when we assume that our known sample statistic (e.g., $\bar{x}$) is the best estimate of our unknown population parameter. In this case, the presumed population parameter around which confidence intervals are constructed has the same value as the alleged claim in hypothesis testing. When a bracket (i.e., *margin of error*) is placed around this hypothesized value, the substantive outcomes of these two procedures are identical.

This description is a bit abstract, so let's look at a basic example to illustrate these ideas. Assume you flipped 100 coins. How many heads would you expect? Most of you answered, "50 heads," right? Well, let's show how this problem would be addressed by the dual methods of constructing confidence intervals and hypothesis testing.

As outlined in the previous chapter, the first steps in developing confidence intervals are selecting a random sample and calculating the sample statistics. Let's assume in our sample we got 50 heads on 100 flips (i.e., $p = .50$ or 50%). Next, we use the sample standard deviation to estimate the standard error ($se = sd / \sqrt{N} = \sqrt{pq / N} = \sqrt{(.5)(.5)/100} = .05$) and select a confidence level. Using a 95% confidence level, this interval ranges from 40% to 60% ($p \pm 1.98se = .40$ to $.60 = 40\%$ to 60%).[1] Thus, this interval tells us that we are 95% confident that the true percent of heads falls somewhere between 40% and 60%.

In hypothesis testing, we start with the assumption that the coin toss is fair ($P_{head} = .50$). Next, we draw out the implications of this assumption through the construction of a sampling distribution of all possible outcomes of an infinite number of flips of 100 coins. This sampling distribution is developed under the assumption that the original claim is true ($P_{head} = .50$). We then estimate the sampling error, using the same formula for constructing confidence intervals (i.e., $se = sd / \sqrt{N} = \sqrt{pq / N} = \sqrt{(.5)(.5)/100} = .05$). If we were now to put a 95% confidence interval around the hypothesized value of .50, we would get the same confidence interval as computed above (i.e., $p \pm 1.98se = .40$ to $.60 = 40\%$ to 60%) Thus, the numbers used in the computations of a confidence interval and hypothesis testing are identical.

Rather than focusing on a particular confidence level (e.g., 95 or 90%), hypothesis testing is based on the probabilities of scores falling outside this interval. This area outside the range of a confidence interval in hypothesis testing is called the **critical region** or **zone of rejection**. When a sample value falls in this critical region, the researcher will reject the original claim (called the **null hypothesis**) in favor of an alternative claim (called the **alternative hypothesis**). Having a sample value fall in

---

1. The t-value of ±1.98 is the critical value of your test at 99 degrees of freedom for a 95% confidence level (or, equivalently, an alpha level of .05 for a two-tailed test). See Appendix B for the critical values for a t-distribution.

the rejection zone or outside the boundaries of a confidence interval is virtually the same thing.[2]

So, here is the basic difference between confidence intervals and hypothesis testing. Confidence intervals focus on estimating the values within an interval of confidence, whereas hypothesis testing places primary importance on whether sample values fall outside that range around the hypothesized value. If our sample value falls within the area defined by a confidence interval, we reach the statistical decision not to reject the hypothesized value. If our sample values fall outside the range of this interval (i.e., they fall in the zone of rejection), we will reject the hypothesized claim.

Although these two types of statistical inference are considered distinct approaches, you can also view the differences between confidence intervals and hypothesis testing as somewhat akin to the "old wine in a new bottle" syndrome. Everything that can be done through confidence intervals (old wine) can also be done through hypothesis testing (new bottle). However, you need to understand the logic of hypothesis testing because it is somewhat more elegant in its demonstration of what is actually being done when you evaluate various "truth" claims. In other words, it is prettier-looking wine in the new bottle, and presentation does matter among informed users and consumers of statistical information.

BASIC TERMINOLOGY AND SYMBOLS

Before the excursion into types of hypothesis testing in Chapter 10, some basic terminology and symbols need to be introduced. The concepts of null and alternative hypotheses, zones of rejection and critical values, and types of errors in decision making are described below.

Types of Hypotheses

Two basic types of hypotheses underlie research in criminology and all other substantive areas: the **null hypothesis** (symbolized as "H_o") and the **alternative hypothesis** (symbolized as "H_a"). We use sample data to

---

2. As will be discussed shortly, there is also a direct parallel between the confidence level and the idea of an error rate in hypothesis testing. This error rate is called various names in hypothesis testing, including the *alpha level* (α), the *significance level of the test*, and/or the *probability of committing a Type I error*. When the alpha level is expressed as a percentage, alpha can be derived from the confidence level by using the following formula: $\alpha = 1 -$ confidence level.

test the null hypothesis and apply decision rules to decide whether or not to reject this hypothesis in favor of the alternative hypothesis.

The null hypothesis is a statement about a population parameter or parameters. This statement may involve one or more population means (μ), population proportions (p), or any other population parameter (e.g., the population correlation coefficient [ρ]). Whatever their particular value or values, the null hypothesis is the claim that someone makes that you assume to be true. In our opening example of criminal trials, the presumption of innocence is the null hypothesis.

To get some idea of how words translate into symbolic representations of a null hypothesis, consider the following examples:

- The average income in the United States is \$32,500. → H_o: $\mu_i = \$32,500$

- The average U.S. education is 12.3 years. → H_o: $\mu_{ed} = 12.3$

- The average arrests for sex offenders is 6.3. → H_o: $\mu_{arrests} = 6.3$

- The average annual number of executions across all countries is 4,534. → H_o: $\mu_{ex} = 4,534$

- The proportion of people who smoke marijuana is 20%. → H_o: $P_s = .20$

- The percent of drivers with a traffic violation is 60%. → H_o: $P_{tv} = .60$

- The percent of students who fail stats courses is 15%. → H_o: $P_f = .15$

- Sex differences in length of prison terms → H_o: $\mu_m - \mu_f = 0 \Leftrightarrow \mu_m = \mu_f$

- Racial differences in prior arrests → H_o: $\mu_{blk} - \mu_{white} = 0 \Leftrightarrow \mu_b = \mu_w$

- Differences between developed and developing countries in their average crime rates → H_o: $\mu_{dev} - \mu_{deving} = 0 \Leftrightarrow \mu_{dev} = \mu_{deving}$

- Gender differences in gun ownership (yes/no) → H_o: $P_m - P_f = 0 \Leftrightarrow P_m = P_f$

- Racial differences in whether or not a driver is ticketed when stopped by the police → H_o: $P_b - P_w = 0 \Leftrightarrow P_b = P_w$

- Differences between teens and adults in approval of premarital sex → H_o: $P_{teen} - P_{adult} = 0 \Leftrightarrow P_{teen} = P_{adult}$

Notice that null hypotheses about group differences in means or proportions are stated with a value = 0. This implies that the means or proportions for each group are identical—that is, the only way you can get a difference of 0 is when the values for each group are the same (e.g., if the mean income for males is $32,000, the mean income for females must also be $32,000 for $\mu_m - \mu_f = 0$). Thus, null hypotheses about differences in means or proportions can be expressed as differences that equal the value of 0 (e.g., $H_o: \mu_m - \mu_f = 0$) or as a direct equality (e.g., $H_o: \mu_m = \mu_f$). These are identical expressions of the same thing (i.e., the group means are identical).

From the standpoint of statistical inference, the null hypothesis is the proverbial "top dog" and/or center of the cosmic universe. Everything we do in hypothesis testing derives from the basic assumption that the null hypothesis is true. This includes the establishment of a sampling distribution and the development of a range of likely sample outcomes under this presumption. In the language of the street, we "throw down" the H_o as truth, establish its "turf," and then rivals come along and challenge that "rep." The rivals are the alternative hypotheses (H_a). The *rep* of the H_o is challenged by testing it through the collection and analysis of a random sample of data. OK, I'm not hip, but hopefully you get the point.

In contrast to the H_o that we assume to be true, the alternative hypothesis (H_a) represents what we really expect to find based on theory, existing research, and/or common sense. For example, in a patriarchal and/or sexist society, do you really expect men and women to have the same number of arrests over their criminal careers? The null hypothesis says, "Yes" (i.e., $H_o: \mu_m = \mu_f$), but most people would really expect to find gender differences in this context. In fact, depending on your own ideological bias or theoretical position, there are three possible alternative hypotheses in this example:

1. Men have more arrests than women ($H_a: \mu_m > \mu_f$),

2. Women have more arrests than men ($H_a: \mu_m < \mu_f$), or

3. We do not know who has more arrests, but we nevertheless expect to find a gender difference ($H_a: \mu_m \neq \mu_f$).

Each of these forms of the alternative hypothesis (i.e., <, >, and ≠) is possible for any substantive problem.

Because it is the expected outcome from theory and prior research, the alternative hypothesis is also called the *substantive* or *research hypothesis* in many disciplines. It is also sometimes symbolized numerically (e.g., H_1). Regardless of its particular name or symbolic form, the alternative hypothesis is always the expected outcome. The formal logic of hypothesis testing dictates that we actually test the null hypothesis and then decide on the basis of sample data whether or not to reject or not reject this claim (H_o) in favor of our alternative expectation (H_a).

Zone of Rejection and Critical Values

When we test the null hypothesis with real data, we have to establish a decision rule. This decision rule defines in advance of our actual statistical test what constitutes rare or common outcomes if the null hypothesis is true. For example, if we want to evaluate the null hypothesis that a coin flip is fair, we have to decide how many heads we would have to get in 100 flips to reject this claim. Possible answers may be more than 80 heads or fewer than 20 heads. Under this rule, we decided to reject the H_o about a fair coin when the number of heads falls outside this range of 20 to 80 heads. In the language of statistics, you have established *critical values* (i.e., ≤ 20 and ≥ 80) that define the *zone of rejection* for the evaluation of the null hypothesis.

The **zone of rejection** is not nearly as ominous as the name implies. Instead, it simply refers to the range of sample outcomes that are going to lead you to reject the claim underlying the null hypothesis. More technically, this rejection zone is an area on a standardized distribution (e.g., normal curve, t-distribution) that defines a "rare" outcome if the null hypothesis is true. The **critical value(s)** refers to the particular point(s) that define the beginning boundary or boundaries of this zone of rejection.

The nature and size of the zone of rejection (also called the *critical region* of a test statistic) depend on three factors. These three factors include the following:

- The type of sampling distribution (e.g., normal curve, t-, χ^2, and F-distributions). The critical values that define the range of "rare" outcomes under the H_o depend on the particular type of standardized comparative distribution utilized when raw scores are converted into standard scores.

- The nature of the alternative hypothesis (H_a). If H_a specifies that the expected value is less than the hypothesized value (e.g., H_a: $P_{heads} < .50$), then you have only one area of rejection that falls in the lower tail of the distribution. If H_a specifies that the expected value is more than the hypothesized value (e.g., H_a: $P_{heads} > .50$), then you have only one area of rejection that falls in the upper (right) tail of the distribution. This is called a **one-tailed test**. However, if H_a is nondirectional (e.g., H_a specifies that the expected value is not equal to the hypothesized value [e.g., H_a: $P_{heads} \neq .50$]), then you have two rejection zones. One of these zones is in the upper tail of the distribution and the other is in the lower tail in these **two-tailed tests**.

- The total area covered by the zone of rejection is based on the **significance level** or the **alpha level** of your test. This alpha level (α) is defined by the total area of this rejection zone.

Significance Levels and Errors in Decision Making

Before testing a null hypothesis with sample data, the research analyst must make two decisions. First, previous research and theory are used to decide on the nature of the alternative hypothesis. As just mentioned, your three options here are deciding that the expected value (H_a) is not equal to, greater than, or less than the value specified in the null hypothesis (H_o). Second, the analyst must decide on what is a rare outcome if the null hypothesis is true. These rare outcome(s) are those that have a low probability of occurring by chance alone if the null hypothesis is true.

Several interchangeable terms are used to describe these rare outcomes, including the statistical test's *significance level, alpha value* (α), and the probability of making a *Type I error*. In each of these cases, we are talking about sample outcomes that have such a low probability of occurrence that the null hypothesis can be rejected with confidence. A big difference between an observed sample outcome and the hypothesized value is considered statistically *significant* because it casts doubt on the accuracy of the null hypothesis. This is the primary reason why the alpha value (α) of a test is also called its **significance level**.

Conventional significance levels in criminological research include alpha values of .01 and .05, meaning that in 1 time out of 100 or 5 times out of 100, you are willing to live with the possibility of making the incorrect decision of rejecting a true hypothesis. Symbolically, these significance levels are expressed as $\alpha = .01$ and $\alpha = .05$, respectively.

Within this realm of hypothesis testing, there are strong links among the concepts of null and alternative hypotheses, sampling distributions and standardized scores (e.g., z- and t-scores), critical value(s), zone(s) of rejection, significance levels/alpha values, and statistical inferences. The nature of interconnections among these concepts is graphically illustrated in Figure 9.1 and summarized by the following observations:

- Critical value(s) establish the beginning boundaries for the zone(s) of rejection. Two critical values (e.g., z = ±1.96) and zones of rejection are present when the alternative hypothesis (H_a) is non-directional (Panel A in Figure 9.1). One critical value (e.g., z = +1.64) and rejection zone is present when the alternative hypothesis (H_a) is directional (Panel B in Figure 9.1). These critical value(s) are expressed as standard scores (i.e., t- or z-scores). They are z-scores when the sample(s) are large ($N > 50$), whereas t-scores are the standard scores in small sample applications.

- The significance level or alpha value ($\alpha = .05$ in Figure 9.1) is established by the research analyst and represents the combined probability of the areas defined by the zone(s) of rejection. If the H_o is true and a large random sample is used, there is only a 5% probability of getting a standard z-score more extreme than ±1.96. In Panel A, this 5% probability is found by summing the probabilities in each tail of the normal distribution (i.e., .025 + .025 = .05 → 5%). Under the alternative hypothesis in Panel B, there is a 5% probability of getting a standard z-score more extreme than +1.64 if the H_o is true. These critical value(s) that are associated with particular alpha levels are derived from column C of the normal curve table in Appendix A.[3]

- Hypothesis testing involves the selection of random sample(s) and the computation of sample statistics to evaluate the presumed accuracy of the hypothesized population values. Convert these sample statistics into standard scores (e.g., z- or t-scores).

- Compare the obtained standard score from the sample with the critical value expected at the predetermined alpha level. If the obtained value falls in the zone of rejection, it exceeds the critical value established by the H_a and the α level.

- Decide whether to reject or not reject the H_o. In Panel A of Figure 9.1, observed z-scores more extreme than ±1.96 will lead to the rejection of the null hypothesis (H_o). In Panel B, observed z-scores greater than +1.64 will serve as the basis for rejecting the null hypothesis. All other values will lead to the retention of the null hypothesis (i.e., the failure to reject H_o).

---

3. If this stuff sounds like a foreign language to you, you should probably go back to Chapter 6 and reread the sections on z-scores and converting z-scores to percentiles.

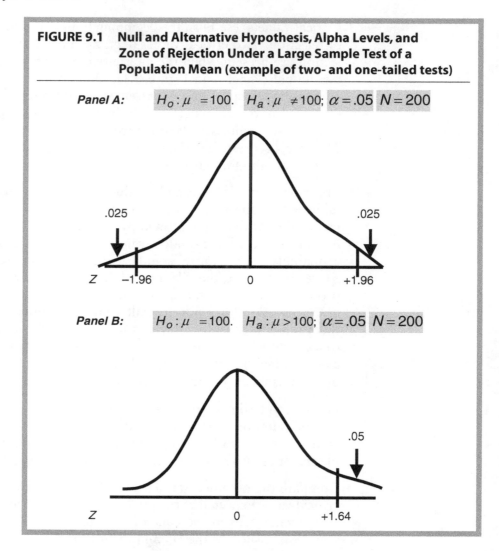

FIGURE 9.1 Null and Alternative Hypothesis, Alpha Levels, and Zone of Rejection Under a Large Sample Test of a Population Mean (example of two- and one-tailed tests)

Panel A: $H_o : \mu = 100.$ $H_a : \mu \neq 100;$ $\alpha = .05$ $N = 200$

.025   .025

Z -1.96 0 $+1.96$

Panel B: $H_o : \mu = 100.$ $H_a : \mu > 100;$ $\alpha = .05$ $N = 200$

.05

Z 0 $+1.64$

When testing statistical hypotheses, sample data is used to estimate population parameters. However, because of sampling error, there is always a chance that our decisions based on a sample may not accurately represent the true state of affairs in the population. As illustrated in the example of criminal trials, we reach a correct decision when guilty people are convicted and innocent people are exonerated. Unfortunately, our decisions are faulty when innocent people are judged to be guilty and guilty people are considered innocent. These four different outcomes, involving the true state of nature or reality, and our decisions about this reality, are summarized in Table 9.1.

As shown in Table 9.1, there are two fundamental errors that are possible when testing statistical hypotheses. These are identified as Type I error and Type II error.

A **Type I error** occurs when we have inadvertently rejected a true null hypothesis. If the null hypothesis in criminal trials is that the person is innocent, we have committed a Type I error when we convict an innocent person. The probability of making this type of error is established by the significance level or alpha value (α) of the test. For example, an alpha value of .01 means that 1 time out every 100, we are willing to make a Type I error of rejecting a true null hypothesis.

TABLE 9.1	Decision Making About Null Hypotheses and Types of Inference Errors (Type I versus Type II error)	
Our Decision	**Actual State in Nature and Reality**	**The Consequences of Our Decision**
Retain H_o	H_o is true.	Correct decision
Reject H_o	H_o is true.	Type I error (α)
Reject H_o	H_o is false.	Correct decision
Retain H_o	H_o is false.	Type II error (β)

A **Type II error** (symbolized as β [beta]) involves situations of retaining or not rejecting a false null hypothesis. A criminal verdict that leads to the acquittal of guilty people is an example of a Type II error.

Although it makes sense that researchers would want to minimize both types of error, the problem is that these errors are interrelated. In particular, efforts to minimize Type I error (by using an extremely small alpha level [e.g., $\alpha = .001$]) will increase the risks of a Type II error and vice versa. For example, increasing the burden of proof requirement to a level of near certainty (rather than "beyond a reasonable doubt") will dramatically reduce the likelihood of innocent people being convicted (Type I error). However, this same decision rule will increase the chances of guilty people being acquitted (Type II error). As balancing points between these two types of errors, conventional practices in the social sciences often involve setting the significance level of a hypothesis test at an alpha value of either .01 and .05.

The analyst's choice of a significance level in hypothesis testing ultimately depends on the relative gravity of making either type of error. In criminal trials, what is the worse of the two evils: executing an innocent person (Type I error) or letting a murderer go free (Type II error)? Our legal standard of "beyond a reasonable doubt" suggests that we place more emphasis on minimizing the risks of a Type I error. However, in other situations, making a Type II error may be the worse case scenario (e.g., letting a serial killer go free), so we weaken the burden of proof standards and thus increase the risks of committing a Type I error by executing innocent people.

These decision-making errors are found in all applications of statistical inference. Although the analyst may choose to minimize one type of error (e.g., by using .01 rather than .05 alpha level to reduce the risks of a Type I error), it is technically impossible to eliminate both of them at the same time. The choice of the significance level of one's test should be based on sound logic and a clear recognition of the relative dangers of committing either Type I or Type II errors in the particular substantive area within criminology and criminal justice.

SUMMARY OF MAJOR POINTS

- Hypothesis testing involves the use of sample data to evaluate claims about population parameters. It is done in research for purposes of statistical inference.

- The null hypothesis (H_o) is a claim about population means or population proportions that is tested with a random sample of data.

- The alternative hypothesis (H_a) is also called the research hypothesis or the substantive hypothesis. It represents what we really expect to find about the population parameter(s) based on existing theory, previous research, and/or logical reasoning. The H_a may be nondirectional (e.g., H_a: $\mu_1 \neq \mu_2$) or directional (e.g., H_a: $\mu_1 > \mu_2$; H_a: $\mu_1 < \mu_2$), depending upon what outcome is expected.

- Sampling distributions are used in hypothesis testing to determine the distribution of all possible outcomes of a test statistic under the assumption that the null hypothesis is true. Under this assumption, sample estimates of the population value specified in the null hypothesis will converge on that hypothesized population value, and a fixed proportion of them will be within a given number of standard errors from this value.

- The appropriate sampling distribution for hypothesis tests involving large samples ($N > 50$) is the normal probability distribution (i.e., the normal curve). In these cases, sample statistics and hypothesized values are converted into z-scores, and a z-test is performed to evaluate whether the obtained standard z-score derived from the sample statistics is a rare or common outcome if the null hypothesis is true.

- The appropriate sampling distribution for hypothesis tests involving small samples ($N < 50$) and unknown population standard deviations is the t-distribution. In these cases, sample statistics and hypothesized values are converted into t-scores and a t-test is performed to evaluate whether the obtained standard t-score derived from the sample statistics is a rare or common outcome if the null hypothesis is true.

- The zone of rejection is the area under a sampling distribution that defines a rare outcome if the null hypothesis is true. This "rejection region" is determined by (1) the type of sampling distribution (i.e., z- or t-tests), (2) the nature of the alternative hypothesis (i.e., is the H_a directional or nondirectional?), and (3) the significance level or alpha value (i.e., the probability of rejecting a true H_o that is considered acceptable by the researcher). If an obtained test statistic falls within this zone of rejection, the null hypothesis is rejected in favor of the alternative hypothesis. If the obtained test statistic does not exceed the critical values that define this rejection zone, the null hypothesis cannot be rejected on the basis of the sample data.

- When performing hypothesis testing, the researcher establishes (1) the particular null hypothesis, (2) the alternative hypothesis, (3) the comparative sampling distribution, (4) the alpha level for the test, and (5) the subsequent nature and area of the zone of rejection. After we transform our sample value(s) into appropriate standard scores, we then compare our obtained values with those expected under the null hypothesis and the decision rules that establish the rejection zone to reach a conclusion about rejecting or not rejecting our initial null hypothesis.

KEY TERMS

Alpha Level (α)   Sampling Distributions
Alternative Hypothesis (H_a)   Significance Level
Critical Value(s)   Type I Error
Margin of Error   Type II Error
Null Hypothesis (H_o)   z-Tests (normal distribution)
One- Versus Two-Tailed Test   Zone(s) of Rejection

APPLYING WHAT YOU HAVE LEARNED

1. Which of the following statements is true about the process of hypothesis testing?

   a. The null hypothesis is assumed to be true, and we collect sample data to evaluate the accuracy of this claim.

   b. The research analyst develops an alternative hypothesis.

   c. A zone of rejection is established that identifies the sample outcomes that will lead to the reject of the null hypothesis.

   d. All of the above are true.

2. The null hypothesis

   a. involves a claim about a population parameter or population parameters.

   b. is the hypothesis that is actually tested in criminological research.

   c. is the expected result based on previous research and criminological theory.

   d. all of the above are true about the null hypothesis.

   e. only a and b are true.

3. The alternative hypothesis

   a. is the expected results derived from previous research and criminological theory.

   b. is expressed symbolically as values that are greater than, less than, or not equal to the value of the null hypothesis.

    c. is used in conjunction with the alpha level to establish the zone of rejection in the testing of the null hypothesis.

    d. all of the above are true about the alternative hypothesis.

4. Hypothesis testing is similar to the estimation of confidence intervals in that

    a. both involve the computation of sample statistics.

    b. both involve the use of sampling distributions to establish critical values and boundaries to determine rare and common outcomes.

    c. both assume random sampling from a population.

    d. all of the above are true.

5. The zone of rejection in hypothesis testing

    a. identifies the range of sample values that will lead to the rejection of the null hypothesis.

    b. is established on the basis of the alternative hypothesis and the significance level of the test.

    c. has combined areas equal to alpha (α), the probability of making a Type I error.

    d. all of the above are true.

6. Assume that an observed sample value of a statistical test falls in the zone of rejection. What statistical inferences can be made from this observation?

    a. This is an extremely rare outcome if the null hypothesis is true.

    b. There is a significant difference between the sample value and the value specified in the null hypothesis.

    c. This is an extremely rare outcome if the alternative hypothesis is true.

    d. All of the above are true.

    e. Only a and b are true.

7. There is more than one possible alternative hypothesis for any given research question.

    a. True

b. False

8. The critical values in hypothesis testing refer to the particular scores that define the beginning boundary or boundaries of the zone of rejection.

   a. True

   b. False

9. Sampling distributions are crucial in hypothesis testing because they allow us to

   a. identify the probabilities of receiving any given sample values under the assumption that the null hypothesis is true.

   b. use these probabilities of various outcomes to establish critical regions (i.e., zone[s] of rejection) that represent the risks of making a Type I error.

   c. make statistically based decisions about rejecting or retaining a null hypothesis.

   d. all of the above are true.

10. Assume that the null hypothesis is that treatment programs for sex offenders are ineffective. Which of the following statements would represent making a Type I error in this case?

    a. Deciding that treatment programs are effective when they really are not effective.

    b. Deciding that treatment programs are ineffective when they really are effective.

    c. Deciding that treatment programs are effective when they really are effective.

    d. Deciding that treatment programs are ineffective when they really are ineffective.

11. Which of the following alpha (α) values represents the highest probability of making a Type I error?

    a. $\alpha = .10$

    b. $\alpha = .05$

    c. $\alpha = .01$

d. $\alpha = .001$

12. A two-tailed test of significance

   a. has two zones of rejection.

   b. is associated with a nondirectional alternative hypothesis.

   c. has a higher probability of making a Type I error than a one-tailed test.

   d. all of the above are true.

   e. only a and b are true.

13. Which of the following is an example of a null hypothesis about a population mean that is expressed in symbolic form?

   a. $H_o: \mu_i = \$100,000$

   b. $H_o: P_s = .20$

   c. $H_o: \mu_m - \mu_f = 0$

   d. $H_o: P_b - P_w = 0$

14. Which of the following is an example of a null hypothesis about a population proportion that is expressed in symbolic form?

   a. $H_o: \mu_i = \$100,000$

   b. $H_o: P_s = .20$

   c. $H_o: \mu_m - \mu_f = 0$

   d. $H_o: P_b - P_w = 0$

15. Which of the following is an example of a null hypothesis about differences in population means that is expressed in symbolic form?

   a. $H_o: \mu_m - \mu_f = 0$

   b. $H_o: \mu_m = \mu_f$

   c. $H_o: \mu_i = \$100,000$

   d. All of the above are true.

   e. Only a and b are true. ✦

10 Hypothesis Testing for Means and Proportions

Hypotheses in criminology and criminal justice come in different forms. They may involve one or more population parameters, tested with small or large random samples, and involve means, proportions, or any other descriptive statistic.

Regardless of their form, the process of testing hypotheses is largely identical across applications. As described in the previous chapter, the analyst begins this process by establishing (1) the particular null hypothesis, (2) the alternative hypothesis, (3) the comparative sampling distribution, (4) the alpha level for the test, and (5) the subsequent nature and area of the zone of rejection. After selecting a random sample, the obtained sample values are then compared to those expected under the null hypothesis. Decision rules that establish the rejection zone are applied to reach a substantive conclusion about rejecting or not rejecting the null hypothesis.

This chapter further describes the logic and procedures in testing hypotheses by focusing on various tests of population means and proportions. It will illustrate the basic steps and computational methods used in these types of hypothesis testing. Detailed examples are used to illustrate how we actually do hypothesis testing under different conditions (e.g., one- or two-sample tests, tests of means or proportions, and large or small sample tests).

TYPES OF HYPOTHESIS TESTING

When evaluating statistical hypotheses about means and proportions, there are four basic types of hypothesis tests. These tests involve (1) one-sample tests of a population mean, (2) one-sample tests of a population proportion, (3) two-sample tests of differences in population means, and (4) two-sample tests of differences in population proportions.[1] The symbolic representations of the null hypothesis (H_o) and alternative hypothesis (H_a) for each of these types of statistical tests are summarized in Table 10.1. These particular tests are described below.

TABLE 10.1   Types of Hypothesis Testing

- One-Sample Tests of a Population Mean:

  H_o: $\mu = some\ value\,(v)$

  H_a: $\mu \neq (v)\ that\ value\ in\ \mathrm{H}_o$

  H_a: $\mu > (v)\ that\ value\ in\ \mathrm{H}_o$

  H_a: $\mu < (v)\ that\ value\ in\ \mathrm{H}_o$

- One-Sample Tests of a Population Proportion:

  H_o: $\rho = some\ value\,(v)$

  H_a: $\rho \neq (v)\ that\ value\ in\ \mathrm{H}_o$

  H_a: $\rho > (v)\ that\ value\ in\ \mathrm{H}_o$

  H_a: $\rho < (v)\ that\ value\ in\ \mathrm{H}_o$

- Two-Sample Tests of Differences in Population Means:

  H_o: $\mu_1 = \mu_2$ or H_o: $\mu_1 - \mu_2 = 0$

  H_a: $\mu_1 \neq \mu_2$ H_a: $\mu_1 > \mu_2$ H_a: $\mu_1 < \mu_2$

- Two-Sample Tests of Differences in Population Proportions:

  H_o: $\rho_1 = \rho_2$ or H_o: $\rho_1 - \rho_2 = 0$

  H_a: $\rho_1 \neq \rho_2$ H_a: $\rho_1 > \rho_2$ H_a: $\rho_1 < \rho_2$

One-Sample Tests of the Population Mean

The easiest way to demonstrate the process of hypothesis testing involves situations in which we are evaluating a claim about a single population parameter. In this particular case, we are evaluating a claim about the population mean (μ). I will show the steps for testing a null hypothesis about a population mean by using the t-distribution to establish the appropriate critical value(s) and the zone(s) of rejection for the test. The t-distribution is used here because the population standard deviation is

---

1. We will discuss other types of hypothesis tests in later chapters. For example, the procedure called *analysis of variance* (Chapter 12) is used to test the null hypothesis that the means for two or more groups are identical. The statistical tests in the current chapter are limited to comparisons of one or two samples or groups.

unknown in most criminological research. If the unlikely event occurs that the population standard deviation is known and a large random sample is available, the normal curve and z-scores would be our comparative standard. However, regardless of whether you use t- or z- scores, the logic of hypothesis testing is the same.

Suppose you were interested in the prior criminal behavior of incarcerated sex offenders. Based on their analysis of 10,000 sex offenders released from prison, Miethe, Olsen, and Mitchell (2006) claim that the average sex offender had 6.8 previous arrests. You have serious doubts about their claim, but you don't know whether the average number of prior arrests is higher or lower than their number. Thus, you decide to draw a small random sample of 25 released sex offenders and computed sample statistics (e.g., $\bar{x}$ and sd) to test this hypothesis about the average prior arrests of sex offenders.

Given a small random sample and an unknown population standard deviation (i.e., σ is unknown), the appropriate test statistic involves a t-test of a population mean. The steps involved in converting raw scores into t-scores, establishing critical values and the zone of rejection, and evaluating the null hypothesis include the following:

- Draw a random sample from the population. The sample size in this case is 25 released sex offenders ($N = 25$).

- Develop a null hypothesis and an alternative hypothesis. H_o: $\mu_{parrest} = 6.8$ (because this is the claim made in the previous study) and H_a: $\mu_{parrest} \neq 6.8$ (because we do not know if the number of prior arrests is above or below this alleged number—we just expect based on theory and past research that 6.8 cannot be correct).

- Develop a decision rule for deciding what sample outcomes will lead you to reject the H_o in favor of the H_a. Given a sample size of 25, a nondirectional alternative H_a, and the selection of an alpha level of .05 ($\alpha = .05$), the critical value of the test is a t-value of ±2.064. This critical value of t = ±2.064 is found by looking at a table of area under a t-distribution (see Appendix B) and looking for the specific value that corresponds to 24 degrees of freedom ($N - 1 = 25 - 1 = 24$) and an alpha value of .05 for a two-tailed test. Any observed value more extreme than t = ±2.064 will fall in the zone of rejection, thereby leading to the rejection of the H_o in favor of the H_a. Note that you picked an alpha level of .05 because that is a conventional significance level in criminological research.

- Compute sample statistics ($\bar{x}$ or sd) and an estimate of the standard error of the mean (se). This estimate of the standard error is determined by $sd / \sqrt{N}$. Assume you have the following sample values: $\bar{x} = 8.6$, $sd = 3.0$. With these sample statistics, your estimate of the standard error is .6 (i.e., $se = sd / \sqrt{N} = 3 / \sqrt{25} = .6$).

- Convert the sample mean into a standardized t-score by using the following formula: $t = (\bar{x} - \mu) / se$. $\bar{x}$ is your sample mean, and μ is the hypothesized population mean. In this example, the obtained t-value = +3.00 (i.e., [8.6 – 6.8] / .6 = +3.00).

- Compare the observed t-value with the expected t-statistic under the decision rule for defining rare or common outcomes if the H_o is true. In this example, compare the observed t-value of +3.00 with the expected t-value of ±2.064.

- Reach a decision about whether the sample data leads to a rejection or nonrejection of the H_o. Since the obtained t-value of +3.00 exceeds the critical value of t = ±2.064, we would reject the H_o that the average number of prior arrests for sex offenders is 6.8 in favor of the alternative that is different than this number. Thus, based on your sample, you would make the inference that sex offenders have a significantly higher arrest record than alleged from the previous study. You can make this inference because your sample is a random sample from the population of sex offenders and you have adjusted for an estimate of sampling error (i.e., standard error of this test statistic [se]).

If the same sample mean and standard deviation were present and we used the normal curve for the comparative basis, the substantive conclusion from this study would be identical. In this particular situation, we would convert our sample mean into a z-score (rather than t-score) using the same basic conversion formula (i.e., $z = (\bar{x} - \mu) / se$). The critical value of the z-statistic at the .05 alpha level would be z = ±1.96. When this expected z-value is compared with the observed z-value, we would reach the same conclusion about rejecting the H_o in favor of the H_a. This shows the parallel forms between t- and z-tests for a population mean.

One-Sample Test of a Population Proportion

The only real difference between a one-sample test of a population proportion and the test of a population mean is the computation of the standard deviation. Other than this slight computational difference and the use of different symbols (ρ's rather than μ's), the steps in testing these hypotheses are identical.

As an illustration of the test of a population proportion, assume that we are interested in evaluating the success of drug courts. According to data compiled and reported by the National Drug Court Clearinghouse, about 22% of drug court graduates are rearrested upon graduation from drug court. As a skeptical person, you have doubts about the accuracy of this claim of only a 22% "failure" rate because you suspect that there may be some vested interest in showing a lower rate of failure (e.g., to support a political agenda for more economic funding for these "successful" drug court programs).

To evaluate this claim about the success rate of drug courts, you need to draw a random sample of drug court participants and compare your computed sample statistics with the presumed population value. The steps involved in this one-sample test of a proportion are similar to all other types of hypothesis testing and include the following:

- Draw a random sample from the population. Let us assume you selected a random sample of 120 graduates from drug court ($N = 120$) and looked at their official police records to determine what proportion of them "failed" (i.e., were rearrested for a crime within 3 years of their graduation from drug court).

- Develop a null hypothesis and an alternative hypothesis. H_o: $P_{fail} = .22$ (because this is the claim derived from the National Drug Court Clearinghouse's data) and H_a: $P_{fail} > .22$ (because you suspect an underreporting of the failure rate of drug court for political reasons).

- Develop a decision rule for deciding what sample outcomes will lead you to reject the H_o in favor of the H_a. Given a sample size of 120, a directional alternative H_a, and the selection of an alpha level of .01 ($\alpha = .01$), the critical value of the test is a z-value of +2.33. We use a z-score because we have a large sample and the central limit theorem tells us that the sampling distribution of repeated large random samples will be normally distributed regardless of the shape of the population distribution. The critical value of z = +2.33 is found by looking at a table of the area under a normal curve and finding the closest z-score that corresponds to the alpha level of .01 (i.e., look in Column C of Appendix A for .01, then move across until you see the z-value of 2.33). Under this decision rule, any obtained z-value greater than +2.33 will fall in the zone of rejection, thereby leading you to reject the H_o in favor of the H_a with a probability of .01 of making a Type I error (i.e., rejecting the claim that drug courts are 22% effective when they are in fact that effective).

- Compute sample statistics (p_{sample}, sd) and the standard error of the proportion (se). Assume that the proportion of failures in our sample was .40 (i.e., p_{sample} = .40). With our sample p = .40, then the sample standard deviation is .49 (i.e., $\sqrt{p(1-p)} = \sqrt{.4(.6)} = .49$). The standard error is .04 (i.e., $se = sd / \sqrt{N} = .49 / \sqrt{120} = .04$).

- Convert the sample proportion into a standardized z-score by using the following formula: $z = (p_{sample} - P_{pop}) / se$. In this case, the obtained z-value = +4.50 (i.e., z = [.40 − .22] / .04 = +4.50).

- Compare the observed z-value with the expected critical value of the z-statistic under the decision rule for defining rare or common outcomes if the H_o is true. In this example, compare the observed z-value of +4.50 with the critical value of z = +2.33.

- Reach a decision about whether the sample data leads to a rejection or nonrejection of the H_o. Since the obtained z-value of +4.50 exceeds the critical value of z = +2.33, we would reject the H_o that the proportion of drug court graduates who fail is .22 in favor of the alternative that the failure rate is higher than this value. An obtained z-value of 4.50 is an extremely rare outcome if the H_o is true. In fact, if you look in a normal curve table (see Appendix A, Column A), you will not even find a z-score of 4.50 or greater—that is, its omission from this table is telling you that the likelihood of getting such a z-value is even less than the probability of 1 out of 1,000 that is associated with a z-score of +4.00 or greater. Thus, you are very confident that your sample results cast serious doubt on the claimed success rate for drug courts in the population. In other words, based on your sample, you would conclude that the failure rate in drug courts is considerably higher than the average failure rate derived from data reported by the National Drug Court Clearinghouse. Hmm! Any conspiracy theorists out there?

If you want some practice doing this type of hypothesis testing, do this same problem over again. However, this time assume that you are using the t-distribution rather than the normal probability distribution (i.e., z-scores). The only difference you will find is that your critical value for defining the zone of rejection will be a t-value of +2.35 (for a one-tailed test at $\alpha = .01$, $df = 119$ [i.e., $N - 1 = 120 - 1 = 119$] $\Rightarrow t \cong +2.35$). This t-value is approximately 2.35 because I used 200 as the approximate degrees of freedom in the t-table in Appendix B. Converting the sample proportion of .40 into a t-score will result in the same value found before with the z-score ($t_{obt} = +4.50$). You will also reach the same substantive conclusion to reject the H_o in favor of the H_a.

Two-Sample Test of Differences in Population Means

By now, you should have mastered the logical steps of hypothesis testing for one-sample tests of either a population mean or proportion. The extension of these tests to questions about group differences in population parameters is merely a slight modification of this basic theme. The only new twist is that you have to draw two random samples (or have two groups to compare within the same sample) and compute a pooled or combined estimate of sampling error (i.e., the standard error). Everything else remains the same.

As an illustration of hypothesis testing involving two population means, let us assume you were interested in gender differences in self-reported delinquency (i.e., number of delinquent acts reported in a survey). Contrary to various claims about gender equality in various aspects of social life, you expect girls in the United States to have lower levels of delinquency than boys because of (1) historical legacies of greater parental supervision of girls and (2) other factors (e.g., higher testosterone or more delinquent peers among boys).

To evaluate these claims and counterclaims, you need to draw random samples of boys and girls and compute their sample statistics. By establishing decision rules for defining rare and common outcomes, you can then use this sample data to reach a conclusion about gender differences in self-reported delinquency. Here is how we do a two-sample test of differences in population means when we have small samples:

- Draw two random samples from the population. Let us assume you do not have a lot of money so you could only take a random sample of 36 girls ($N_g = 36$) and a random sample of 26 boys ($N_b = 26$). Each juvenile was asked about the number of delinquent acts that he or she committed in the last month.

- Develop a null hypothesis and an alternative hypothesis. H_o: $\mu_g - \mu_b = 0 \Leftrightarrow \mu_g = \mu_b$ (i.e., the claim is that there are no gender differences in the frequency of delinquent acts). The alternative hypothesis is H_a: $\mu_g - \mu_b < 0 \Leftrightarrow \mu_g < \mu_b$ (i.e., you expect to find girls to have lower numbers of self-reported delinquent acts than boys due to various factors and theories about gender differences).

- Develop a decision rule for deciding what sample outcomes will lead you to reject the H_o in favor of the H_a. Given small sample sizes and unknown population standard deviations, the appropriate comparative distribution is the t-distribution. The number of degrees of freedom (*df*) in this two-sample test of differences is 60. This is found by adding together the number of *df*'s in the girl sample ($N_g - 1 = 36 - 1 = 35$) and the number of *df*'s in the boy sample ($N_b = 26 - 1 = 25$). Let's select an alpha level of .01 ($\alpha = .01$). Under these conditions and a directional H_a (i.e., $\mu_g < \mu_b$), the critical value for our t-test is –2.39. This value is found by looking in the table of the t-distribution (see Appendix B) for the t-value that corresponds to a one-tailed test with $\alpha = .01$ and 60 *df*'s. Under this decision rule, any obtained t-value less than –2.39 will fall in the zone of rejection, thereby leading you to reject the H_o in favor of the H_a.

- Compute sample statistics for each sample ($\overline{x}_g$, sd_g; $\overline{x}_b$, sd_b), and estimate the standard error of differences in means (*se*). Assume you had the following sample statistics: $\overline{x}_g = 13.2$; $sd_g = 2.1$; $\overline{x}_b = 13.7$; $sd_b = 2.2$. If we assume that the population standard deviations are equal, we can use a pooled estimate of the standard error of the difference in means. The computing formula for the *se* is a monster, but it just requires a little math:

$$se_{\overline{x}-\overline{x}} = se = \sqrt{\frac{(N_1 - 1)sd_1^2 + (N_2 - 1)sd_2^2}{N_1 + N_2 - 2}} \sqrt{\frac{(N_1 + N_2)}{N_1(N_2)}}$$

$$se_{\overline{x}-\overline{x}} = se = \sqrt{\frac{(N_g - 1)sd_g^2 + (N_b - 1)sd_b^2}{N_g + N_b - 2}} \sqrt{\frac{(N_g + N_b)}{N_g(N_b)}}$$

$$se_{\overline{x}-\overline{x}} = se = \sqrt{\frac{(36-1)2.1^2 + (26-1)2.2^2}{36+26-2}} \sqrt{\frac{(36+26)}{36(26)}}$$

$$se = \sqrt{4.6} \sqrt{.07} = (2.14)(.26) = .56$$

- Thus, the estimate of the standard error of the differences in means is equal to .56.

- Convert the sample differences in means into standardized t-scores by using the following formula: $t = (\bar{x}_g - \bar{x}_b) / se$. In this case, the obtained t-value = −.89 (i.e., t = [13.2 − 13.7] / .56 = −.89).

- Compare the observed t-value with the expected t-statistic under the decision rule for defining rare or common outcomes if the H_o is true. In this example, compare the observed t-value of −.89 with the expected t-value of −2.39.

- Reach a decision about whether the sample data leads to a rejection or nonrejection of the H_o. Since the obtained t-value of −.89 does not exceed the critical value of t = −2.39, we would not reject the H_o that girls and boys in the United States commit the same number of delinquent acts. Girls in our sample committed a slightly lower number of delinquent acts than boys (13.2 versus 13.7), which is in a direction consistent with our expectations based on the alternative hypothesis (H_a). However, this difference is not large enough to represent a rare outcome under our decision rule, thereby we could not reject the H_o's claim of gender equality in delinquency. An obtained t-value of −.89 would occur substantially more than 1 time out of 100 if the null hypothesis is true. Thus, our sample data provides no solid empirical evidence to challenge the H_o of gender equality in delinquency.

If you assumed that the standard deviations of these small samples were unequal, the formula for the t-statistic is of the same form, but the estimate of the standard error of the differences in means is different. In the case of unequal sample standard deviations, the appropriate formula for the t-test is

$$t = (\bar{x}_1 - \bar{x}_2) / se, \text{ where } se = \sqrt{\frac{sd_1^2}{N_1} + \frac{sd_2^2}{N_2}}$$

Finally, when the samples are large (N's > 50), the appropriate test of the differences in population means is a z-test using the normal distribution. The critical value(s) to define the zone of rejection at the particular alpha level will be a z-value, and the sample means will be converted into a z-statistic using the following formula:

$$Z = (\bar{x}_1 - \bar{x}_2) / se, \text{ where } se = \sqrt{\frac{\sigma_1^2}{N_1} + \frac{\sigma_2^2}{N_2}}$$

Regardless of the particular formula used to convert the differences in sample means into t-scores or z-scores, the logic of the process of hypothesis testing is the same. The major difference involves differences in the comparative distribution (i.e., t- or normal distribution), the critical values that establish the rejection region under these sampling distributions, and the computation and/or estimation of the standard error (*se*).

Two-Sample Tests of Differences in Population Proportions

Another type of hypothesis testing of group differences involves comparisons of population proportions. In these situations, we have two groups (e.g., males versus females, or Democrats versus Republicans), and we are interested in finding out whether there are group differences on some attribute (e.g., favor or oppose gun control or capital punishment). As you should expect, we go through basically the same "song and dance" when doing these types of hypothesis testing. The math is again relatively easy, although the hand calculation and estimation of the standard error of the differences in proportions remain the major computational nightmare.

Suppose you were interested in racial differences in the support for capital punishment. As a criminologist, you may be aware that minority group members are clearly overrepresented relative to their population as persons who get the death penalty in the United States. Blacks are also disproportionately represented as victims of homicide, the only state-level capital crime in this country. Under these conditions, you might not have a clear prediction about whether blacks are more or less likely than whites to favor capital punishment. Because you are curious about these possible racial differences, you decide to collect and analyze random samples of residents to assess this research question.

The General Social Survey (GSS) asks random samples of Americans their attitudes and beliefs about a wide variety of social issues. This data is available for secondary analysis through the Inter-University Consortium for Political and Social Research (ICPSR) at the University of Michigan. The 2000 GSS Survey provides information from a random sample of 383 black and 2,050 white U.S. adults on their attitude toward the death penalty for murder (coded as *favor* or *oppose*). The sample data and the steps in testing hypotheses about group differences in population proportions include the following:

- Draw random samples from the population. As a random sample of U.S. residents, the GSS sample can also be viewed as yielding random samples for each racial group as well. The sample size for each racial group includes $N_w = 2,050$ and $N_b = 383$.

- Develop a null hypothesis and an alternative hypothesis. H_o: $P_w - P_b = 0 \Leftrightarrow P_w = P_b$ (i.e., there are no differences in the proportion of whites (w) and blacks (b) that support the death penalty). H_a: $P_w - P_b \neq 0 \Leftrightarrow P_w \neq P_b$ (i.e., you expect to find some racial differences, but you have conflicting theories or ideas about whether blacks will have higher or lower support of capital punishment than whites).

- Develop a decision rule for deciding what sample outcomes will lead you to reject the H_o in favor of the H_a. Given large sample sizes, the normal distribution is the appropriate comparative distribution for converting differences in proportions into standard z-scores. Let us select an alpha level of .01 ($\alpha = .01$). With this alpha level and a nondirectional H_a, the critical value for our z-test of differences in proportions is $z = \pm 2.58$. Under this decision rule, any obtained z-value more extreme than ± 2.58 will fall in the zone of rejection, thereby leading us to reject the H_o of no racial differences in favor of the H_a.

- Compute sample statistics for each sample (ρ_w, sd_w; ρ_b, sd_b), and estimate the standard error of differences in proportions (se). The GSS survey yields the following sample statistics: $\rho_w = .74$ $sd_w = .44$ (i.e., $sd_w = \sqrt{p_w(1 - p_w)} = \sqrt{(.74)(.26)} = .44$); $\rho_b = .43$; $sd_b = .50$. If we assume that the population standard deviations are equal, we can use a pooled estimate of the standard error of the difference in proportions. The computing formula for the se requires two distinct steps:

  1. Develop a weighted proportion estimate of P (the pooled proportion in category P) and a weighted proportion estimate of the pooled proportion in category Q (i.e., $1 - P$):

     $$P_{wt} = (N_1\rho_1 + N_2\rho_2)/[N_1 + N_2] \text{ and } Q_{wt} = 1 - P_{wt}$$

  2. Plug in values of P_{wt} and Q_{wt} into the formula for standard error (se):

     $$SE_{(p1-p2)} = se = \sqrt{P_{wt}Q_{wt}\,[(N_1 + N_2)/(N_1N_2)]}$$

Applied to this sample data, we have

$$P_{wt} = (N_1\rho_1 + N_2\rho_2)/[N_1 + N_2] =$$

$$P_{wt} = (N_w\rho_w + N_b\rho_b)/[N_w + N_b] =$$
$$[2050\,(.74) + 383\,(.43)]/[2050 + 383] = 1681.7\,/\,2433 = .69$$

$$Q_{wt} = 1 - P_{wt} = 1 - .69 = .31$$

Plug the values of P_{wt} and Q_{wt} into the formula for standard error (*se*):

$$SE_{(pw-pb)} = se = \sqrt{P_{wt}Q_{wt}\,[(N_w + N_b)/(N_w N_b)]}$$

$$se = \sqrt{(.69)(.31)\,[(2050 + 383)/(2050\,(383))]}$$
$$= \sqrt{(.21)(.003)} = \sqrt{.0006} = .03$$

Thus, the estimate of the standard error of the differences in population proportions is equal to .03.

- Convert the sample differences in proportions into standardized z-scores by using the following formula: $z = (\rho_w - \rho_b)/se$. In this case, the obtained z-value = +10.33 (i.e., z = [.74 − .43] / .03 = +10.33).

- Compare the observed z-value with the expected z-statistic under the decision rule for defining rare or common outcomes if the H_o is true. In this example, compare the observed z-value of +10.33 with the expected z-value of ±2.58.

- Reach a decision about whether the sample data leads to a rejection or nonrejection of the H_o. The obtained z-value of +10.33 far exceeds the critical value of z = ±2.58, so we reject the H_o that white and black citizens have the same level of support for capital punishment. A z-value of +10.33 is an incredibly rare outcome if the H_o is true—it has a probability far below 1 time out of 1,000 (the last entry in a normal curve table for a Z of > 4.00). Thus, our sample data provides solid empirical evidence of major racial differences in attitude toward capital punishment for murderers. Less than 50% of black adults favor the death penalty compared to nearly 75% of white adults.

Small sample tests of differences in population proportions can also be conducted. In this case, the t-distribution is the comparative sampling distribution. The logic of these small sample tests of proportions is identical to the processes described for all statistical tests in this chapter. The difference between small sample and large sample tests for differences in proportions again focuses on the sampling distribution utilized (i.e., the t-distribution rather than the normal distribution) and the need to estimate the standard error associated with the t-statistic because the population standard deviation is unknown.

ISSUES IN TESTING STATISTICAL HYPOTHESES

When performing any type of statistical tests of hypotheses about population means and proportions, it is always important to remember that statistical results are only as good as the assumptions underlying their construction. This problem with the *GIGO* syndrome is just as crucial here as in any other type of social statistics.

The primary source of "garbage" in statistical inference is the lack of random sample(s) of the population. Claims of a "random sample" are one of the most dubious assertions that are made in social science research. Survey data from mail or telephone interviews and official data reports on various social indicators (such as crime and unemployment) are rarely if ever random samples because of problems with (1) sampling bias (e.g., using outdated lists or telephone directories when a sizeable minority of people have unlisted phone numbers), (2) nonresponse and missing data from survey items or official documents, and/or (3) various constraints (e.g., legal, ethical, and economic) that prohibit the selection of a random sample.

For purposes of statistical inference, the problem with nonrandom sampling is that it provides a major rival explanation for the observed pattern of results. In particular, if we decide to reject H_o, the rare sample outcome(s) that lead to this decision may be due to H_o really being wrong (as we typically assume when we reject H_o), or the rare outcome may have resulted from a biased sample. To eliminate this rival explanation, it is of fundamental importance that samples be as representative of their populations as possible.

When random sampling is used in a research study, we can actually compute the probability of making a Type I error (i.e., rejecting a true null hypothesis) and make adjustments in our choice of an alpha level to minimize this type of error that is inherent in sampling. This is not possible if we have sampling bias. So, random sampling from a population is a basic assumption that must be accomplished to have any faith in the statistical inferences drawn from a sample of data.

Another issue in hypothesis testing involves the effect of sample size on substantive conclusions about "significant" findings. In particular, all of the types of hypothesis testing done in this chapter are influenced by sample size. The nature of the effect of sample size is through its impact on the standard error of the estimates. Given that formulas for the standard error involve the ratio of a standard deviation to the square root of the sample size (i.e., $se = \sigma / \sqrt{n}$ or $se = sd / \sqrt{n}$), it should be obvious that

1. large samples yield smaller standard errors,

2. smaller standard errors result in a larger test statistic (i.e., obtained t-value or z-value), and

3. larger test statistics lead to a greater probability of rejecting the H_o.

Thus, if you really want to reject the H_o for political or other nefarious reasons, just increase the sample size until even the most trivial difference in absolute magnitude becomes statistically significant.

The question about sample size adversely affecting the results of hypothesis testing is both troubling and reassuring. On the one hand, we should have greater confidence in large sample sizes (as long as they are random samples) because those samples in the long run will lead to sample estimates that more closely group around the true population value. In contrast, "statistically significant" results from large samples may yield trivial substantive differences (e.g., a 1 percent difference in social attitudes across groups). Under these conditions, the researcher really has to ask whether this difference is substantively important (what some call **substantive significance**). Good practice in social statistics often involves finding a balance between **statistical significance** and substantively important research conclusions.

Another basic issue in hypothesis testing involves the selection of the particular alpha level (i.e., the significance level) for the statistical test procedure. Conventional levels of statistical significance (e.g., $\alpha = 0.5$ or $\alpha = 0.1$ for one- or two-tailed tests) have been used in this chapter. However, any significance level may be used, depending upon the particular research question. When the research wants to minimize Type I error (i.e., the probability of rejecting a true H_o), a more extreme alpha level (like .01 rather than .05) is used. However, by minimizing this type of error, the researcher increases the risk of affirming a wrong H_o (i.e., making a Type II error). The probability of making a Type II error is given by $1 - \alpha$.

If you stick with the conventional levels of statistical significance (i.e., .05 or .01), you will be on solid statistical footing for reaching conclusions about rejecting or not rejecting the H_o. For some types of exploratory research on small samples, more probable outcomes (e.g., .10) are often used in decision rules. Regardless of the particular significance level chosen, however, good research practice involves striking an appropriate balance between the statistical and substantive significance of the obtained findings.

As mentioned in the beginning of Chapter 9, both confidence intervals and hypothesis testing will result in the same substantive conclusions. For example, the 95% confidence interval is identical to the .05 alpha level in hypothesis testing for a two-tailed test. If a sample estimate of the population parameter falls outside the confidence interval, it is defined as a rare outcome if the null hypothesis is true, thereby leading us to reject the null hypothesis.

The importance of the parallel between these two types of statistical inferences is that the informed consumer or user can use either approach for evaluating hypotheses about human behavior. If the logic of hypothesis testing makes no sense to you, go back to Chapter 8 and read again about confidence intervals. Similarly, if the chapter on confidence intervals was a bit foggy, maybe this chapter has made more sense. If you understand both types of statistical inference, you have got the best of both worlds.

My last comment on hypothesis testing is a plea to examine the nature of the sample data before computing any formal statistical tests. Given that all types of hypothesis testing derive from the sample statistics, informed users and consumers should begin their analysis by looking at these descriptive statistics. For example, large differences in sample means or proportions are probably going to translate into significant differences that will result in the rejection of the H_o. This is most obvious in the example of racial differences in the support for capital punishment, where the differences in the sample proportions are so large (43% of blacks support the death penalty versus 74% among whites) that anyone would probably conclude that there are substantial racial differences in these attitudes. In other cases, however, looking at the sample data may not be as telling. In these situations, the formal test of the H_o is required to determine whether this difference is large enough to reject this claim once we take into account sampling error (i.e., the standard error). Again, good practice in social statistics involves both informal and visual impressions and inspections of the data *and* formal testing of the presumed claims.

SUMMARY OF MAJOR POINTS

- There are four different types of hypothesis tests for means and proportions: (1) one-sample test of a population mean, (2) one-sample test of a population proportion, (3) two-sample tests of differences in population means, and (4) two-sample tests of differences in population proportions. These hypotheses may be evaluated using either z-tests or t-tests, depending upon the sample size.

- Regardless of the particular type of hypothesis testing, the process of evaluating a null hypothesis is identical. The appropriate sequence in this process involves (1) establishing the null and alternative hypotheses; (2) developing a decision rule for evaluating the null hypothesis (i.e., establish a zone of rejection based on the type of sampling distribution, the alpha level, and the nature of the alternative hypothesis); (3) drawing a random sample(s) from the population, computing sample statistics, and estimating the standard error for the test statistic; (4) comparing the observed standard score (z- or t-value) with the expected standard score under the null hypothesis; and (5) reaching a decision about rejecting or not rejecting the null hypothesis based on whether your observed test-statistic falls within the zone of rejection.

- Similar to other statistical calculations, hypothesis testing is susceptible to the "garbage in, garbage out" syndrome. The assumption of a random sample is crucial in hypothesis testing—without a random sample, you have no way of estimating sampling error and no way to determine whether a rare outcome derived from hypothesis testing is due to the null hypothesis being wrong or the result of a biased sample.

- Tests of statistical significance are strongly affected by the sample size. As the sample size increases, the standard error of the test statistic decreases. Under these conditions, small numerical differences between observed and hypothesized values may be statistically significant (i.e., we reject the null hypothesis in favor of an alternative hypothesis) but relatively unimportant for substantive conclusions. Good practices among informed consumers and users of social statistics involve paying attention to both the statistical and substantive significance of research findings.

KEY TERMS

Alpha Level (α)	Standard Error of Estimate
Alternative Hypothesis (H_a)	Statistical and Substantive Significance
Critical Values	t-Tests (t-distribution)
Null Hypothesis (H_o)	Type I Error
One- and Two-Tailed Test	Type II Error
Random Sample	z-Tests (normal distribution)
Sampling Distributions	Zone of Rejection

MAJOR FORMULAS AND SYMBOLIC REPRESENTATIONS

One-Sample Test of a Population Mean:

H_o: $\mu = some\ value\ (v)$

H_a: $\mu \neq (v)$ *that value in* H_o

H_a: $\mu > (v)$ *that value in* H_o

H_a: $\mu < (v)$ *that value in* H_o

t-test (small sample, σ unknown):

$t = (\overline{x} - \mu) / se$, where $se = sd / \sqrt{N}$

z-test (large sample [$N > 50$]):

$z = (\overline{x} - \mu) / se$, where $se = \sigma / \sqrt{N}$

One-Sample Test of a Population Proportion:

H_o: $\rho = some\ value\ (v)$

H_a: $\rho \neq (v)$ *that value in* H_o

H_a: $\rho > (v)$ *that value in* H_o

H_a: $\rho < (v)$ *that value in* H_o

t-test (small sample, σ unknown):

$t = (\rho_{sample} - \rho_{Ho}) / se$, where $se = sd / \sqrt{N}$ and $\rho_{Ho} =$ the hypothesized value of p.

z-test (large sample [$N > 50$]):

$z = (\rho_{sample} - \rho_{Ho}) / se$, where $se = \sigma / \sqrt{N}$ and $\rho_{Ho} =$ the hypothesized value of p.

Two-Sample Tests of Differences in Population Means:

H_o: $\mu_1 = \mu_2$

H_a: $\mu_1 \neq \mu_2$; H_a: $\mu_1 > \mu_2$; H_a: $\mu_1 < \mu_2$

t-test (small samples, σ unknown, sample sd's assumed equal):

$$t = (\overline{x}_1 - \overline{x}_2) / se, \text{ where } se = \sqrt{\frac{(N_1 - 1)sd_1^2 + (N_2 - 1)sd_2^2}{N_1 + N_2 - 2}} \sqrt{\frac{(N_1 + N_2)}{N_1(N_2)}}$$

t-test (small samples, σ unknown, sample sd's assumed unequal):

$$t = (\overline{x}_1 - \overline{x}_2) / se, \text{ where } se = \sqrt{\frac{sd_1^2}{N_1} + \frac{sd_2^2}{N_2}}$$

z-test (large samples, σ's known):

$$z = (\overline{x}_1 - \overline{x}_2) / se, \text{ where } se = \sqrt{\frac{\sigma_1^2}{N_1} + \frac{\sigma_2^2}{N_2}}$$

Two-Sample Tests of Differences in Population Proportions:

$H_o: \rho_1 = \rho_2$

$H_a: \rho_1 \neq \rho_2; H_a: \rho_1 > \rho_2; H_a: \rho_1 < \rho_2$

z-test (large samples, σ's known):

$$z = (\rho_1 - \rho_2) / se, \text{ where } se = \sqrt{P_{wt} Q_{wt} \left[(N_1 + N_2) / (N_1 N_2) \right]} \text{ and}$$
$$P_{wt} = (N_1 \rho_1 + N_2 \rho_2) / [N_1 + N_2] \text{ and } Q_{wt} = 1 - P_{wt}.$$

SPSS Applications (*optional section*)

All of the types of hypothesis testing described in this chapter can be conducted through **SPSS**. The particular procedures are found under the menu marked **Analyze**. SPSS uses the t-distribution for all statistical tests of population means and proportions. However, given that the t-distribution is appropriate for small samples and that it converges with the normal distribution as the sample size(s) increases, the restriction to t-values is not problematic.

To conduct one-sample t-tests of a population mean or population proportion, perform the following steps on an SPSS data file.

- Click on the menu marked **Analyze**.

- Scroll down to **Compare Means**, and click on this phrase.

- Click on the option marked **One-Sample T-Test**.

- Select, in the list of variables, the variable that you are interested in. This is your dependent variable. Click on that variable so that it shows in the box marked **Test Variable(s)**.

- Look at the box marked **Test Value**, and insert the value that you have specified as the null hypothesis by clicking in this box. For example, if your hypothesized mean value is 60, you would insert **60** in this space for the Test Value.

- Click the menu button marked **OK**, and SPSS will run this test using the data file and variable(s) you have provided.

- The SPSS output from this procedure will provide the t-value, the degrees of freedom, and the probability value for this test. If that probability value is smaller than the alpha value you selected for your study (i.e., you picked $\alpha = .05$ and the probability from the SPSS output is .049 or smaller), you would reject your null hypothesis. If the SPSS probability value is greater than your decision rule (i.e., the SPSS probability value is .06 or larger), you would decide not to reject the null hypothesis.

For conducting a hypothesis test about differences in population means or proportions using SPSS, perform the following steps:

- Click on the menu marked **Analyze**.

- Scroll down to **Compare Means**, and click on this phrase.

- Click on the option marked **Independent Samples T-Test**.

- Select, in the list of variables, the variable that you are interested in. Click on that variable so that it shows in the box marked **Test-Variable(s)**.

- Look at the box marked **Group Variable**, and insert the independent variable that you are using for comparing groups. For example, if you were interested in testing gender differences in educational attainment, your group variable would be *gender*. Once you selected this group variable, click on the box marked **Define Groups**, and then insert the codes to define Group 1: ____ and Group 2: ____. For example, if you coded gender in your data file as 0 = male and 1 = female, you would insert the value *0* in the box for Group 1 and the value *1* in the box of Group 2. Click on **Continue** and then **OK** to generate the SPSS output for this procedure.

- The SPSS output from this procedure will provide the t-value, the degrees of freedom, and the probability value for this test. If that probability value is smaller than the alpha value you selected for your study, you would reject your null hypothesis about no differences in group means or group proportions in the population. If the SPSS probability value is greater than your chosen alpha level, you would not reject the null hypothesis.

APPLYING WHAT YOU HAVE LEARNED

1. When an obtained sample value falls in the zone of the rejection of a test statistic, the typical conclusion is that we

   a. reject the null hypothesis.

   b. do not reject the null hypothesis.

   c. reject the alternative hypothesis.

   d. have committed a Type II error.

2. The major differences between hypothesis tests of means versus proportions is

   a. the sampling distribution utilized.

   b. the formula for estimating the standard error of the estimate.

   c. the alpha level of the tests.

   d. the size of the zones of rejection.

3. The probability of making a Type I error in hypothesis testing is indicated by

   a. the alpha level of the test.

   b. the significance level of the test.

   c. the area contained in the zone of rejection for the test.

   d. all of the above are true.

4. Alpha levels in hypothesis testing are similar to the idea of _____ in confidence intervals.

   a. standard errors

   b. confidence levels

   c. population values

   d. substantive significance

5. Statistically significant differences are always substantively significant.

   a. True

   b. False

6. The results of hypothesis testing are affected by

    a. sample size.

    b. the magnitude of sampling error.

    c. the GIGO syndrome.

    d. all of the above.

7. Express each of the following statements in symbolic form as null hypotheses:

    a. The proportion of drug offenders who relapse is .40. H_o: _____

    b. The success of a drug treatment center is 40%. H_o: _____

    c. The average score on the LSAT is 150. H_o: _____

    d. The average amount of alcohol consumed per person in the United States per year is 50 gallons. H_o: _____

    e. The comparative number of executions in Western and non-Western societies. H_o: _____

    f. Gender differences in the proportion of students who fail courses in statistics. H_o: _____

    g. Differences between Americans and Canadians in the percentage of citizens who have ever smoked marijuana. H_o: _____

    h. The average IQ of your college instructors is 0. H_o: _____

8. Given the following information, determine the appropriate critical value(s) that would lead to the rejection of the null hypothesis H_o in favor of the alternative hypothesis H_a.

    a. $(H_o: u_w = 85; H_a: u_w \neq 85; N_w = 500; \alpha = .05)$
       Critical Value(s) = _____

    b. $(H_o: u_1 = 85; H_a: u_1 > 85; N_1 = 500; \alpha = .05)$
       Critical Value(s) = _____

    c. $(H_o: u_1 = 85; H_a: u_1 < 85; N_1 = 500; \alpha = .05)$
       Critical Value(s) = _____

    d. $(H_o: p_1 = .55; H_a: p_1 \neq .55; N_1 = 150; \alpha = .05)$
       Critical Value(s) = _____

e. $(H_o: \rho_1 = .55; H_a: \rho_1 < .55; N_1 = 150; \alpha = .05)$
Critical Value(s) = _____

f. $(H_o: u_w = 85; H_a: u_w \neq 85; N_1 = 21; \alpha = .05)$
Critical Value(s) = _____

g. $(H_o: u_1 = 85; H_a: u_1 > 85; N_1 = 21; \alpha = .05)$
Critical Value(s) = _____

h. $(H_o: u_1 = 85; H_a: u_1 < 85; N_1 = 21; \alpha = .05)$
Critical Value(s) = _____

i. $(H_o: \rho_1 = .55; H_a: \rho_1 \neq .55; N_1 = 45; \alpha = .05)$
Critical Value(s) = _____

j. $(H_o: \rho_1 = .55; H_a: \rho_1 > .55; N_1 = 45; \alpha = .05)$
Critical Value(s) = _____

k. $(H_o: \rho_1 = .55; H_a: \rho_1 < .55; N_1 = 45; \alpha = .05)$
Critical Value(s) = _____

l. $(H_o: u_1 - u_2 = 0; H_a: u_1 - u_2 \neq 0; N_1 = 75; N_2 = 65; \alpha = .01)$
Critical Value(s) = _____

m. $(H_o: u_1 - u_2 = 0; H_a: u_1 - u_2 < 0; N_1 = 75; N_2 = 65; \alpha = .01)$
Critical Value(s) = _____

n. $(H_o: u_1 - u_2 = 0; H_a: u_1 - u_2 > 0; N_1 = 75; N_2 = 65; \alpha = .01)$
Critical Value(s) = _____

o. $(H_o: p_1 - p_2 = 0; H_a: p_1 - p_2 > 0; N_1 = 75; N_2 = 65; \alpha = .01)$
Critical Value(s) = _____

p. $(H_o: u_1 - u_2 = 0; H_a: u_1 - u_2 \neq 0; N_1 = 15; N_2 = 16; \alpha = .01)$
Critical Value(s) = _____

q. $(H_o: p_1 - p_2 = 0; H_a: p_1 - p_2 < 0; N_1 = 18; N_2 = 24; \alpha = .01)$
Critical Value(s) = _____

9. Decide whether to reject or not reject the following statistical tests. You are given in each case information about the H_o, H_a, the alpha level (α), the critical values (abbreviated z_{cv} and t_{cv}) that establish the boundaries for rejecting H_o in favor of H_a, and the obtained z-values or t-values computed from our sample data.

a. [H_o: u = 80; H_a: u ≠ 80; α = .05; $z_{cv} = \pm 1.96$; $z_{obtained} = +2.23$]
Do you reject or not reject H_o? _____ Why? _____

b. $[H_o: u = 80; H_a: u > 80; \alpha = .05; z_{cv} = +1.64; z_{obtained} = +2.23]$
Do you reject or not reject H_o? _____ Why? _____

c. $[H_o: p = .65; H_a: p > .65; \alpha = .01; z_{cv} = +2.33; z_{obtained} = -2.40]$
Do you reject or not reject H_o? _____ Why? _____

d. $[H_o: p = .65; H_a: p < .65; \alpha = .01; z_{cv} = -2.33; z_{obtained} = -2.40]$
Do you reject or not reject H_o? _____ Why? _____

e. $[H_o: u = 80; H_a: u \neq 80; \alpha = .05; t_{cv} = \pm2.042; t_{obtained} = +2.23]$
Do you reject or not reject H_o? _____ Why? _____

f. $[H_o: u = 80; H_a: u < 80; \alpha = .05; t_{cv} = -1.697; t_{obtained} = -1.58]$
Do you reject or not reject H_o? _____ Why? _____

g. $[H_o: p = .65; H_a: p < .65; \alpha = .01; t_{cv} = -2.485; t_{obtained} = -2.50]$
Do you reject or not reject H_o? _____ Why? _____

h. $[H_o: u_1 = u_2; H_a: u_1 < u_2; \alpha = .05; z_{cv} = -1.64; z_{obtained} = -1.58]$
Do you reject or not reject H_o? _____ Why? _____

i. $[H_o: p_1 = p_2; H_a: p_1 \neq p_2; \alpha = .01; t_{cv} = \pm2.66; t_{obtained} = -2.80]$
Do you reject or not reject H_o? _____ Why? _____

j. $[H_o: p_1 = p_2; H_a: p_1 > p_2; \alpha = .01; t_{cv} = +2.39; t_{obtained} = +2.48]$
Do you reject or not reject H_o? _____ Why? _____

10. What effect does sample size have on hypothesis testing? ✦

11 Statistical Association in Contingency Tables

When criminologists make cause-and-effect statements (like marijuana is the gateway drug for more serious drug abuse) or note some other connection between two or more variables, they are talking about the idea of a statistical association. The easiest way to assess the nature and strength of this association for qualitative variables is to construct a cross-tabulation of the variables and explore the pattern of joint occurrence of particular attributes within it. How to develop these contingency tables and interpret the interrelationships among variables within them is the major focus of the current chapter.

After exploring the frequency distribution and descriptive statistics for individual variables, the typical statistical analysis then proceeds by examining the interrelationship among the variables. Is variation in income related to the level of one's education (e.g., to get a good paying job, do you need a good education?)? Are differences in a country's retention of the death penalty associated with their level of economic development, their primary religion, and/or their degree of political stability? For these and other questions, the informed analyst is concerned with measuring the magnitude of covariation between two variables or the joint occurrence among attributes. The concept of **statistical association** is used by statisticians to describe these interrelationships between two or more variables.

The current chapter examines statistical associations that involve the joint occurrence of attributes and quantitative variables with a limited number of categories. These statistical associations will be measured and assessed through the analysis of a **contingency table**—that is, a table that displays the joint distribution of these attributes. Rules for constructing these tables and interpreting their substantive results will be developed and discussed. The **chi-square test (χ^2)** will also be described as a formal way of testing the null hypothesis that there is no statistical association between two variables in the contingency table. The "why" and "how" questions surrounding statistical associations among these types of variables are discussed below.

THE IMPORTANCE OF STATISTICAL ASSOCIATION AND CONTINGENCY TABLES

We can learn a lot about our world by simply looking at the univariate distribution of a variable or sets of variables. Summary descriptive statistics like means, medians, and modes provide the typical profile in a sample or population, enabling consumers to use this information in their daily lives. For example, information about the crime rate, the median family income, unemployment rates, the political party of incumbents, population density, the average number of business establishments, and other types of descriptive statistics often serve as social indicators of the quality of life and the perceived attractiveness of the places where we live.

Once this average profile based on individual variables is summarized, however, the next natural or logical question is what accounts for variation within each of these profiles. For example, do cities that are above average in their crime rates also fall above average in their unemployment rates—a finding that you might expect under the "poverty causes crime" assumption? Similarly, is the average number of premarital sexual partners reported by interview respondents affected by their political party preference (e.g., are Republicans or Democrats more sexually active?). Providing descriptive summaries of the distribution of these variables is important, but it is the joint distribution of them that provides more insight for understanding the variation in human behavior.

So, why is the search for statistical associations important? Let me give you a couple basic answers:

- First, variables, by definition, vary, and it is important for various theoretical and practical reasons to identify the sources of this variation. For example, most of us want to know what contributes to our personal differences from the "average American." However, you cannot answer this question unless you explore the sources of variation around this average by assessing the statistical association between this particular variable and other variables that may be related to it.

- Second, a necessary condition for making any causal inference is that there must be an empirical relationship (i.e., statistical association) between the presumed causal variable (X) and the effect variable (Y). Under this condition, the pursuit of causal relations also requires that we determine the nature and magnitude of the statistical association among variables.

THE STRUCTURE OF A CONTINGENCY TABLE

A **contingency table** displays the individual and combined distributions of two categorical variables. One of these variables is arranged in columns, and the other variable is arranged in rows. The dimensions of the contingency table are defined by the number of categories for the row variable (R) and the number of categories of the column variable (C). For example, a 3×2 contingency table has 3 rows and 2 columns. A 10×50 table has 10 rows and 50 columns. The basic structure of a contingency table and the symbolic notation for the two types of distributions within it are summarized in Table 11.1.

TABLE 11.1   Structure of a Contingency Table and Notation

Row (r) Variable	Column (c) Variable			Row (R) Marginals
	c1	c2	c3	
r1	r_1c_1	r_1c_2	r_1c_3	R1
r2	r_2c_1	r_2c_2	r_2c_3	R2
Column (C) Marginals	C1	C2	C3	$\Sigma C \equiv \Sigma R \equiv N$

As illustrated in Table 11.1, the **marginal distributions** in a contingency table simply reflect the frequency distributions for the row and column variables treated separately or individually. For example, the value of *R1* designates the total number of observations in the first category of the row variable, whereas *C3* represents the total number of observations in the third category of the column variable. The sum of the row marginal totals is equal to the sum of the column marginal totals. The sum of either of these marginal totals is also equal to N *(the total number of observations)*.

The key elements in a contingency table are the **joint distributions** of the categories considered simultaneously. These joint distributions are symbolized by the notation r_ic_j (interpreted as the number in the *i*th row *and* *j*th column). These joint frequencies are also called the *cells* of a contingency table. The joint category or cell labeled r_2c_3 designates the number of observations in the second category of the row variable *and* the third category of the column variable. Similarly, the joint distribution

r_1c_1 defines the number of observations in the first category of both the row and column variables.

To make this less abstract, let's look at an example of a cross-tabulation of two real variables: *gender* (coded 1 = Female, 2 = Male) and *race/ethnicity* (coded 1 = White, 2 = Black, 3 = Hispanic). Table 11.2 displays the joint and marginal distributions for these two variables.

TABLE 11.2   Example of a Contingency Table (2 rows × 3 columns)

Gender	Race/Ethnicity			
	1 = White	2 = Black	3 = Hispanic	Row Total
1 = Female	500	200	100	800
2 = Male	400	150	50	600
Column Total:	900	350	150	1,400

Note: *Gender* is the row variable and *race/ethnicity* is the column variable.

It should be fairly easy to identify various joint and marginal distributions of the variables *gender* and *race/ethnicity* in Table 11.2. For example, the row totals indicate that 800 females and 600 males were included in this sample, representing a total of 1,400 people (i.e., N = 1,400). In the symbols identified in Table 11.1, the marginal frequency of 800 females would be designated as *R1*, while the symbol *R2* defines the marginal frequency of the 600 males (i.e., males are the second category of the row variable). The same logic applies to the column marginal frequencies. For example, the 900 white people in the sample would be designated by the symbol *C1* (i.e., the total for column 1).

The joint distribution of the person's gender and race is represented by the numbers within the cells of the table. These joint frequencies and the notation for each category include the following: 500 white females(r_1c_1), 200 black females (r_1c_2), 100 Hispanic females (r_1c_3), 400 white males (r_2c_1), 150 black males (r_2c_2), and 50 Hispanic males (r_2c_3).

There are no technical limits on the numbers of categories of the row variable and column variable in a contingency table. For example, if one were interested in the cross-tabulation of the 63 racial categories used by the Census Bureau and the 50 U.S. states, the contingency table would have 63 rows and 50 columns (i.e., a total of 3,150 distinct cells [63 × 50 = 3,150]). However, when actually interpreting contingency tables, it is often advisable to reduce substantially the number of categories of both the row and column variables. In the case of the joint distribution of racial categories and states, we may want to reclassify race into three to five categories and combine states into nine geographical regions. Issues surrounding the recoding and reclassifying of variables for developing simplified contingency tables are discussed in the last section of this chapter.

DEVELOPING TABLES OF TOTAL, ROW, AND COLUMN PERCENTAGES

For most analyses of contingency tables for categorical variables, the raw counts or tallies of the number of people or objects in particular cells of the table are often less important than the relative proportion of people or objects in the cells expressed within a standardized form. The types of standardization of contingency tables involve converting these counts and joint tallies into percentages.

There are three separate types of percentage distributions that may be used in a contingency table analysis. These involve tables of total percentages, row percentages, and column percentages. Table 11.3 illustrates how these particular percentage tables are computed from the original table of joint and marginal frequencies.

The difference between the types of percentage tables illustrated in Table 11.3 depends entirely on the base categories for computing the percentages. For example, the **table of total percentages** is derived from dividing each joint frequency $(r_i c_j)$ by the total number of observations (N). The **table of row percentages** is found by dividing each joint frequency $(r_i c_j)$ by the total number of observations in a particular row (R_i). Similarly, the **table of column percentages** is found by dividing each joint frequency $(r_i c_j)$ by the total number of observations in a particular column (C_j). These percentage tables are often given more attention than the frequency table in this type of analysis because the percentages are standardized by their base size and thus offer a common basis for making relative comparisons within and across categories.

THE RULES FOR INTERPRETING A CONTINGENCY TABLE

You do not have to be a rocket scientist to interpret most contingency tables. In fact, by following just a couple of basic rules, it is easy to interpret the pattern of results underlying them. For all contingency tables, you begin by looking at the **marginal distributions** for each

TABLE 11.3   Converting Observed Marginal and Cell Frequencies in Tables of Total, Row, and Column Percentages

Table of Marginal and Joint Frequencies

Gender	Race/Ethnicity			Row Total
	1 = White	2 = Black	3 = Hispanic	
1 = Female	500	200	100	800
2 = Male	400	150	50	600
Column Total:	900	350	150	1,400

Table of Total Percents (computed by taking $r_i c_j$ / N)

Gender	Race/Ethnicity			Row Total
	1 = White	2 = Black	3 = Hispanic	
1 = Female	36% (500/1,400)	14% (200/1,400)	7% (100/1,400)	800
2 = Male	29% (400/1,400)	11% (150/1,400)	4% (50/1,400)	600
Column Total:	900	350	150	1,400

Table of Row Percents (computed by taking $r_i c_j$ / R_i)

Gender	Race/Ethnicity			Row Total
	1 = White	2 = Black	3 = Hispanic	
1 = Female	62.5% (500/800)	25% (200/800)	12.5% (100/800)	100% (800)
2 = Male	67% (400/600)	25% (150/600)	8% (50/600)	100% (600)
Column Total:	900	350	150	1,400

Table of Column Percents (computed by taking $r_i c_j$ / C_j)

Gender	Race/Ethnicity			Row Total
	1 = White	2 = Black	3 = Hispanic	
1 = Female	56% (500/900)	57% (200/350)	67% (100/150)	800
2 = Male	44% (400/900)	43% (150/350)	33% (50/150)	600
Column Total:	100% (900)	100% (350)	100% (150)	1,400

variable, and then explore the nature of their **joint distributions**. The particular procedures and rules for interpreting these tables are summarized below.

For the original table of frequencies and the table of total percentages, primary attention focuses on the identification of the cells with the most and least number and/or proportion of observations. The modal cell is the particular joint combination of attributes that represents the most cases or the largest proportion of cases in the table of total percentages. In the example in Table 11.3, this modal cell is *White Females*. The 500 white females in this cell category [r_1c_1] represent about 36% of the total sample. The next most common category is *White Males*, accounting for 400 cases or 29% of the total sample. Hispanic males are the least prevalent gender-race combination in this example. Only 4% of the total sample falls within this cell of the contingency table. You have just completed the interpretation of the tables of total frequencies and percentages.

Now, when interpreting the table's row and column percentages, attention focuses on the joint distributions relative to their marginal distributions. The "golden rule" for interpreting the table of row percentages is the following:

- *Percentage within each row, and compare within the categories of the column variable.*

When interpreting a table of column percentages, this golden rule is as follows:

- *Percentage within each column, and compare within the categories of the row variable.*

Let's apply these rules to interpret the examples in Table 11.3:

- *Row percentage interpretation:* About 62% of the females in the sample are white, and about 67% of the males in the sample are white. Thus, the majority of both females and males in this study are white, but whites represent a slightly higher percentage among males than females.

- *Column percentage interpretation:* Two-thirds of the Hispanics in this study are females, and females account for about 56% of the sample among the other racial and ethnic groups. Thus, the majority of people within each racial and ethnic group in this sample are females, and females make up a higher proportion among Hispanics than any other racial and ethnic groups.

So, what did we learn about the statistical association between race and gender in this example? Here are the conclusions based on the various tables:

- White females are the most common race-gender category in this sample, followed by white males. Hispanic males are especially underrepresented in this example. This is the conclusion from the total percent table.

- Among both males and females, roughly two-thirds of the sample is white. This is the conclusion from the row percent table.

- Among all racial and ethnic groups, the majority of people in the sample are female, and this is especially true among Hispanics. This is the conclusion from the column percent table.

SPECIFYING CAUSAL RELATIONS IN CONTINGENCY TABLES

Contingency table analysis is cumbersome when you have to interpret four different tables for any two variables. Fortunately, your interpretative labors are reduced considerably if we can apply the causal language of **independent variables** and **dependent variables** to these analyses. Under these conditions, only one of the marginal tables is subject to analysis and interpretation.

When applied to the causal relationships between an independent and dependent variable, the "golden rule" for constructing and interpreting the appropriate contingency table is more specific. This new rule basically states that you

- *percentage within categories of the independent variable and compare these percentages for each category of the dependent variable.*

As an illustration of this interpretive rule for causal relations in contingency tables, consider the relationship between exposure to pornography and sexual violence. In this case, exposure to pornography is thought to cause sexual violence. Accordingly, pornography is the independent variable and sexual violence is the dependent variable. Table 11.4 provides the joint frequency distributions and the appropriate table of percentages for a sample of hypothetical data.

The top half of Table 11.4 indicates that the majority of people in this hypothetical sample had watched pornography (170/230) and the most common criminal offense of all people in this sample involved sexual violence (n = 95). These marginal distributions are the initial focus for any contingency table analysis. However, our primary interest is the joint distribution of the two variables. In this particular case, the major concern is whether sex offenders are more prevalent among those who have been exposed to pornography than those who have not.

The standard method for interpreting contingency tables in causal analyses involves computing percentages within categories of the independent variable and comparing these percentages for each category of the dependent variable. Applying this rule to the data arranged in Table 11.4 results in a table of column percentages. The interpretation of this bottom panel of cell percentages in Table 11.4 indicates that

---

TABLE 11.4   Assessing the Causal Association Between Exposure to Pornography and Sexual Violence (hypothetical data)

Joint Frequency Table

Dependent Variable (type of criminal act)	Independent Variable (exposure to pornography)		
	No	Yes	Total
Alcohol Offense	25	50	75
Property Offense	20	40	60
Sexual Violence	15	80	95
Total	60	170	230

Column Percent Table

Dependent Variable (type of criminal act)	Independent Variable (exposure to pornography)		
	No (%)	Yes (%)	Total
Alcohol Offense	42	29	75
Property Offense	33	24	60
Sexual Violence	25	47	95
Percent	100	100	
Total	(60)	(170)	(230)

- sex offenders represent nearly one-half of the offenders in this study who have watched pornography, but they account for only one-quarter of those who have not been exposed to pornography; and

- both alcohol and property offenders represent a higher proportion of those offenders not exposed rather than exposed to pornographic materials.

Given the arrangement of the frequency data in Table 11.4, the interpretation of only the column percentage table is sufficient to derive substantive conclusions about pornography and sex offenders. Based on this hypothetical data, we would conclude that these two variables are statistically associated. In particular, sex offenders are more prevalent among those who view pornography than those who do not. An opposite conclusion is found for the non-sex offenders in this example—that is, they have a relatively higher prevalence among those who have not been exposed to pornography.

ASSESSING THE MAGNITUDE OF BIVARIATE ASSOCIATIONS IN CONTINGENCY TABLES

There are two different methods for assessing the magnitude or strength of a **bivariate association** in a contingency table. One is a more visual and intuitive approach, whereas the other method relies upon formal statistical tests. Similar to our discussion in the last chapter about substantive and statistical significance, the informed analyst and consumer of social statistics will use both methods as the "best" practice. Each approach is described below.

Visual and Intuitive Approach

The most basic way to assess the strength or magnitude of a **statistical association** among categorical variables is to simply inspect the size of the percentage differences in the cell percentages across categories of the variables. Larger percentage differences across categories are reflective of stronger statistical associations between the variables.

Table 11.5 reveals some general guidelines for substantive conclusions about "no/weak," "moderate," and "strong" associations based on the relative size of the percentage differences. It also provides examples to illustrate the magnitude of these differences across comparative categories in a 2 × 2 table.

TABLE 11.5   Intuitive Guidelines for Assessing "Weak," "Moderate," and "Strong" Bivariate Associations in Contingency Tables

1. No/Weak Relationship = 0 to 10 Percentage Point Differences

Example:		Male (%)	Female (%)	
Drug Addict?	No	33	34	
	Yes	67	66	(1% point difference)
	Total	100	100	

2. Moderate Relationship = 10 to 30 Percentage Point Differences

Example:		Male (%)	Female (%)	
Drug Addict?	No	13	34	
	Yes	87	66	(21% point difference)
	Total	100	100	

3. Strong Relationship = >30 Percentage Point Differences

Example:		Male (%)	Female (%)	
Drug Addict?	No	13	54	
	Yes	87	46	(41% point difference)
	Total	100	100	

4. Perfect Relationship = 100 Percentage Point Differences

Example:		Male (%)	Female (%)	
Drug Addict?	No	0	100	
	Yes	100	0	(100% point difference)
	Total	100	100	

Although the intuitive rules offer guidance for interpreting the magnitude of the relationship between two variables in a contingency table, they are merely informal rules. Depending upon the particular research question or sample size, small percentage point differences between categories may be considered substantial or reflective of a "strong" relationship. Similarly, even large percentage differences may be considered relatively unimportant if they are derived from extremely small sample sizes. Nonetheless, it is important to look at these percentage differences across categories in any analysis of a contingency table because the formal tests we conduct to assess the statistical significance of the relationship between two variables derive from the same type of comparisons of the joint distributions across different categories.

The Chi-Square Test of Statistical Independence (χ^2)

The formal approach to assessing the magnitude of an association among categorical variables in a contingency table involves the **chi-square test**. This statistical procedure provides a formal test of the null hypothesis that the two variables are not related (i.e., they are statistically independent).

If two variables are independent, the outcome of one variable does not affect the other. More precisely, when two variables are independent, there is no relationship between them, and their **observed cell frequencies** will be identical to their **expected cell frequencies**. If the variables are related, the observed cell frequencies will depart from the expected cell frequencies based on their marginal distributions.

Similar to other types of hypothesis testing, the chi-square test (χ^2) involves the comparison of observed and expected outcomes under a null hypothesis. The χ^2 test has a sampling distribution in which the critical value for rejecting the null hypothesis of independence is based on the alpha level (i.e., the probability of making a Type I error) and the degrees of freedom (df). Within contingency table analyses, the degrees of freedom of the χ^2 test are represented by the product of $r-1$ and $c-1$, where r is the number of rows and c is the number of columns. For example, a 5 × 3 table has 8 degrees of freedom ($[(r-1)(c-1)] = [(5-1)(3-1) = 8]$).

Appendix C provides the critical values for the χ^2 test for given degrees of freedom and several conventional alpha levels for this test (e.g., $\alpha = .05$; $\alpha = .01$). If the obtained χ^2 exceeds this expected χ^2 value for the specified degrees of freedom and alpha level, we decide to reject the null hypothesis that the variables are not related (i.e., we conclude that they are related). This is the same logic we used in testing a null hypothesis about population means or proportions. The major difference, however, is that the comparative distribution is χ^2 rather than the normal curve or t-distribution. The obtained χ^2 value is computed by using the following formula:

$$\chi^2 = \sum \frac{(f_o - f_e)^2}{f_e},$$

where f_o = the observed frequency in each cell and f_e = the expected frequency in each cell.

To show the computational details for the χ^2 test, consider the bivariate relationship between race and type of criminal penalties for convicted drug offenders. Criminal penalties involve three categories (i.e., 1 = fine, 2 = probation, 3 = jail) and the offender's race is coded into two categories (1 = white, 2 = black). The 3 × 2 tables of observed and expected cell frequencies are shown in Table 11.6. This table also shows how the expected cell frequencies are calculated.

As demonstrated in Table 11.6, the **expected cell frequencies** are found by multiplying the particular row and column marginals and dividing this product by the sample size (N). When this table of expected cell frequencies is converted into a table of column percentages, it is easy to see how the assumption of independence between the variables translates into a finding of no difference across the categories. For example, based on the expected cell frequency, the proportion of blacks who are expected to receive a jail sentence (39/100 = 39%) is identical to the proportion of whites who are expected to receive a jail sentence (21/54 =

TABLE 11.6	Observed and Expected Cell Frequencies for Racial Differences in Criminal Penalties for Drug Offenders (hypothetical data)					
	Observed Cell Frequencies			**Expected Cell Frequencies**		
	White1	**Black2**	**Total**	**White1**	**Black2**	**Total**
Fine1	30	20	50	17.5	32.5	50
Probat2	16	28	44	15.4	28.6	44
Jail3	8	52	60	21.0	39.0	60
Total	54	100	154	$\cong 54$	$\cong 100$	154

Computing Expected Frequencies	
Fine1	White1 = fe_{11} = (R1 × C1) / N = (50 × 54) / 154 = 17.5
Probat2	White1 = fe_{21} = (R2 × C1) / N = (44 × 54) / 154 = 15.4
Jail3	White1 = fe_{31} = (R3 × C1) / N = (60 × 54) / 154 = 21.0
Fine1	Black2 = fe_{12} = (R1 × C2) / N = (50 × 100) / 154 = 32.5
Probat2	Black2 = fe_{22} = (R2 × C2) / N = (44 × 100) / 154 = 28.6
Jail3	Black2 = fe_{32} = (R3 × C2) / N = (60 × 100) / 154 = 39.0

39%). It is in this way that the expected cell frequencies become representative of the null hypothesis of no relationship between the variables in a contingency table.

After computing the expected cell frequencies, the next steps in the computation of the χ^2 value involve

1. subtracting the expected frequency from the observed frequency for each cell,

2. squaring each of these differences,

3. dividing each squared difference by the expected frequency for that cell, and

4. adding all these numbers for all cells.

For the observed and expected cell frequencies in Table 11.6, the χ^2 value is defined by the following:

$$\chi^2 = \sum \frac{(f_o - f_e)^2}{fe} = \sum (fo_{11} - fe_{11})^2 \, / \, fe_{11} + \ldots \ldots (fo_{32} - fe_{32})^2 \, / \, fe_{32} =$$

$$= [(30-17.5)^2 \, / \, 17.5] + [(16-15.4)^2 \, / \, 15.4] + [(8-21.0)^2 \, / \, 21.0] +$$
$$[(20-32.5)^2 \, / \, 32.5] + [(28-28.6)^2 \, / \, 28.6] + [(52-39.0)^2 \, / \, 39.0]$$
$$= 8.93 + .02 + 8.05 + 4.81 + .01 + 4.33$$

$$= \chi^2 = 26.15$$

At 2 degrees of freedom (i.e., $(3-1) \times (2-1) = 2 \, df$) and an alpha level of .05, the critical value of χ^2 for rejecting the null hypothesis of independence is 5.991. Since the observed χ^2 value of 26.15 far exceeds the critical value of 5.991 under the assumption of independence, we conclude that these variables are related.

A significant χ^2 value allows the analysts to conclude that variables are related, but the χ^2 test does not identify the pattern of that relationship. In the example in Table 11.6, we determined that race and criminal penalties were statistically associated, but we do not know from this test what racial group is given the most and least severe punishments. To answer this question, the researcher has to interpret the actual table of row or column percents.

When the observed cell frequencies in Table 11.6 are converted to a table of column percents, it is easy to demonstrate the nature of the race-punishment relationships. In particular, this column percent table would show that 52% of blacks (52/100) got a jail sentence compared to only 15% among whites (8/54). Given the magnitude of the differences in these percentages and the previously reported results of the χ^2 test, we would conclude from this study that

- there is a strong and statistically significant relationship between race and criminal penalties for drug offenders, and

- blacks are far more likely than whites to receive a jail sentence.

The informed consumer should also recognize the specific bases for these conclusions and the importance of both statements to accurately describe the race-punishment relationship. In particular, the conclusion that this relationship is "strong" derives from our guidelines for interpreting percentage differences (see Table 11.5), whereas the claim of "statistical significance" is based on the χ^2 test. The description of the nature of the racial differences (i.e., blacks are more likely to be incarcerated than whites) is derived from the interpretation of the contingency table and, in particular, the table of column percents. This same logic of conducting formal χ^2 tests and then interpreting the nature of the relationship applies to all types of contingency table analysis.

ISSUES IN CONTINGENCY TABLE ANALYSIS

The examination of a contingency table is the fundamental basis of the search for a **bivariate association** between categorical variables. However, there are several specific issues that arise in the construction and analysis of these tables. The χ^2 test also has some major limitations for evaluating the hypothesis of independence. Alternative measures of the bivariate relationship among qualitative variables are also available. These issues are discussed below.

How Many Categories for Categorical Variables?

Technically, a contingency table can be developed for any two variables, regardless of the number of categories within them. For example, users of the 2000 U.S. Census data can cross-tabulate up to 63 possible racial categories by 50 states to create an enormous 63 × 50 contingency table for assessing racial differences within states. Similarly, if age is coded into 10-year intervals and there are 196 countries in the world, this 10 × 196 contingency table for age differences in countries would contain 1,960 unique cells.

These massive contingency tables are in sharp contrast to the 2 × 2 and 3 × 2 tables that have been used in this chapter. However, regardless of the number of categories, the computational method and rules for interpreting the contingency table analysis remain the same. What differs is the decreased ability to provide a succinct summary of the results and the greater possibility of distorted percentage differences across categories with small cell frequencies when there are a large number of categories. When expected cell counts involve less than five observations (a common problem with small sample sizes but large numbers of categories), the probabilities associated with the χ^2 test also become increasingly inaccurate.

For both practical (i.e., ease of interpretation) and statistical (e.g., the robustness of the formal tests) reasons, social analysts using contingency tables often restrict the number of categories for each variable. This is done by either (1) collapsing across categories (e.g., combining the 10 age intervals into five categories or even three categories [< 21, 21–65, over 65]), or (2) getting rid of some of the categories and cases in them entirely (e.g., focusing your analysis of census data on only persons who report a single race [six categories] and deleting those who fall within any of the 57 multiple race categories).

The answer to the question of "how many categories" to include in a contingency table depends on several factors. The primary factor is your particular research question. For example, if you are really interested in state differences on some other variable (e.g., whether or not they have the death penalty), then you need to have 50 categories to represent the "state" variable. However, if the particular geographical unit is not that crucial for your analysis, you could combine states into nine regions or even four time zones to reduce the number of categories. Similarly, depending on the research question, a variable like age may be reduced to only two categories (e.g., adults versus nonadults, senior citizens versus others).

Another basis for deciding the number of categories involves the use of various statistical "rules of thumb" about minimum cell size (e.g., 5 cases per cell, 10 per cell). For example, if you picked an average minimum cell frequency of 10 observations and you had a sample size of 200, the maximum number of cells in your contingency table would be 20 (i.e., 200 sample size / 10 minimum = 20 cells). Various size tables would fit this requirement (e.g., 4 × 5, 6 × 3, 8 × 2, 4 × 4, 3 × 4, etc.) as long as cases were roughly dispersed equally across these cells. While these "rules of thumb" provide a general statistical guide, your choice of the number of categories should be based primarily on your particular substantive research questions, previous theory, and sound logical reasons.

GIGO and the Value of Theory in Identifying Other Important Variables

As mentioned earlier, you do not have to be a rocket scientist to crunch out the numbers in a contingency table. Anyone can do that. However, you do have to be a rocket scientist to make sure that numbers about gravitational pull and fuel consumption make sense. In a similar vein, sound statistical practice in the social sciences requires at least some theoretical knowledge of the subject matter. If not, you run the great risk of the dastardly problem of "garbage in, garbage out."

To illustrate the value of substantive theory in contingency table analysis, consider the example of racial differences in criminal penalties used earlier (see Table 11.6). The major conclusion derived from this table was that blacks were substantially and significantly more likely than whites to receive a jail sentence upon a drug conviction.

Before you conclude from this hypothetical data that the criminal justice system discriminates against black defendants, however, you need to know something about existing substantive theory on factors associated with sentencing decisions. In this particular case, existing theory and previous research would inform you that the type of legal punishments for drug offenders is strongly influenced by the type of drug involved (e.g., marijuana users get lighter penalties than crack users) and the type of drug activity (e.g., users get lighter penalties than sellers).

So, what does this substantive knowledge tell us about the bivariate contingency table between race and criminal penalties? Well, it tells us that black drug offenders may get jail sentences more often other racial groups because (1) they may be more likely to be charged for "crack" offenses and/or (2) they may be more likely to be charged with selling rather than mere possession. In other words, rather than race itself, it may be the differences in drug behaviors associated with race (i.e., the differential propensities of blacks to be charged with selling or using crack cocaine) that account for the more severe punishment for black offenders in this hypothetical data.

These multiple interpretations of the racial differences in criminal sentences are reflective of a more general problem in bivariate contingency table analysis. This problem is the possible distortion of substantive findings by focusing exclusively on the two variables in the contingency table and ignoring other factors that may influence both variables. Statisticians refer to this problem as *misspecification* of the relationship between variables, and its remedy is to incorporate these other variables into the statistical model or design.

How do you assess the impact of other variables on the primary bivariate relationship in a contingency table analysis? The short answer is that you conduct a **multivariate analysis** that controls for the impact of these other variables. In the example of racial differences in criminal sentences of drug offenders, a simple method of multivariate analysis would involve two basic steps:

- Break down your sample into four different groups: (1) marijuana users, (2) marijuana sellers, (3) crack users, and (4) crack dealers.

- Construct and analyze the contingency table involving race and criminal sentence for each of the four groups.

If the same findings are found across these different groups, you would be more confident in your substantive conclusions about racial disparities in the sentencing of drug offenders. By doing this type of multivariate analysis, you have minimized some of the threat of the GIGO syndrome adversely affecting the substantive conclusions derived from a bivariate contingency table analysis.

Sample Size and Significance Tests

Similar to other statistical tests (e.g., t-tests of means and proportions), the chi-square test of independence is strongly affected by the sample size. In fact, the larger the sample size, the greater the likelihood of rejecting the null hypothesis of independence.

This relationship between sample size and statistical significance is demonstrated in Table 11.7. As revealed in the column percents, the visual method of assessing the magnitude of bivariate associations in contingency tables would indicate a moderately strong relationship between gender and drug addiction across each sample (i.e., the 20% point difference across categories represents a "moderate" relationship). However, the statistical significance of this relationship is strongly affected by the sample size even when the cell proportions based on the column percentages are identical. This hypothetical relationship between gender and drug addiction is statistically insignificant with $N = 50$, significant at $\alpha < .05$ with $N = 100$, and achieving a higher statistical significance ($\alpha < .001$) for $N = 500$. Given this property of χ^2 tests, it is important that the informed analyst explore both the statistical and substantive significance of the observed results.

Other Measures of Association for Categorical Variables

The chi-square test is only one of many measures of the relationship between two categorical variables. Some of these other measures of associ-

TABLE 11.7   Effects of Sample Size on Statistical Significance of χ^2 Test

Drug Addict?	Gender		
	M	**F**	
No	40	60	
Yes	60	40	
Total %	100%	100%	
N =	25	25	(50)

$$\chi^2 = 2.00, \alpha > .05$$

Drug Addict?	Gender		
	M	**F**	
No	40	60	
Yes	60	40	
Total %	100%	100%	
N =	50	50	(100)

$$\chi^2 = 4.00, \alpha < .05$$

Drug Addict?	Gender		
	M	**F**	
No	40	60	
Yes	60	40	
Total %	100%	100%	
N =	250	250	(500)

$$\chi^2 = 20.0, \alpha < .001$$

ation are simply a chi-square value adjusted for the effects of the number of cases (e.g., Pearson's coefficient of contingency) or the number of rows and columns (e.g., Cramer's *V*). Another measure of association derived from chi-square and Cramer's *V* is the phi (ϕ) coefficient for 2 × 2 tables.

When nominal variables can be viewed causally as independent and dependent variables, Guttman's coefficient of predictability (called lambda [λ]) is another measure of association. The two-sample test of differences in population proportions discussed in the last chapter is an alternative way of evaluating the statistical association among two nominal variables. Common measures of association for variables with ordinal categories include gamma, Somer's D, Kendall's tau-b, and tau-c.

For those interested in more details about these other measures of association for nominal and ordinal variables, I strongly encourage you to pick up another statistics book and read about their relative strengths and limitations. I have focused on the chi-square test in this chapter because (1) of its widespread use in contingency table analysis, (2) other measures derive from it, and (3) it has direct parallels to the visual methods of interpreting tables (e.g., a finding of 0 differences in percentage points when making comparisons across categories is equivalent to a χ^2 value of 0).

SUMMARY OF MAJOR POINTS

- A contingency table represents the cross-classification of two categorical variables. It displays the joint and marginal distributions of these two variables.

- The major components of a contingency table are the marginal frequency distributions and the joint distributions. The marginal frequency distributions represent the frequency distribution of each variable treated separately. The joint distributions are the "cells" of the contingency table, and they represent the particular combinations of the two variables considered simultaneously.

- The dimensions of a contingency table are determined by the number of categories of the row variable (R) and the number of categories of the column variable (C). For example, a 3 × 2 table has three rows and two columns. The number of cells of the table is the product of the number of rows and the number of columns (i.e., $R \times C$ = cells). A 4 × 5 table has 20 cells (i.e., 20 unique combinations of categories of the two variables).

- There are four distinct types of tables in every contingency table analysis: (1) a table of observed marginal and joint frequencies, (2) a table of total percentages (representing the proportion of the total number of cases within each cell of the table), (3) a table of row percentages (representing the percent of cases in a particular row found in each column), and (4) a table of column percentages (representing the percent of cases in a particular column found in each row).

- The primary rule for developing and interpreting a percentage table is to "*percent within categories of one variable and compare within categories of the other variable(s).*" When the two variables are considered causally related (i.e., as "independent" and "dependent" variables), the appropriate rule is to "*percent within categories of the independent variable and compare these percentages for each category of the dependent variable.*"

- There are two different ways to assess the magnitude of association in a contingency table. One method involves a visual comparison of the percentage differences across categories of the variables. "Strong" relationships are indicated by percentage differences of 30% points or greater across the categories. The second method involves a formal test of statistical association using the chi-square test (χ^2). A significant χ^2 value leads to the rejection of the null hypothesis of independence (i.e., we conclude that the variables are statistically related).

- The χ^2 test is affected by sample size and the number of cases within each cell. It is most appropriate when the expected cell frequency for any cell is five or more cases. The larger the sample size, *ceteris paribus*, the greater the likelihood of finding a statistically significant value for the χ^2 test.

- Being aware of the substantive theory and previous research is important when conducting bivariate contingency table analysis. This theory and previous research will help identify other factors that may influence the relationship between these two variables and minimize the likelihood of distorting the actual nature of this relationship by the failure to consider these other factors.

- There are numerous alternative measures of association for nominal and ordinal variables. This chapter focuses on the chi-square test because of its widespread use in social research, its role as the source for other derivative measures of association, and its parallels to the visual methods for assessing the magnitude of a statistical association in a contingency table.

KEY TERMS

Bivariate Association and Analysis
Chi-Square Test (χ^2)

Contingency Table
Dependent Variables

Expected Cell Frequencies
Independent Variables
Joint Distributions
Marginal Distributions
Observed Cell Frequencies

Statistical Association
Table of Column Percentages
Table of Row Percentages
Table of Total Percentages

MAJOR FORMULAS

$$\chi^2 = \sum \frac{(f_o - f_e)^2}{fe},$$

where f_o = the observed frequency in each cell and f_e = the expected frequency in each cell.

SPSS Applications (*Optional Section*)

Contingency tables are easily constructed and assessed within SPSS. The basic procedure for conducting this type of tabular analysis is called *Crosstabs*. This procedure is available through SPSS by performing the following steps on a data file:

- Click on the **Analyze** menu.

- Click on **Descriptive Statistics**.

- Select the procedure **Crosstab**.

- Select a particular variable as the **Row Variable** and **Column Variable**.

- Click on the **Statistics** button.

- Click on the box in front of the chi-square to select this procedure.

- Click on **Continue**.

- Select the box marked **Cells**.

- Click on the **Count** options you want to display (observed and/or expected) and the percentages required (total, row, and/or column).

- Click on **Continue**.

- Click on **OK** to generate the contingency table.

APPLYING WHAT YOU HAVE LEARNED

1. A cross tabulation or contingency table displays

   a. the marginal distributions of two variables.

   b. the joint distribution of two variables.

   c. the standard deviation of the variables.

   d. all of the above are true.

   e. only a and b are true.

2. Contingency table analysis is most appropriate for examining the relationship between

   a. two qualitative variables measured on a nominal or ordinal scale.

   b. two quantitative variables measured on an interval or ratio scale.

   c. one qualitative and one quantitative variable.

3. The observed cell values in a contingency table are also called the

   a. marginal frequencies.

   b. marginal percents.

   c. joint frequencies.

   d. expected cell frequencies.

4. The marginal distributions in a contingency table are the same as the frequency distribution for each variable when they are treated separately.

   a. True

   b. False

5. Within a table of row percentages,

   a. the sum of the joint (cell) percentages in any given row is 100%.

   b. the sum of the joint (cell) percentages in any given column is 100%.

   c. the sum of all of the joint (cell) percentages in the table equals 100%.

6. Within a table of total percentages,

    a. the sum of the joint (cell) percentages in any given row is 100%.

    b. the sum of the joint (cell) percentages in any given column is 100%.

    c. the sum of all of the joint (cell) percentages in the table equals 100%.

7. Suppose you were interested in the relationship between gender and the most serious type of index crime committed by 500 offenders. Gender has two categories (1 = Male and 2 = Female), and eight different types of index crime are used in the FBI's crime classification. If this information were summarized in a contingency table, how many cells would be in this table?

    a. 2 cells

    b. 8 cells

    c. 10 cells

    d. 16 cells

8. The dimensions of a contingency table are defined by the

    a. number of rows and number of columns.

    b. sample size.

    c. chi-square value.

9. In a study of the bivariate relationship between gender and the likelihood of being a victim of identity theft,

    a. gender is the independent variable, and identity theft is the dependent variable.

    b. gender is the dependent variable, and identity theft is the independent variable.

    c. both gender and identity theft are independent variables.

    d. both gender and identity theft are dependent variables.

10. If variables in a contingency table analysis can be classified as independent and dependent variables, the "golden rule" for interpreting the table is to

    a. focus on the table of total percents.

    b.   percent within categories of independent variable and compare these percentages for each category of the dependent variable.

    c.   percent within categories of dependent variable and compare these percentages for each category of the independent variable.

    d.   hire someone else to interpret the tables for you.

11. When the dependent variable is the row variable and the independent variable is the column variable, the primary focus of the analyst should be on the interpretation of the

    a.   table of observed frequencies.

    b.   table of total percents.

    c.   table of column percents.

    d.   table of row percents.

12. As a general rule in interpreting the magnitude of the statistical association in a contingency table, a "strong" relationship is indicated by

    a.   0 to 10 percentage point differences across categories.

    b.   10 to 30 percentage point differences across categories.

    c.   greater than 30 percentage point differences across categories.

13. A statistically significant chi-square value means that

    a.   there is a relationship between the two variables.

    b.   the observed chi-square value exceeded the expected chi-square value.

    c.   there is no relationship between the two variables.

    d.   both a and b are true.

14. If two variables are not related to each other at all (i.e., they are statistically independent),

    a.   the chi-square value will be 0.

    b.   the observed and expected cell frequencies will be identical.

    c.   the percentage differences across categories will be identical (e.g., the percent of all males who use illegal drugs is the same as the percent of all females who use illegal drugs).

    d.   all of the above are true.

15. Compared to a small sample, which of the following is generally true when you have a large sample size?

    a. It is more difficult to achieve a statistically significant chi-square value.

    b. It is easier to achieve a statistically significant chi-square value.

    c. There are more problems with small cell frequencies (i.e., more cells of the table with less than five observations).

16. The primary factor in determining the number of categories for each variable in a contingency table analysis is

    a. the research questions underlying the study.

    b. the sample size.

    c. the ease of interpretation of the relationships.

17. The test of the differences in two sample proportions is an alternative to a chi-square test as a way of evaluating the statistical significance of the association between two nominal variables.

    a. True

    b. False

18. Use the following 2 × 3 contingency table to answer these questions:

Property Crime Victim?	Place of Residency			
	1 = Town	2 = Suburb	3 = City	Total
1 = No	60	50	20	130
2 = Yes	35	30	100	165
Total	95	80	120	295

    a. Using the table notation discussed in this chapter, what is the value of R1? _____ R2? _____ C1? _____ C2? _____ C3? _____

    b. What is the value of cell r_1c_1? _____ cell r_1c_2? _____ cell r_1c_3? _____ cell r_2c_1? _____ cell r_2c_2? _____ cell r_2c_3? _____

c. If your place of residency is said to influence the likelihood of property crime victimization, what is the dependent variable in this example? _____ What is the independent variable? _____

d. Given the arrangement of the table above, what type of percentage table would you use (total, row, or column percent) to assess the presumed causal relationship between residency and property victimization? _____

e. Interpret this table of the relationship between place of residency and property crime victimization risks. Interpret both the marginal and joint distributions using the appropriate rules for interpreting tables. _____

f. Based on the visual method of interpreting the magnitude of an association in a contingency table, would you consider the relationship between residency and property victimization to be "weak," "moderate," or "strong"? _____ How large a percentage point difference did you find between town dwellers and city residents in their victimization experiences? _____

g. How many degrees of freedom are there for this problem? _____

h. If you wanted to use chi-square (χ^2) to test the hypothesis of independence between these two variables, what critical value of χ^2 would be necessary to reject this hypothesis at the .05 alpha level? _____

i. Compute the χ^2 value for this example. What is this obtained χ^2 value? _____

j. What conclusion do you reach from this χ^2 test about the relationship between place of residency and property victimization? _____ ✦

12

The Analysis of Variance (ANOVA)

A *controversial treatment for sex offenders involves the use of drugs to induce chemical castration. To evaluate its effectiveness, a basic experimental design would involve the random assignment of offenders to different groups (e.g., a control group given a placebo [sugar pill] and an experimental group given the inhibiting drug) and the subsequent monitoring of the physiological response of each group to sexually arousing materials.*

Under these conditions, the presumed effectiveness of chemical castration reduces to two basic questions: (1) Are the average physiological responses to sexually explicit material lower for the experimental group than the control group? And (2) how much variation in these physiological responses is explained by group membership? The statistical procedure that provides direct answers to these questions is called the analysis of variance (ANOVA).

As mentioned in previous chapters, variation is a major fact of human life, and a primary goal of social research involves trying to account for it. For example, how much of the variation in the length of prison terms for convicted drug offenders is due to differences in their type of drug activity (i.e., whether they are users, buyers, or manufacturers)? Are differences in the crime rates across U.S. cities explained by differences in their geographical region (e.g., South, Midwest, Northeast, or West)? For virtually every question in criminological research, the primary concern is in the analysis of this variance. Not surprisingly, a statistical technique called **analysis of variance (ANOVA)** is designed to address these types of research questions.

This chapter describes the logic and applications of the *ANOVA* statistical technique. It begins with a description of the conditions in which *ANOVA* is used (e.g., interval/ratio-measurement of a dependent variable and nominal/ordinal measurement of an independent variable) and then addresses how total variation is partitioned into two major components (i.e., between-group and within-group variation). Measures of statistical association (e.g., eta-squared [η^2]) and the *F*-test for evaluating the hypothesis of equal group means are also discussed. As with previous chapters, detailed examples are used to illustrate the logic of ANOVA and the computational methods underlying this statistical technique and its related components.

OVERVIEW OF ANOVA AND WHEN IT IS USED

As its name implies, **ANOVA** is a statistical technique for the analysis of variance. This variation is the variation in some quantitatively measured dependent variable. Among pure statisticians, it is assumed that the dependent variable is measured on an interval or ratio scale, but you will often see applications of ANOVA with only ordinal or even nominal measurement of the dependent variable. If you do not have at least interval-level measurement, the basic idea of ANOVA (i.e., to explain variation around a central value [i.e., the overall mean]) doesn't make a whole lot of sense because the mean is fairly meaningless with nominal measures or ordinal scales with only a couple categories. Accordingly, the best practice is to use ANOVA only when your dependent variable is measured on an interval or ratio scale.

In addition to the dependent variable, ANOVA also requires at least one independent variable. This independent variable can involve any level of measurement (i.e., nominal, ordinal, or interval/ratio), but the categories of the independent variable represent distinct "groups." As distinct groups, the typical ANOVA application will rarely include more than ten categories of the independent variable. When the independent variable has only two categories, ANOVA provides substantive results that are equivalent to those achieved from a two-sample test of differences in population means (see Chapter 10).

With sufficiently large sample sizes, there are virtually no limits on the number of independent variables that may be included in an ANOVA research design. When there is only one independent variable, the type of analysis is referred to as **One-Way ANOVA**. For two independent variables, it is called a **Two-Way ANOVA**. In the more general case, it is called an **N-Way ANOVA**, where N refers to the number of independent variables.

Because this textbook covers only elementary statistics, I will focus my attention on *one-way ANOVA* (i.e., situations of one dependent variable and one independent variable). Unless specified otherwise, I will use the generic term *ANOVA* through the rest of the chapter as an acronym for a one-way analysis of variance.

Although employed in diverse research studies, ANOVA is most widely applied in experimental and quasi-experimental designs. Within this context, the independent variable represents "treatment" and "control" groups, and the primary research question involves an assessment of how much variation in the dependent variable (i.e., some outcome measure) is explained by knowledge of group membership.

In experimental research and other applications of ANOVA, the total variation in the dependent variable is broken down or partitioned into two distinct components:

1. variation attributed to group differences (e.g., differences in the mean scores *between* the treatment group and control groups), and

2. variation attributed to individual differences *within* each group (e.g., departures of individual's scores from their group mean).

The logic of this partitioning of the total variation into the between-group and within-group components is the essence of ANOVA and is discussed in detail below.

PARTITIONING VARIATION INTO BETWEEN- AND WITHIN-GROUP DIFFERENCES

To understand the logic of ANOVA, it is necessary to get the basic idea of partitioning variation. We categorize juveniles as *nondelinquents, sporadic offenders*, or *chronic delinquents*; college professors as *boring* or *annoying*, and drug violators as *recreational users* or *addicts*. In the same way, ANOVA takes all people and/or professors, notices their variation in some variable (e.g., criminal careers, victimization experiences, and safety precautions), and then compartmentalizes this total variation into two components:

1. variation between groups of people (i.e., differences between recreational drug users and addicts), and

2. variation within these groups of people (e.g., differences among users and addicts).

The more of this total variation that is attributed to between-group differences, the better able we are to explain our primary variable of interest.

Here is a more straightforward example of variation and its components. Suppose you took a sample of 15 men and asked them about their adult criminal careers (e.g., the number of times they have been arrested as adults). You also asked them to identify which of the following three categories best describes their juvenile criminal history: 1 = *nondelinquent* (*nondelinq*), 2 = *sporadic*, and 3 = *chronic*. The number of adult arrests and the juvenile history for each person in the sample are presented in Table 12.1. Assume in this example that you are trying to explain variation in adult arrests (your dependent variable) by group membership (i.e., the person's self-defined juvenile record as *nondelinquent*, *sporadic*, or *chronic*).

TABLE 12.1 Adult Arrest History and Juvenile Record for 15 Males (coding of juvenile record: 1 = nondelinquent, 2 = sporadic, 3 = chronic)

Unsorted Data File		Sorted Data File		
# Adult Arrests	Juvenile Record	# Adult Arrests	Juvenile Record	
3	2 (sporadic)	0	1 (nondelinq)	
0	1 (nondelinq)	0	1 (nondelinq)	
5	3 (chronic)	1	1 (nondelinq)	$\bar{x}_{nondel} = 1.0$
0	1 (nondelinq)	1	1 (nondelinq)	
4	2 (sporadic)	3	1 (nondelinq)	
9	3 (chronic)	3	2 (sporadic)	
10	3 (chronic)	4	2 (sporadic)	
1	1 (nondelinq)	4	2 (sporadic)	$\bar{x}_{sporadic} = 5.0$
4	2 (sporadic)	4	2 (sporadic)	
11	3 (chronic)	10	2 (sporadic)	
1	1 (nondelinq)	5	3 (chronic)	
4	2 (sporadic)	9	3 (chronic)	
15	3 (chronic)	10	3 (chronic)	$\bar{x}_{chronic} = 10.0$
10	2 (sporadic)	11	3 (chronic)	
3	1 (nondelinq)	15	3 (chronic)	

Overall Mean = Grand Mean = $\bar{x}_{Grand} = 5.3$

A visual inspection of the unsorted data file in Table 12.1 provides a general view of the variation in adult arrests and a somewhat vague impression of the patterns of juvenile records within each group. When you go down the columns of this unsorted data, you will see that

1. the frequency of adult arrests ranges from 0 to 15 times,

2. the lowest arrest frequencies (e.g., 0 and 1 timers) involve those males with "nondelinquent" juvenile records, and

3. the most prolific adult offenders (i.e., those with over 10 arrests) are linked to those who said they had "chronic" juvenile records.

You should also notice from this unsorted data file that there is variation around the overall mean value of 5.3 adult arrests.

An easier way to visualize variation in a data file and identify patterns within it involves grouping together (i.e., "sorting") the data on the basis of the categories of the independent variable (i.e., the "groups" variable in ANOVA). When this is done in Table 12.1, the pattern of variation within and between each group is more clearly evident. These patterns include the following trends:

- The "non–juvenile delinquents" had the lowest adult arrest histories, and there is little variation in the number of adult arrests within this group. The group mean is one arrest, and the most prolific adult offender in this group had three adult arrests. Everyone else in the group had one or fewer arrests.

- The "sporadic delinquent" had on average 5 adult arrests—an arrest frequency close to the overall *grand mean* of 5.3. There is some variation around the mean arrest frequency for this group, with most having around 3 adult arrests, but one self-defined "sporadic delinquent" had 10 adult arrests.

- Males with the highest frequency of adult arrests are those who viewed themselves as "chronic delinquents" as juveniles. The mean number of adult arrests for this group was 10, and there is wide variability within this group. Most self-defined "chronics" had around 10 adult arrests, but one of them with only 5 arrests had a substantially lower frequency of adult offending than other "chronics." Another offender in this group was especially prolific, with 15 adult arrests.

Guess what? You have just completed your first "visually based" ANOVA statistical analysis. The summary above tells you that there is variation in adult arrest frequency for these 15 guys and that there is a clear pattern of differences in mean ratings between these 3 groups. There is also some but relatively less variation within each group. As you will see shortly, this pattern of relatively high between-group variation and relatively low within-group variation is the recipe for obtaining a strong and statistically significant association between the dependent variable and independent variable in an ANOVA analysis.

Calculating the Total Variation in a Dependent Variable

The goal of ANOVA is to provide a statistical summary of the amount of variation in a dependent variable that is accounted for by group membership or categories of an independent variable. How we measure this total variation is easy—it is simply the variance in scores that is not standardized by dividing by the number of observations. So, if you remember how to compute the population variance (σ^2) in Chapter 6, you have mastered the math for computing the total variation.

Similar to the population variance, the total variation in a dependent variable is reflective of the sum of the squared deviations from the overall mean score. This overall mean is called the **grand mean**. The **total variation** is denoted in ANOVA by the following computing formula and symbols:

$$\text{Total Variation} = SS_{total} = \Sigma(X_i - \overline{X}_{Grand})^2, \text{ where}$$

SS_{total} = sum of the squared deviations from the grand mean,
X_i = the individual score on the dependent variable, and
$\overline{X}_{Grand}$ = the overall mean across all cases.

The basic steps to compute the total variation in the dependent variable involve the following:

- Compute the grand mean ($\overline{x}_{grand}$) by summing up all scores and dividing by N (i.e., the total number of observations).

- Compute the deviation of each individual score (x_i) from the overall or grand mean ($x_i - \overline{x}_{grand}$).

- Square each deviation score ($x_i - \overline{x}_{grand})^2$.

- Sum up all of these squared deviations ($\sum(x_i - \overline{x}_{grand})^2$).

When the formula for the total variation is applied to the data in Table 12.1, the obtained value of SS_{total} is 293.3. This is the total amount of variation that we will attempt to explain by taking into account the amount of variation between groups or categories of the independent variable. In particular, the technique of ANOVA breaks down this total variation into two separate components:

1. $SS_{Between}$ (between-group sum of squared deviations), and

2. SS_{Within} (within-group sum of squared deviations)

As an equation, this decomposition or partitioning of total variation is given by the following formula:

$$SS_{Total} = SS_{Between} + SS_{Within}$$

Calculating the Between-Group Variation

The **between-group variation** is the amount of variation in the dependent variable that is accounted for or explained by the mean scores for each group. This component of the total variation is denoted as $SS_{Between}$, and it represents the sum of the squared deviations of each group's mean from the grand mean. Symbolically, this between-group variation is expressed by the following formula:

$$SS_{Between} = \sum N_g (\overline{x}_g - \overline{x}_{grand})^2, \text{ where}$$

N_g = number of observations in the gth group,
$\overline{x}_g$ = the mean for gth group or category of the independent variable, and
$\overline{x}_{grand}$ = the mean for the entire sample.

Applying this formula for the between-group variation to the arrest records in Table 12.1 yields the following value for $SS_{Between}$:

$$SS_{Between} = \sum N_g (\overline{x}_g - \overline{x}_{grand})^2$$

$$= N_{g1}(\overline{x}_{g1} - \overline{x}_{grand})^2 + N_{g2}(\overline{x}_{g2} - \overline{x}_{grand})^2 + N_{g3}(\overline{x}_{g3} - \overline{x}_{grand})^2$$

$$= 5(1-5.3)^2 + 5(5-5.3)^2 + 5(10-5.3)^2 = 203.3$$

By comparing this value of $SS_{Between}$ (i.e., 203.3) with the previous calculated value of SS_{Total} (i.e., 293.3), you will notice that over two-thirds of the total variation in adult arrests is due to group differences in their self-defined juvenile classifications as *nondelinquents*, *sporadic offenders*, and *chronic delinquents* (i.e., 203.3 / 293.3 = .693 ≅ two-thirds). Under these conditions, if you only knew someone's juvenile classification, you could be fairly accurate in predicting his or her adult arrest frequency by just using the mean score for his or her group.

Calculating the Within-Group Variation

As you will notice by looking at the sorted data file in Table 12.1, there is variation in the adult arrests around each group of males. For example, most "sporadic" delinquents had 4 adult arrests, but one of them had 10. Similarly, most self-defined "chronic" delinquents had around 10 adult arrests, but 1 of them had only 5 arrests in adulthood.

This variation around each group mean is called the **within-group variation**. This sum of the squared deviations of the individual scores from their respective group mean is denoted as SS_{Within}. It is also called *error variance* (i.e., SS_{Error}) because it is the amount of error when using just the group means to predict the overall variation in a dependent variable. The within-group variation is represented by the following formula:

$$SS_{Within} = \sum(x_i - \overline{x}_g)^2, \text{ where}$$

x_i = the individual's score on the dependent variable, and
$\overline{x}_g$ = the mean value on the dependent variable for the gth group or category of the independent variable.

Applying this formula for the within-group variation to the sorted data file in Table 12.1 yields the following value for SS_{Within}:

$$SS_{Within} = \sum(x_i - \overline{x}_g)^2$$

$$= \sum[(x_i - \overline{x}_{g1})^2 + (x_i - \overline{x}_{g2})^2 + (x_i - \overline{x}_{g3})^2]$$

$$\begin{aligned}=&[(0-1)^2 + (0-1)^2 + (1-1)^2 + (1-1)^2 + (3-1)^2] + \\ &[(3-5)^2 + (4-5)^2 + (4-5)^2 + (4-5)^2 + (10-5)^2] + \\ &[(5-10)^2 + (9-10)^2 + (10-10)^2 + (11-10)^2 + (15-10)^2] = 90.0\end{aligned}$$

This within-group variation is also commonly computed simply by subtracting the between-group variation from the total variation. In other words, $SS_{Within} = SS_{Total} - SS_{Between}$. For this example on adult arrests, SS_{Total} is 293.3 and $SS_{Between}$ is 203.3, so SS_{Within} equals 90.0 (i.e., 293.3 − 203.3 = 90.0). It does not matter whether SS_{Within} is calculated by summing up the squared deviations of individual scores from their respective mean score or by the method of subtraction ($SS_{Within} = SS_{Total} - SS_{Between}$). However, the subtraction method is often quicker and less error prone, especially when you have a large sample size.

When all is said and done, ANOVA reduces to the investigation of the total variation and its sources. These sources are variation between groups and variation within groups. You have the basic knowledge necessary for performing an ANOVA on any data if you understand the logic of computation of the following formula:

$$SS_{Total} = SS_{Between} + SS_{Within}$$

HYPOTHESIS TESTING AND MEASURES OF ASSOCIATION IN ANOVA

ANOVA is similar to other statistical procedures in that it is used for hypothesis testing and for assessing the magnitude of association between variables. These related functions of ANOVA are described below.

Testing the Hypothesis of Equality of Group Means

ANOVA involves the comparison of group means, so it makes sense that hypothesis testing within this context would be a statement about these mean differences. In fact, this is exactly what the null hypothesis involves in ANOVA. Specifically, the null hypothesis (H_o) is that the population means for each group are identical and equal in numerical value to the overall mean of the population. The symbolic form of this null hypothesis in ANOVA is

$$H_o: \mu_{g1} = \mu_{g2} = \mu_{g3} = \mu_{g4} = \ldots \mu_{gk} = \mu_{grand}, \text{ where}$$

μ_{g1} = the population mean for group 1 and the same notation for all other groups 1 to k, and
μ_{grand} = the overall population mean.

When sample data is used to estimate population parameters, the null hypothesis (H_o) is expressed in terms of the equality of sample means. In symbolic form, this H_o about sample means is expressed as

$$H_o: \overline{x}_{g1} = \overline{x}_{g2} = \overline{x}_{g3} = \overline{x}_{g4} = \ldots \overline{x}_{gk} = \overline{x}_{grand}$$

Now, think about what this null hypothesis about the equality of groups implies about the magnitude of between-group and within-group variation. If the group means are the same and they all have the same value as the total mean, there is no between-group variation ($SS_{Between} = 0$), and the total variation is represented entirely by within-group variation ($SS_{Total} = SS_{Within}$). In this situation, knowledge of one's group membership does not help account for the total variation in the dependent variable because the groups have the same mean value.

The formal procedure for testing the hypothesis of equal means in ANOVA involves a comparison of the ratio of between-group and within-group variation. However, because of differences in the number of observations in the calculation of $SS_{Between}$ (i.e., the number of groups [k]) and SS_{Within} (i.e., the number of individual scores), these dual sources of variation need to be standardized for comparative purposes. Accordingly, each component is divided by its respective degrees of freedom and converted into what is called (1) *mean sum of squares between groups* (**MS**$_{Between}$) and (2) *mean sum of squares within groups* (**MS**$_{Within}$). The specific formulas for converting sums of squares (SS) to mean squares (MS) are

$$MS_{Between} = SS_{Between} / k - 1, \text{ where}$$

k = the number of groups.

$$MS_{Within} = SS_{Within} / N - k, \text{ where}$$

k = the number of groups, and N = the number of observations.

After the sources of variation are standardized by their degrees of freedom, the formal test of the hypothesis of equal means is conducted by examining the ratio of $MS_{Between}$ and MS_{Within} variance. This ratio is called the **F-ratio**, and it is the value of this test statistic that is used to evaluate the null hypothesis. The F-ratio formula is defined as

$$\text{F-ratio} = MS_{Between} / MS_{Within}$$

Similar to other test statistics explored in this book (e.g., z-test, t-test, and χ^2), the test of this *F-ratio* has a sampling distribution that defines rare or common outcomes if the null hypothesis is true. The critical value of this F-test depends on the alpha level (i.e., the selected probability of making a Type I error) and the degrees of freedom associated with the between-group and within-group components. Appendix D provides a table of critical values of the F-test for various degrees of freedom and the .05 alpha level.

When applied to our example of adult arrests among 15 males in Table 12.1, the critical value of the F-test would be 3.885 for an alpha level of .05. This value is obtained by recognizing that there are $K - 1 = 2$ degrees of freedom associated with the $MS_{Between}$ (i.e., $k = 3$ groups) and 12 degrees of freedom associated with the MS_{Within} (i.e., $N - k = 15 - 3 = 12$). The critical F-value of 3.885 is found by looking for the value in Appendix D that intersects 2 and 12 degrees of freedom. Under this decision rule, we will reject the null hypothesis that the three groups of guys have the same adult arrest frequency if our obtained F-value exceeds our critical value of 3.885.

Although the visual inspection of the group means in Table 12.1 suggests that nondelinquent juveniles, sporadic juvenile offenders, and

chronic delinquents are substantially different in their adult arrest records, the test of the F-ratio provides a formal statistical evaluation of
the hypothesis of equal means. The ANOVA summary table that provides the essential information for testing this hypothesis about group
differences in arrest histories is presented in Table 12.2.

TABLE 12.2 ANOVA Summary Table for Adult Arrest Frequency by Type of Juvenile Record (groups = nondelinquent, sporadic, and chronic) *N* = 15 Males

Source	Sum of Squares	df	Means Sum of Squares	F-Value	P(alpha)
Between Groups	203.3	2	101.7	13.56	< .01
Within Groups	90.0	12	7.5		
Total	293.3	14			

When the observed F-value is compared with the expected F-value
under our decision rule, the results in Table 12.2 indicate that we would
reject the null hypothesis of equal means. By looking at the mean values
for each group, we would be able to further specify the nature of the
between-group differences. In this particular example, the rejection of
the null hypothesis of equal means is due primarily to a high mean
level of adult arrests by "chronic" delinquents relative to the "nondelinquents" when they were juveniles. Thus, the formal test provided by
the F-ratio and the visual comparison of the nature of the differences in
means for different groups are the methods utilized to evaluate hypotheses within an ANOVA framework.

Measures of Association in ANOVA

The primary measure of association used in ANOVA applications focuses on the ratio of the between-group and total variation. This ratio is
called by various names in the research literature. It is most often referred to as **eta squared** (η^2), but is also called the *correlation ratio*. The
computing formula for η^2 is very simple—it is the ratio of between-group variation to total-group variation and is expressed as the
following equation:

$$\text{Eta squared} = \eta^2 = SS_{Between} / SS_{Total}$$

This measure of association can be interpreted in at least two different ways. First, it is often viewed as a *proportional reduction of error* (PRE) measure because it describes the proportion by which errors in guessing the scores on the dependent variable are reduced by knowledge of the independent variable. Second, it is treated as the proportion of the variation in the dependent variable explained by the independent variable. Although social scientists often prefer the second interpretation of η^2, the two expressions are equivalent representations of basically the same thing.

When applied to the ANOVA summary table for adult arrests (see Table 12.2), the η^2 value is .69 (i.e., $SS_{Between} / SS_{Total} = 203.3 / 293.3 = .69$). As a PRE measure, this finding suggests that the errors in predicting adult arrest frequencies solely based on the overall mean are reduced by 69% by knowledge of the particular group membership of each male in the sample. Similarly, we can also say that group membership explains about 69% of the variation in adult arrest prevalence.

As you might expect because they share a common interest in the ratio of variances, there is a strong relationship between the size of η^2 and the likelihood of finding a statistically significant F-ratio. Large ratios of between- to within-group variation will result in large values of η^2 and often yield statistically significant F-ratios if the sample size is sufficiently large ($N > 50$). However, with very large sample sizes ($N > 1,000$), relatively small η^2 values (e.g., $\eta^2 < 2\%$) may also yield statistically significant F-ratios. Thus, for ANOVA and other analytic techniques, the informed consumer or user often balances the formal conclusions of statistical significance with the substantive importance of the observed group differences. Statistically significant findings in some cases may be substantively trivial.

ISSUES IN THE ANALYSIS OF VARIANCE

ANOVA is a statistical approach for examining group differences on a quantitatively measured dependent variable. It provides a statistical answer to the question about whether knowledge of group membership helps us explain variation in this dependent variable.

To use ANOVA wisely, several assumptions are required. Aside from interval or ratio measurement of the dependent variable, hypothesis testing about population means requires random sampling from the population(s). The categorical means for the independent variable are assumed to be independent (i.e., unrelated to each other). It is also assumed that the dependent variable is normally distributed in the population and that the distributions of the dependent variable within categories of the independent variable have equal variances in the population. Fortunately, ANOVA is able to handle some departures from these assumptions (e.g., normal distributions and equal variances) if the sample size(s) are large.

Similar to the problems with a bivariate contingency table analysis, the use of one-way ANOVA in nonexperimental research is also susceptible to the problems of misspecification by failing to include other variables in the analysis. ANOVA can be easily extended to include multiple independent variables to better isolate the unique or conditional impact of group membership on the dependent variable once these other factors are taken into account. In experimental research, the impact of these other factors is controlled by design through random assignment to "treatment" and "control" groups. However, for researchers who use one-way ANOVA in nonexperimental settings, it is extremely important to be aware of existing theory and previous research. Knowledge of the substantive area will help reduce the dreaded GIGO problem that arises from uninformed statistical analysis using ANOVA or any other procedure.

SUMMARY OF MAJOR POINTS

- The analysis of variance (ANOVA) is a popular statistical approach for examining group differences on a quantitatively measured dependent variable.

- ANOVA involves the decomposition or partitioning of the total variation in a dependent variable into two independent components: (1) between-group variation and (2) within-group variation.

- The between-group variation reflects the sum of the squared deviations of each group's mean from the overall or grand mean. The within-group variation is the sum of the squared deviations of each individual's score from the mean for their respective group.

- The null hypothesis (H_o) in ANOVA is that there are no differences in the group means in the population. We test this hypothesis using sample means as our best estimates of the population means.

- The statistical significance of the mean differences in ANOVA is tested by the examination of the ratio of the between-group and within-group variation. These sources of variation are converted to variances by adjusting for their degrees of freedom. The subsequent ratio of these mean square components is called an *F-test*. By comparing our observed F-ratio with the expected F-ratio based on our decision rules (i.e., alpha level and degrees of freedom), we reach a conclusion about rejecting or not rejecting the H_o of equal means.

- The primary measure of association in ANOVA is eta squared (η^2). Eta squared provides a descriptive summary of the proportion of variation in a dependent variable that is explained by the independent variable. It is also interpreted as the proportion by which errors in guessing the scores on the dependent variable on the basis of the overall mean are reduced by knowledge of one's membership in particular categories of the independent variable.

- ANOVA requires interval or ratio measurement of the dependent variable, a normal distribution, random sampling, independence of the categories of the independent variables, and equal population variances in the distribution of the dependent variable within categories of the independent variables. When large samples are used, slight departures from some of these assumptions (e.g., normal distributions and equal variances) do not nullify the value of ANOVA as a statistical method.

- ANOVA involving one dependent variable and one independent variable is called *one-way ANOVA*. ANOVA can be easily extended to multiple independent variables. For users of one-way ANOVA, informed analysis requires knowledge of substantive theory and previous research to minimize the chances of misspecifying the magnitude of group differences on the dependent variable. Substantive theory and previous research will tell the researcher what other variables to include in the analysis.

KEY TERMS

Analysis of Variance (ANOVA)
Between-Group Variation
Eta Squared (η^2)
F-Ratio
Grand Mean
$MS_{Between}$ Versus MS_{Within}

N-Way ANOVA
One-Way ANOVA
Total Variation
Two-Way ANOVA
Within-Group Variation

MAJOR FORMULAS AND SYMBOLIC REPRESENTATIONS

$Total\ Variation = SS_{total} = \Sigma(X_i - \overline{X}_{Grand})^2$, where
SS_{total} = sum of the squared deviations from the grand mean,
X_i = the individual score on the dependent variable, and
$\overline{X}_{Grand}$ = the overall mean across all cases.

$SS_{Total} = SS_{Between} + SS_{Within}$

$SS_{Between} = \sum N_g(\overline{x}_g - \overline{x}_{grand})^2$, where
N_g = the number of observations in the *g*th group,
$\overline{x}_g$ = the mean for *g*th group or category of the independent variable, and
$\overline{x}_{grand}$ = the mean for the entire sample.

$SS_{Within} = \sum(x_i - \overline{x}_g)^2$, where
x_i = the individual's score on the dependent variable, and
$\overline{x}_g$ = the mean value on the dependent variable for the *g*th group or category of the independent variable.

$H_o: \mu_{g1} = \mu_{g2} = \mu_{g3} = \mu_{g4} = \ldots \mu_{gk} = \mu_{grand}$, where
μ_{g1} = the population mean for group 1 and the same notation for all other groups 1 to *k*, and
μ_{grand} = the overall population mean.

$MS_{Between} = SS_{Between} / k - 1$, where
k = the number of groups.

$MS_{Within} = SS_{Within} / N - k$, where
k = the number of groups, and *N* = the number of observations.

F-ratio = $MS_{Between} / MS_{Within}$

Eta squared = $\eta^2 = SS_{Between} / SS_{Total}$

SPSS Applications (*Optional Section*)

SPSS provides procedures for conducting one-way ANOVA and ANOVA with multiple independent variables. The steps involved in conducting a one-way ANOVA in SPSS include the following:

- Click on the **Analyze** menu.

- Click on **Compare Means**.

- Select the procedure **One-Way ANOVA**.

> - Select a particular variable as the dependent variable, and click in the box marked **Dependent Listing**. Select a particular variable as the independent variable, and click in the box marked **Factor**.
> - Click on the button labeled **OK** to generate the SPSS output that contains the ANOVA Summary Table.

APPLYING WHAT YOU HAVE LEARNED

1. ANOVA is the appropriate statistical procedure for bivariate relationships when

   a. the dependent variable is measured on an interval or ratio scale, and the independent variable is measured on a nominal or ordinal score.

   b. the dependent variable is measured on an nominal scale.

   c. it is unclear what variable is the independent variable and what variable is the dependent variable.

2. The null hypothesis under ANOVA is that the mean scores on the dependent variable are

   a. equal for all groups or categories of the independent variable.

   b. different across categories of the independent variable.

3. ANOVA breaks down variation in the dependent variable into

   a. total variation.

   b. between-group variation.

   c. within-group variation.

   d. all of the above are true.

4. The F-ratio in ANOVA compares the relative sizes of the

   a. total and within-group variation.

   b. total and between-group variation.

   c. between-group and within-group variation.

   d. sample size and the population size.

5. If group membership significantly influences the dependent variable, which of the following ANOVA outcomes would you expect?

   a. An observed F-ratio that exceeds the expected F-value under the null hypothesis.

   b. A large eta-square value (η^2).

   c. Large between-group differences relative to the within-group variation.

   d. All of the above are true.

For each of the following sets of group means, indicate whether you think group membership would have a weak, moderate, or strong impact on explaining variation in the dependent variable. Assume small within-group variation and sample sizes of about 20 people in each group.

6. $\bar{x}_1 = 2; \bar{x}_2 = 4; \bar{x}_3 = 40 \rightarrow$ weak, moderate, or strong impact? _____

7. $\bar{x}_1 = 48; \bar{x}_2 = 36; \bar{x}_3 = 32 \rightarrow$ weak, moderate, or strong impact? _____

8. $\bar{x}_1 = 100; \bar{x}_2 = 101; \bar{x}_3 = 100 \rightarrow$ weak, moderate, or strong impact? _____

9. $\bar{x}_1 = 100; \bar{x}_2 = 101; \bar{x}_3 = 100; \bar{x}_4 = 5 \rightarrow$ weak, moderate, or strong impact? _____

10. $\bar{x}_1 = 48; \bar{x}_2 = 46; \bar{x}_3 = 50 \rightarrow$ weak, moderate, or strong impact? _____

Are there social class differences in the number of traffic violations? Here are the sample means and standard deviations for the number of tickets given for each group: lower class (mean = 3.2, *sd* = 1.4), middle class (mean = 14.2, *sd* = 4.3), and upper class (mean = 4.5, *sd* = 1.1). You have 50 drivers in each group in your sample.

11. If you evaluate these social class differences in an ANOVA procedure, what is the null hypothesis?

   a. H_o: u1 = u2 = u3, where *u1* = the mean tickets for lower-class drivers, *u2* = the mean tickets for middle-class drivers, and *u3* = the mean tickets for upper-class drivers.

   b. H_o: u1 < u2 < u3, where *u1* = the mean tickets for lower-class drivers, *u2* = the mean tickets for middle-class drivers, and *u3* = the mean tickets for upper-class drivers.

    c. The null hypothesis cannot be specified because there is no dependent variable.

12. If you were to conduct an ANOVA on this data, what do you think you would find?

    a. An insignificant F-ratio because of large between-group and large within-group variation

    b. An insignificant F-ratio because of small between-group and large within-group variation

    c. A significant F-ratio because of large between-group and small within-group variation

    d. A significant F-ratio because of large between-group and large within-group variation

13. What does this sample data show about social class differences in getting tickets?

    a. Middle-class drivers get more tickets than either lower- or upper-class drivers.

    b. There is greater variability in the number of tickets received by middle-class drivers than is true of either lower- or upper-class drivers.

    c. Both a and b are true.

14. Which of the following factors may explain these social class differences in getting traffic tickets?

    a. Middle-class drivers may be worse drivers than other social class groups.

    b. Police may target middle-class drivers for traffic violations more than other groups.

    c. The samples may be biased against middle-class drivers (i.e., making middle-class drivers look like they are worse drivers).

    d. Lower-class and upper-class drivers may be more likely to lie about their bad driving records than middle-class drivers.

    e. All of the above are possible explanations for these results.

15. You conduct an analysis of variance (ANOVA) on the effectiveness of various types of treatment (e.g., drug therapy, electric shock, chemi-

cal castration, and cognitive-behavioral therapy) on the risks of recidivism for sex offenders. Your coefficient of determination (eta-squared) is .90, or 90%. What does this coefficient tell you in this example?

a. It means that chemical castration is the most effective treatment for sex offenders.

b. It means that about 90% of the variation in the risks of recidivism is explained by differences in the type of treatment received by sex offenders.

c. It means that about 90% of the variation in the type of sex offender treatment is explained by differences in recidivism.

d. It means that there are relatively small differences in recidivism risks based on the type of treatment and relatively large within-treatment differences in recidivism risks.

e. Only a and b are true.

16. Here is some hypothetical data on the number of bribes taken by 10 politicians. Five of these officials are Democrats (D), and five are Republicans (R).

Number of Bribes Taken by Democrat (D) and Republican (R) Politicians (hypothetical data for 10 politicians)	
Political Bribes	Party
2	D
3	R
5	D
6	D
5	R
7	R
7	D
10	R
10	D
15	R

a. What is the dependent variable in this example? _____

b. What is the independent variable in this example? _____

c. By visually inspecting the data in the above table, do you think there are major or minor differences in the average number of bribes taken by Democrats and Republicans? _____ Explain why you expect this conclusion. _____

d. What is the SS_{total} in this bribery data? _____

e. What is the $SS_{Between}$ in this bribery data? _____

f. What is the SS_{Within} in this bribery data? _____

g. Complete the following ANOVA Summary Table for the bribery data:

Source	Sum of Squares	df	Mean Sum of Squares	F-value
Between Groups				
Within Groups				
Total				

h. If you were to test the hypothesis that the means are equal, what critical value of the F-test would be necessary to reject the H_o about the .05 significance level? F-critical value at .05 level = _____

i. What conclusion do you reach about political party differences in taking bribes based on this F-test? _____

j. What is the value of eta-squared (η^2) in this example? _____ Show how you derived this value from the data in the ANOVA summary table. _____

k. Interpret the value of eta squared (η^2) in this example. _____ ✦

13 *Correlation and Regression*

*M*any important substantive questions in criminology focus on the relationship between two quantitative variables and how changes in an independent variable affect a dependent variable. For example, each of the following variables is thought to decrease crime rates under the deterrence doctrine: (1) increases in police expenditures and number of police officers per 1,000 residents, (2) increases in clearance rates, (3) increases in the number of "three-strikes" convictions, (4) increases in the number of capital sentences, and (5) increases in the number of citizens who own firearms. Other applications of the relationship between two quantitative variables include (1) hours of police sensitivity training and civilian complaints, (2) monetary funding for Head Start programs and the magnitude of decline in long-term welfare and criminal justice expenditures, (3) funding for drug treatment facilities and drug abuse rates, and (4) school dropout rates and juvenile crime rates.

When exploring these types of relationships, the analyst will want to use statistical techniques that (1) summarize the association between the variables and (2) offer a particular measure of how unit changes in one variable affect the other variable. The techniques of bivariate correlation and linear regression are the tools used by criminologists to answer these types of research questions.

*T*his chapter describes the primary methods for measuring the nature and magnitude of the statistical association between two quantitative variables that are measured on an interval or ratio scale. These techniques include (1) **correlation** (for measuring the direction and magnitude of association between two variables) and (2) **regression analysis** (for assessing the nature and magnitude of change in a dependent variable for a unit change in an independent variable). Before directly investigating these approaches, however, let us begin with a more intuitive, visual tour of the idea of covariation between two quantitative variables. This visual approach involves the shape and patterning of data points in a scatter diagram (i.e., a scatterplot).

THE SCATTERPLOT OF TWO INTERVAL OR RATIO VARIABLES

Regardless of the type of statistical analysis, the first step is always to look at the data. Visual inspection of the data prior to its complete analysis will tell you whether there are odd observations (i.e., outliers), whether the distribution looks approximately normal (i.e., thereby allowing for z-transformations), and whether the size of the differences in sample means or proportions is likely to result in statistically significant or insignificant results. In addition, a bar chart or pie chart provides immediate visual recognition of the modal category—it is the longest bar or biggest piece of the pie.

When exploring the relationship between two quantitative variables, visual methods have at least the same, if not even greater, importance for subsequent analysis. In fact, by plotting each case's value on the two variables in Cartesian coordinates (x, y), the resulting graph will offer visual evidence of two possible patterns. First, it will demonstrate whether these data points cluster in a particular manner (e.g., low scores on X tend to go with low scores of Y). Second, it will show whether this pattern is indicative of a linear trajectory (e.g., increasing scores on X are associated with increasing scores on Y for all values of X).

This visual representation of the relationship between two quantitative variables is called a **scatter diagram** or, equivalently, a **scatterplot**. It is constructed simply by plotting on a graph the intersection of the scores on variable X and variable Y for each individual observation. What a scatterplot can reveal about the nature and magnitude of the relationship between two quantitative variables is illustrated in Figure 13.1.

A quick look at the scatterplots in Figure 13.1 tells you immediately something about the nature of the relationships between the two sets of variables. In the top scatterplot, the data points exhibit a tightly clustered band that goes from bottom left to top right. Substantively, it suggests that states with higher school dropout rates have higher homicide rates or, equivalently, that low dropout rates are associated with low homicide rates. This relationship is also clearly not a perfect linear relationship because the data points do not fall directly on one single line. However, their clustering in a "cigar-like" ban does suggest that dropout and homicide rates are related.[1]

---

1. If you are thinking that "kids who drop out of school kill people," you are committing the *ecological fallacy* by inferring individual-level behavior from aggregate-level data on states. It could be that dropouts are more prone to kill people (because of frustration, labeling, and various other reasons), but we cannot make this inference from state-level data. Instead, the scatterplot in Figure 13.1 only suggests that these two variables are related within these aggregate units.

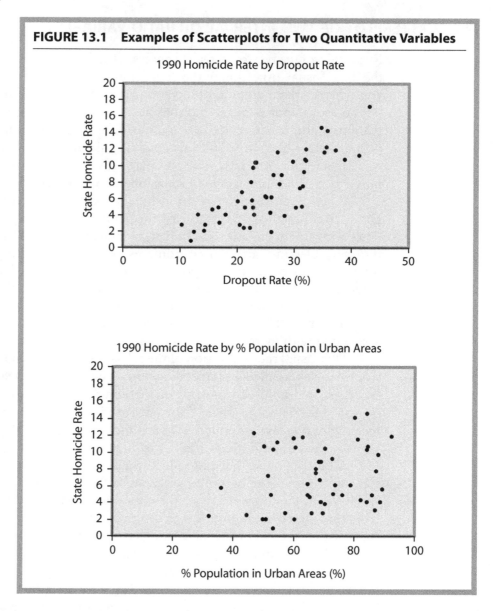

FIGURE 13.1   Examples of Scatterplots for Two Quantitative Variables

The scatterplot in the bottom panel of Figure 13.1 provides a different visual image of the relationship between two quantitative variables. In this case, the data points are more widely spread across the graph in a pattern similar to a "shotgun blast" of a target from a distance. Substantively, this scatterplot suggests that highly urban states do not necessarily have either high or low homicide rates, and the same is true for less urban states. In contrast to the more uniform visual pattern for dropout rates, the random-looking arrangement of the "dots" in this scatterplot indicates a relatively weak relationship between a state's homicide rate and the proportion of its population that lives in an urban area.

So, here are the nuts and bolts on scatterplots. First, you construct them by plotting the intersection of the scores on two variables (i.e., variables Y and X). Each axis of the graph should be arranged from low scores to high scores so that the lowest score on both variable Y and X is represented by the "dot" that is closer than any other point to the lower left-hand corner of the graph. The scatterplots in Figure 13.1 display this proper setup of the Y and X axis. Second, look at the scatter pattern of the data points to determine the direction and magnitude of the relationship between the variables. Some basic rules for deriving the direction and magnitude of this relationship include the following:

- The more the data points form a narrow ellipse, the stronger the relationship between the variables. A "shotgun blast" pattern is indicative of a weak relationship, a "cigar shape" reflects a stronger relationship, a narrower "cigarette shape" is even stronger, and the alignment of all data points on a nonparallel straight line indicates a perfect relationship between the two variables.

- The direction of the relationship is whether it is positive (i.e., as x increases, y increases, or as x decreases, y decreases) or negative (i.e., as x increases, y decreases, or as x decreases, y increases). Variables that are positively related move in the same direction, whereas negative relationships move in the opposite directions (e.g., x increases and y decreases).

- In a properly constructed scatterplot, the scatter of points would indicate a positive relationship if the band of data points is arranged from the lower-left to the upper-right ends of the graph. The scatter pattern for dropout and homicide rates displayed in the top panel of Figure 13.1 illustrates this visual image of a positive relationship. In contrast, a negative relationship is revealed by a band of data points that follow a top-left to lower-right pattern. For both positive and negative relationships, the narrower the band of points, the stronger the relationship between the two variables.

Scatterplots are a most useful visual aid to data analysis when the number of observations or data points is relatively small (i.e., $N < 100$). For large sample problems, the pattern of dots becomes somewhat of a big blur and changing notation does not help much (e.g., using the # sign to represent multiple observations with the same coordinate values).

Even though they are somewhat messy with large N's, it is important to realize that the pattern of data points in a scatterplot provides direct evidence of the appropriateness of the particular statistical measures of association for quantitative variables. For example, correlation and regression analyses assume a **linear relationship** between the variables, an assumption that can be empirically evaluated by looking at the scatterplot. Similarly, a scatterplot will also help identify outliers and other data points that strongly influence the results of these statistical analyses. Given its value for these purposes, you should always look at the scatterplots as a preliminary step in the statistical analysis of bivariate associations among quantitative variables.

THE CORRELATION COEFFICIENT

When most statisticians and criminologists talk about statistical associations between variables, they use the generic term *correlation* to convey this relationship. There are different types of correlation coefficients in statistics (e.g., Spearman's rank-order correlation coefficient, Pearson's product moment correlation coefficient, and canonical correlations).

For our purposes, I will focus entirely on Pearson's correlation coefficient (symbolized as r_{xy}, r_{yx}, or just plain r) because it is, by far, the most commonly used measure of association in social research. I will also use the generic name *correlation* throughout the rest of this chapter to refer to Pearson's correlation coefficient. It is just easier to drop Pearson's name, OK? No disrespect is intended.

The **correlation coefficient** is a measure of the linear association between two variables. It has some well-defined properties. Specifically, it is a symmetrical measure (i.e., $r_{xy} = r_{yx}$), and the value of the coefficient ranges from −1.00 to +1.00. A correlation (r) of −1.00 indicates a perfect, negative relationship between the two variables, and the value of +1.00 indicates a perfect, positive correlation. You will never see a perfect correlation (either r = −1.0 or r = +1.0) unless you have screwed up.[2] An-

---

2. For example, if you correlated the age of 10 people with the age of these same 10 people (i.e., you are correlating *age* with *age*), you should get a perfect positive correlation unless the people cannot reliably remember their age.

other property of the correlation coefficient is that it obtains the value of 0 when there is no linear relationship between the two variables.

What counts as a large correlation? Well, definitely an $r = \pm 1.0$, but outside these limits the answer depends on disciplinary tradition and sample size. As a general "rule of thumb" for moderate to large sample sizes ($N > 50$ and < 500), here are some general guidelines for labeling the magnitude of the correlation (r) between two quantitative variables:

- *Perfect relationship:* $r = \pm 1.00$

- *Strong relationship:* $r = +.70$ to $+.99$ and $r = -.70$ to $-.99$

- *Moderately strong relationship:* $r = +.50$ to $+.69$ and $r = -.50$ to $-.69$

- *Moderate relationship:* $r = +.35$ to $+.49$ and $r = -.35$ to $-.49$

- *Moderately weak relationship:* $r = +.20$ to $+.34$ and $r = -.20$ to $-.34$

- *Weak relationship:* $r = +.10$ to $+.19$ and $r = -.10$ to $-.19$

- *No relationship:* $r = .00$ to $+.09$ and $r = .00$ to $-.09$

The correlation coefficient is a summary measure of the relative nature of the covariation between two continuous variables and their variances. When two variables covary together more than they vary internally to each other, a strong correlation coefficient will be found. Symbolically, these components of the correlation coefficient are expressed in the following manner:

$$r_{xy} = r_{yx} = r = cov(xy) / \sqrt{var(x)\ var(y)} = cov(xy) / sd(x)\ sd(y), \text{ where}$$

$cov(xy)$ = the covariation or cross-product of variables x and y,
$var(x)$ = the variation in variable x,
$var(y)$ = the variation in variable y,
$sd(x)$ = the standard deviation of variable x, and
$sd(y)$ = the standard deviation of variable y.

When the definitional properties of each of these components are expanded, the definitional formula for the correlation coefficient is

$$r = \frac{cov(xy)}{sd(x)sd(y)} = \frac{\sum(x-\bar{x})(y-\bar{y})/n-1}{\sqrt{\dfrac{\sum(x-\bar{x})^2}{n-1}}\sqrt{\dfrac{\sum(y-\bar{y})^2}{n-1}}}$$

A close examination of this formula for the correlation coefficient reveals the process necessary to compute it. The particular steps in this computational process include the following:

- Compute the means for each variable ($\bar{x}$, $\bar{y}$).

- For each individual case or observation, subtract the individual score from the mean score for each variable ($x - \bar{x}$, $y - \bar{y}$) and then square these deviation scores.

- Multiply each deviation score from $\bar{x}$ by each deviation score from $\bar{y}$. This cross-product of the deviation scores is indicated by $(x - \bar{x})(y - \bar{y})$.

- Compute the standard deviation for each variable by summing up the squared deviations from their respective means, dividing by $n - 1$, and taking the square root.

- Compute the covariance of x and y by summing up the cross-product of the deviation scores (i.e., $\sum(x - \bar{x})(y - \bar{y})$) and dividing by $n - 1$.

- Calculate the correlation coefficient by dividing the covariance of x and y by the product of standard deviations of x and the standard deviation of y.

Table 13.1 provides a simple example of computing the correlation between the number of onions consumed per day (x) and the number of friends (y) reported by five college students. The correlation in this case ($r = -.88$) indicates a strong negative relationship between onion consumption and the number of friends. If you want more friends, eat fewer onions. Or, if you want fewer friends, eat more onions. The logic of these computation details applies to any two quantitative variables and to any number of observations.

If you plotted the data on onions and friends, you would notice that the data points fall pretty much on a straight line that goes from the upper-left corner to the bottom right end of the graph (see Figure 13.2). This visual pattern would suggest a strong, negative relationship between the two variables. From this perspective, the correlation coefficient represents a summary measure of the degree to which data points converge on a straight line. The nature of this straight line (i.e., the point where it intersects the Y-axis and its slope) is the foundation for linear regression analysis.

TABLE 13.1 Computing a Correlation Between Two Quantitative Variables
(x = number of onions consumed, y = number of friends, n = 5 students)

x	y	$(x - \bar{x})$	$(y - \bar{y})$	$(x - \bar{x})^2$	$(y - \bar{y})^2$	$(x - \bar{x})(y - \bar{y})$
4	10	1	0	1	0	0
3	8	0	−2	0	4	0
2	12	−1	2	1	4	−2
5	6	2	−4	4	16	−8
1	14	−2	4	4	16	−8
$\sum =$ 15	50	0	0	10	40	−18

Computations:

$$\bar{x} = \sum x / n = 15 / 5 = 3.0; \ \bar{y} = \sum y / n = 50 / 5 = 10.0;$$

$$cov(xy) = \sum (x - \bar{x})(y - \bar{y}) / n - 1 = -18 / 4 = -4.5$$

$$sd(x) = \sqrt{(x - \bar{x})^2 / n - 1} = \sqrt{10 / 4} = \sqrt{2.5} = 1.6$$

$$sd(y) = \sqrt{(y - \bar{y})^2 / n - 1} = \sqrt{40 / 4} = \sqrt{10} = 3.2$$

$$r = cov(xy) / sd(x)sd(y) = -4.5 / (1.6)(3.2) = -.88$$

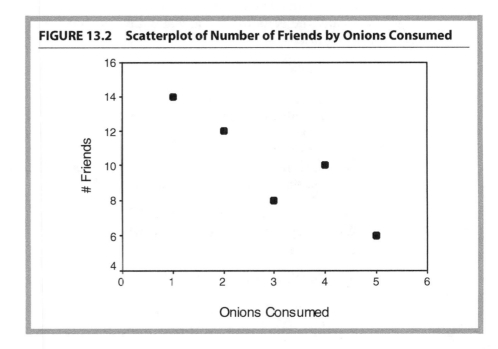

FIGURE 13.2 Scatterplot of Number of Friends by Onions Consumed

REGRESSION ANALYSIS

The correlation coefficient is a symmetrical measure of association between quantitative variables. It does not matter what variable is considered the X variable or the Y variable—you get the same results regardless. However, in many applications of criminological research, we have sufficient information to treat quantitative variables in causal terms by specifying them as independent (causes) or dependent (effects) variables. For these types of analysis, we designate Y as the dependent variable and X as the independent variable(s).

Instead of just summarizing the bivariate association between variables, a regression analysis is conducted in order to assess how changes in the independent variable influence the dependent variable. If, for example, you increase your study time by 1 hour per day, what effect, if any, will this have on your percentile score on the next test? For each additional onion consumed, how many friends will you lose? For every additional execution, how much does the homicide rate change? All of these examples share a common concern with discovering how unit changes in an independent variable affect the nature and level of change in a dependent variable. The **regression coefficient** (i.e., the slope) provides the answer to these questions.

Regression analysis involves the specification of a linear equation that links an independent variable to a dependent variable. This equation is basically the equation for any straight line and is represented by the following notation:

$Y = \alpha + \beta X$, where

Y = the value of the dependent variable,
X = the value of the independent variable,
α = the y-intercept (i.e., the point where the regression line crosses the Y-axis), and
β = the slope coefficient representing the effect of a unit change in X on the value of the dependent variable.

Both α (the **Y-intercept term**) and β (the **slope**) are population values. When they are estimated with sample data, the form of the regression equation is

$Y = a + bX$, where

a = the sample estimate of α, and
b = the sample estimate of β.

The regression equation is based on a **linear relationship**. As a linear formulation, the effect of X on Y is assumed to be identical for every value of X. Alternative nonlinear model specifications are also used within a regression framework (e.g., $Y = a + bX^2$). However, this chapter will focus on linear regression analysis.

As mentioned in the discussion of scatterplots, it is important to look at a visual display of the data before conducting a regression analysis. This preliminary scan of the scatterplot may reveal patterns of non-linear relationships that may be "linearized" through transformations of the data. Such a linear transformation is illustrated in Figure 13.3. This revised coding of the X variable (i.e., $X = log\ X$) may now be included instead of X in the regression equation to assess the effects of the independent variable on the dependent variable. However, in this particular case, the interpretation of the effect of X is in terms of log-unit changes rather than unit changes. These alternative forms and transformations are discussed more fully in more advanced statistics books.

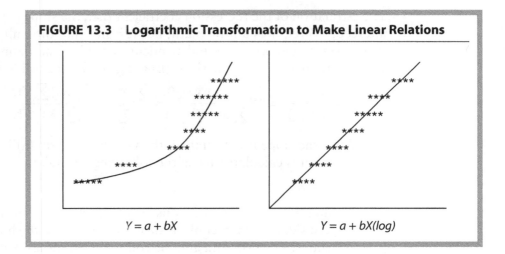

FIGURE 13.3   Logarithmic Transformation to Make Linear Relations

$Y = a + bX$ $Y = a + bX(log)$

The regression equation ($Y = a + bX$) is based on the method of **least squares**. This method involves finding the single best-fitting straight line that serves to minimize the total distance between the data points. Statisticians have shown that this "best-fitting" line occurs when the values of the y-intercept (a) and the slope (b) are determined in such a way to minimize the sum of the squared errors between the observed and predicted scores on the dependent variable. These "least square" errors in predicting Y from X are called the **residual sum of squares** ($SS_{residual}$) and is symbolized as

$$SS_{residual} = \sum (Y_{observed} - Y_{predicted})^2 = \sum (Y - \hat{Y})^2,$$

where $\hat{Y}$ = the predicted value of Y under the least squares estimates of the y-intercept (a) and slope (b).

Now, think about what we are trying to do here. We have got sets of data points for two continuous variables, and we want to assess how changes in one of them (X) influence changes in the other (Y). By looking at the scatterplot, we want to draw a straight line that minimizes the distance between them. That straight line is of the linear form (i.e., $Y = a + bX$). We compute estimates of these coefficients (a, b) that fulfill the "least squares" requirement. Once that line is drawn, departures from this line (either above or below it) are errors in predicting Y on the basis of X (i.e., $Y - \hat{Y}$). If all of the data points fall on this line, the X variable perfectly predicts Y and there is no error in prediction ($SS_{residual} = 0$).

The Computation of the Regression Coefficient and Y-Intercept

The estimation of the regression coefficient (i.e., the slope [b]) and the Y-intercept (a) requires a little math, but it is not that difficult in a simple regression model with one independent variable. The definitional and computing formulas for the slope (b) are given by the following:

$$b = \frac{cov(xy)}{var(x)} = \frac{\sum (x - \bar{x})(y - \bar{y})}{\sum (x - \bar{x})^2} = \frac{\sum XY - (\sum X)(\sum Y)/N}{\sum X^2 - (\sum X)^2/N}$$

After the slope is determined, the y-intercept term (a) in the regression equation is calculated using the following formula:

$$a = \bar{Y} - b\bar{X}$$

To illustrate the computations of the coefficients in a regression analysis, consider the impact of the dropout rate (x) on the homicide rate (y) in 20 states. The raw data and the computations necessary to conduct this regression analysis are displayed in Table 13.2.

The results in Table 13.2 indicate the following regression equation for the effect of dropout rates on homicide rates: $Y_{hom} = -2.9 + .39X_{drop}$. The regression coefficient *(slope)* reveals that for each additional unit increase in the school dropout rate for a state, the state's homicide rate increases by .39 units. In the actual units of measurement for these variables, this regression coefficient translates into a .39 per 100,000 increase in homicide rates for each percentage point increase in the school dropout rate. The y-intercept term represents the homicide rate when the dropout rate is zero (i.e., $X = 0$). In this case, the homicide rate would be

TABLE 13.2 Regression Analysis Predicting Homicide Rates (Y) on the Basis of Dropout Rates (X) for 20 States

	X	Y	X^2	Y^2	XY	$\hat{Y}$	$Y - \hat{Y}$	$(Y - \hat{Y})^2$
AL	35.3	11.6	1,246	135	409	10.8	.8	.6
AK	31.6	7.5	999	56	237	9.4	−1.9	3.5
AZ	27.5	7.7	756	59	212	7.8	−.1	.0
AR	23.3	10.3	543	106	240	6.1	4.2	17.6
CA	32.2	11.9	1,037	142	383	9.6	2.3	5.3
CO	25.9	4.2	671	18	109	7.1	−2.9	8.6
CT	25.1	5.1	630	26	128	6.8	−1.7	2.9
DE	31.5	5.0	992	25	158	9.3	−4.3	18.8
FL	38.9	10.7	1,513	114	416	12.2	−1.5	2.4
GA	37.3	11.8	1,391	139	440	11.6	.2	.0
HI	13.2	4.0	174	16	53	2.1	1.9	3.5
ID	20.6	2.7	424	7	56	5.0	−2.3	5.5
IL	23.4	10.3	548	106	241	6.1	4.2	17.3
IN	25.0	6.2	625	38	155	6.8	−.6	.3
IA	12.5	1.9	156	4	24	1.8	.1	.0
KS	18.0	4.0	324	16	72	4.0	.0	.0
KY	31.0	7.2	961	52	223	9.1	−1.9	3.7
LA	43.3	17.2	1,875	296	745	14.0	3.2	10.4
ME	22.4	2.4	502	6	54	5.7	−3.3	11.2
MD	27.2	11.5	740	132	313	7.6	3.9	14.9
$\sum =$	545.2	153.2	16,107	1,493	4,667	153.2	0	127

Computations:

$$\overline{X} = \sum X / N = 545.2 / 20 = 27.3$$

$$\overline{Y} = \sum Y / N = 153.2 / 20 = 7.7$$

$$b = \frac{\sum XY - (\sum X)(\sum Y) / N}{\sum X^2 - (\sum X)^2 / N} = \frac{4,667 - (545.2)(153.2) / 20}{16,107 - 14,862} = .39$$

$$a = \overline{Y} - b\overline{X} = 7.7 - (.39)27.3 = -2.9$$

Thus, $Y = a + bX \Rightarrow Y = -2.9 + .39X$

a negative –2.9 per 100,000. This y-intercept does not make a whole lot of sense in this case (because you cannot have a negative homicide rate), but this is the correct interpretation of it.

Goodness of Fit of a Regression Equation

So, how well does this regression equation fit the observed data? There are two ways to answer this question. First, you can look at the scatterplot for a visual representation of how the data points are spread around the regression line. Second, several measures of association are available to formally assess the magnitude of the relationship between the two quantitative variables.

As shown in Figure 13.4, the scatterplot of rates of homicide and school dropout illustrates some departures from the regression line. Due to the principles of least squares, you should notice that the regression line is pulled toward the extreme observation (e.g., the data point for Louisiana in the top right corner) and minimizes the distance between that point and the rest of the observations. A positive relationship between the variables is suggested by the patterning of the data points and

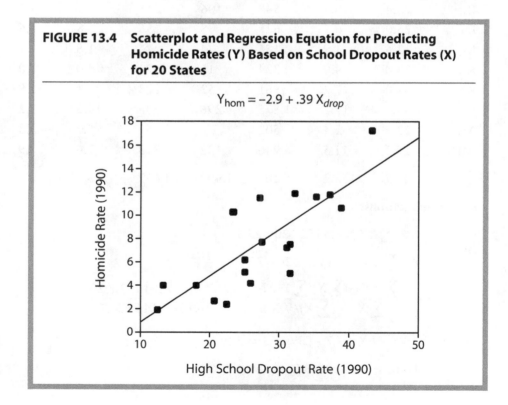

FIGURE 13.4   Scatterplot and Regression Equation for Predicting Homicide Rates (Y) Based on School Dropout Rates (X) for 20 States

$$Y_{hom} = -2.9 + .39\, X_{drop}$$

Homicide Rate (1990)

High School Dropout Rate (1990)

is confirmed by the positive slope for the regression coefficient. The shape of the data points is more like a "football" than a "cigar," but it is still suggestive of a strong positive correlation between these variables.

The statistical method for assessing the magnitude of the overall relationship between two quantitative variables involves the **correlation coefficient** (r) and the **coefficient of determination** (symbolized as R^2). In the case of a bivariate regression analysis (i.e., one dependent variable and one independent variable), the coefficient of determination is simply the square of the correlation coefficient (i.e., $R^2 = r^2$).

Similar to eta squared (η^2) in ANOVA, the coefficient of determination represents the proportion of variation in a dependent variable that is explained by the independent variable(s). Both η^2 and R^2 are also interpretable in terms of the proportional reduction of error in predicting a dependent variable (Y) based on knowledge of the scores on the independent variable (X) rather than based solely on the mean of the dependent variable. The primary differences between these measures of association are that the R^2 assumes a linear relationship between the continuous variables, whereas η^2 makes no assumption about the form of the relationship between categories of the independent variable and the dependent variable.

Based on the homicide and dropout rates in Table 13.2, the value of the correlation coefficient is +.78 and the coefficient of determination is .61 (i.e., $R^2 = .78^2 = .61$). The size of this correlation fits within the general rule category for a "strong" positive relationship. The coefficient of determination indicates that 61% of the variation in states' homicide rates is accounted for by their dropout rates. Thus, the high school dropout rate is a strong predictor of the homicide rate because it explains a substantial proportion of the variation in this variable.

Similar to the problem of defining rules of thumb in other applications, it is difficult to come up with clear substantive guidelines for interpreting weak, moderate, and strong relationships based on the coefficient of determination. In most applications of social research with multiple independent variables, you will rarely find an R^2 value of greater than 25%, especially with large sample sizes (e.g., $N > 200$). Ultimately, this decision about the magnitude of a relationship depends on the balance between its substantive importance and statistical significance.

Hypothesis Testing and Tests of Statistical Significance

Correlation and regression coefficients are similar to other types of descriptive statistics in that they can be the basis for parameter estimation and hypothesis testing. Similar to sample means and proportions, we can develop confidence intervals around correlation and regression coefficients to provide an interval that is likely to capture their true population values. Likewise, t-tests and F-tests are commonly used to evaluate hypotheses about particular population parameters.

The hypothesized values in these formal tests of statistical significance may be about the population correlation (H_o: $Rho = 0$), the regression coefficient (H_o: $\beta = 0$), the Y-intercept (H_o: $\alpha = 0$), and/or the coefficient of determination (H_o: $R^2 = 0$). As is true of all forms of hypothesis testing, the process of hypothesis testing for correlation and regression coefficients involves (1) the comparison of the observed sample values with the expected values under the null hypothesis, and (2) the application of decision rules about the sampling distribution, estimates of sampling error, and significance levels of the test.

When testing hypotheses about bivariate relationships, the test of the correlation coefficient is identical to the test of the regression coefficient. It is also conceptually identical to testing the null hypothesis that the coefficient of determination is zero (i.e., knowledge of the independent variable does not help us accurately predict values of the dependent variable). To conduct hypothesis tests about these bivariate relationships, the following assumptions are required:

- The observations have been randomly selected from the population.

- Both variables are normally distributed—this assumption can be relaxed with large samples ($n > 50$) without dramatically affecting the results.

- Both variables are measured at the interval or ratio level.

- The two variables are related to each other in a linear manner. In other words, a straight line best represents the relationship between Y and X.

- Errors in predicting Y from X are normally distributed, have an expected value of zero, and have a constant variance across all levels of the X variable.

The accuracy of many of these assumptions can be evaluated by looking at the scatterplot and the nature of the residual error variances (i.e., the pattern of discrepancies between the observed and predicted values of Y for different values of the independent variable). An example of these residual errors is shown in the last column of Table 13.2.

If these assumptions are met, the formal test of statistical significance of the correlation or regression coefficient is another example of "old wine in a new bottle." In particular, we test this hypothesis with the following t-statistic:

$$t = r\sqrt{\frac{n-2}{1-r^2}}, \text{ where}$$

n = the sample size and r = the sample correlation.

The critical value for this t-test is based on the significance level and $n - 2$ degrees of freedom. When applied to the sample correlation of .78 for the relationship between homicide and dropout rates in 20 states, this obtained t-value of this test is

$$t = r\sqrt{\frac{n-2}{1-r^2}} = .78\sqrt{\frac{20-2}{1-(.78)^2}} = .78\sqrt{46} = 5.29$$

To reject the null hypothesis of $r = 0$ in the population, Appendix B indicates that critical value of the t-statistic is 2.101 at the .05 significance level for a two-tailed test and 18 degrees of freedom. Given that our obtained t-value of 5.29 greatly exceeds this critical value, we are confident in rejecting this null hypothesis. Our formal test confirms the results of our more intuitive assessment that (1) homicide rates and dropout rates are strongly related, and (2) states' school dropout rates explain a major proportion of the variation in their homicide rates.

Using Regression Analysis for Predicting Outcomes

Given the substantive conclusion that an independent variable helps explain variation in a dependent variable, regression analysis provides an incredibly useful tool for prediction and extrapolations. For these purposes, all you have to do is plug into the regression equation the values of an independent variable (X) that you are interested in and solve the equation. It is easier than you think.

Take, for example, the regression equation for homicide rates and dropout rates. Our estimated regression equation based on the method of least squares is $Y_{hom} = -2.9 + .39X_{drop}$. Suppose we wanted to know the predicted homicide rate if a state had a 50% dropout rate. To get this predicted homicide rate (symbolized as $\hat{Y}$), just plug in the value 50 for X and solve the equation: $\hat{Y} = -2.9 + .39(50) = 16.6$. Thus, if the high school dropout rate was 50%, the expected homicide rate would be 16.6 per

100,000. This predicted homicide rate is more than twice as large as the average homicide rate of 7.7 for these 20 states in 1990.

The predicted value of any dependent variable for any value of an independent variable can be easily determined as long as you know the regression equation. For example, suppose the regression equation for predicting income from one's years of education is $Y_\$ = 4250 + 2000X_{ed}$. With this information, you should be able to figure out how I derived the following predicted incomes for each of these educational levels:

- 8th-grade education ➜ $\hat{Y}_{income}$ = $20,250
- 12th-grade education ➜ $\hat{Y}_{income}$ = $28,250
- 16 years of education ➜ $\hat{Y}_{income}$ = $36,250
- 20 years of education ➜ $\hat{Y}_{income}$ = $44,250
- 50 years of education ➜ $\hat{Y}_{income}$ = $104,250

Although the use of regression analysis for predicting outcomes is an attractive feature of this technique, it is important to emphasize that such predictions are based on several fundamental assumptions. First, they assume that the independent variable is an important predictor of the dependent variable. If the relationship is weak, then the prediction of Y for different values of X is largely meaningless. Second, the relationship is assumed to be linear, meaning the effect of X on Y is the same for all values of X. In other words, if the slope of the regression line is different for a particular value of X, a linear projection of the same slope for all X values is a misspecification of the functional form of the true relationship between X and Y. An examination of the scatterplots provides a method for evaluating the feasibility of both of these assumptions.

ISSUES IN BIVARIATE REGRESSION AND CORRELATION ANALYSIS

Bivariate regression and correlation analyses serve as the fundamental basis of many studies in criminology and the social sciences. If the assumptions are met, they provide useful summary measures of the statistical association between two quantitative variables.

However, in many cases of social research, the most interesting variables are not measured on interval or ratio scales and the world is more complicated than the simple bivariate relationships described by these statistical techniques. Fortunately, the logic of regression analysis can be extended to a wider array of situations than has been described so far in this chapter. Here is a very brief introduction to a couple of ways in which regression analysis has been extended to deal with these situations.

First, the assumption of interval or ratio measurement of both variables can be relaxed by performing different types of regression analysis. For example, a technique called *dummy variable regression* is used to assess the impact of categorical independent variables on a continuous dependent variable. This approach is virtually identical in both method and results to performing an ANOVA analysis. When the dependent variable has only two nominal outcomes (i.e., yes or no, support or oppose), a *logistic regression analysis* is available to assess the impact of an independent variable on the log-likelihood of being in one category rather than another of this dependent variable. These other types of regression analysis are described in full detail in more advanced statistics books.

Second, similar to the addition of other variables in ANOVA problems, multiple independent variables can be included in a regression analysis. This type of situation is called *multiple regression analysis* and allows the researcher to assess the impact of an independent variable(s) on a dependent variable once controls are introduced for the impact of these other variables. By adjusting for the impact of these other variables, multiple regression analysis provides a more rigorous and methodologically sound approach for evaluating the net or conditional effects of an independent variable on a dependent variable.

For those desiring more information about these extensions of regression analysis, the best advice is to take a more advanced statistics class, especially one that focuses on multivariate analysis techniques. These techniques require greater mathematical skill to use and understand them. However, they are indispensable methods for making sound substantive conclusions from the analysis of criminological data.

SUMMARY OF MAJOR POINTS

- Correlation and regression analysis are two statistical procedures for examining the relationship between two quantitative variables. A scatter diagram or scatterplot is a visual representation of the relationship between these variables.

- The strength and direction of the association between two quantitative variables can be visually and intuitively judged by looking at the scattergram. A pattern of data points that looks like a "shotgun blast" from a distance indicates a weak relationship between variables. A "cigar shape" suggests a moderately strong relationship, a "cigarette shape" an even stronger relationship, and a perfect relationship is displayed when all data points fall on a straight line. When the band of data points flows from the lower left corner of the graph to the upper right corner, a positive relationship between the variables is indicated. A clustering band that goes from the upper left corner to the bottom right corner indicates a negative relationship between the variables.

- When variables are positively related, they move in the same direction (both x and y increase together, or x and y decrease together). A negative relationship indicates that variables move in the opposite directions (e.g., as x increases, y decreases; as x decreases, y increases).

- The correlation coefficient (r) is a symmetrical measure of linear association that ranges in value from –1.00 to +1.00. A correlation of greater than ±.50 is considered moderately strong or stronger, whereas a correlation of less than ±.10 is considered "weak" in most situations.

- A linear regression equation represents the relationship between a dependent variable (Y) and an independent variable (X). It is of the form $Y = a + bX$, where a is the y-intercept (i.e., the value of Y when $X = 0$) and b is the regression coefficient or slope indicating the effect of a unit change in X on the dependent variable.

- The values of the y-intercept and slope in a regression equation are estimated by the method of ordinary least squares. This method results in the selection of the values of these parameters that minimizes the sum of the squared errors in predicting Y on the basis of X.

- The coefficient of determination (R^2) represents the proportion of variation in a dependent variable that is accounted for by the independent variable(s). In the case of a bivariate regression analysis, the coefficient of determination is simply found by squaring the value of the correlation coefficient (i.e., $R^2 = r^2$).

- Both visual inspection of the scatterplot and the computation of R^2 are different ways of assessing the "goodness of fit" of a regression model. The more data points converge on a straight line or extremely narrow ellipse, the better the fit of the regression equation. Similarly, the higher the R^2 value, the better the fit (i.e., the more X explains the levels of Y).

- Similar to other summary statistics (like means and proportions), sample estimates of correlation and regression coefficients can be used to develop confidence intervals around the likely true population parameters and to test statistical hypotheses. A t-test is used to evaluate the null hypothesis about the values of a correlation coefficient ($Ho: r = 0$) and the regression coefficient ($Ho: b = 0$). In the case of bivariate analyses, the test of the statistical significance of the correlation coefficient is identical to the test of the regression coefficient.

- Regression analysis is a useful tool for purposes of prediction and extrapolation. If the relationship between X and Y is linear and X is a substantively and statistically important predictor of Y, predicted values of Y can be determined for any value of X.

- Simple bivariate regression analysis can be extended to situations in which the variables do not have to be measured on an interval or ratio scale. The techniques of *dummy regression analysis* and *logistic regression* are examples of these extensions. Additional variables can also be included in the regression model using a technique called *multiple regression analysis*. These techniques are described in more advanced statistics books. The motivated student who wants to learn more about these techniques should take an additional statistics course, especially one that focuses on multivariate analysis.

KEY TERMS

Coefficient of Determination (R^2)	Regression Analysis
Correlation	Regression Coefficient, or Slope (b)
Correlation Coefficient (r)	Residual Sum of Squares
"Least Squares" Method	Scatterplot or Scatter Diagram
Linear Relationship	Y-Intercept Term (a)

MAJOR FORMULAS AND SYMBOLIC REPRESENTATIONS

Pearson's Correlation Coefficient (r):

$$r = \frac{cov(xy)}{sd(x)sd(y)} = \frac{\sum(x - \bar{x})(y - \bar{y}) / n - 1}{\sqrt{\dfrac{\sum(x - \bar{x})^2}{n - 1}} \sqrt{\dfrac{\sum(y - \bar{y})^2}{n - 1}}}$$

Regression Equation (population parameters):

$$Y = \alpha + \beta X$$

Regression Equation (sample estimates of population parameters):

$$Y = a + bX$$

Residual Sum of Square Errors in Prediction:

$$SS_{residual} = \sum(Y_{observed} - Y_{predicted})^2 = \sum(Y - \hat{Y})^2$$

Slope or Regression Coefficient (b):

$$b = \frac{cov(xy)}{var(x)} = \frac{\sum(x - \bar{x})(y - \bar{y})}{\sum(x - \bar{x})^2} = \frac{\sum XY - (\sum X)(\sum Y) / N}{\sum X^2 - (\sum X)^2 / N}$$

Y-Intercept (a):

$$a = \bar{Y} - b\bar{X}$$

Coefficient of Determination (R^2) for Bivariate Analysis:

$$R^2 = r^2$$

Significance Test of Bivariate Correlation or Regression Coefficient:

$$t = r\sqrt{\frac{n - 2}{1 - r^2}}$$

SPSS Applications (*Optional Section*)

Scatterplots, correlation, and regression are separate procedures within the SPSS program. Assuming you have an active data file, here is a quick summary of the steps involved in each of these procedures.

Scatterplot

A basic bivariate scatterplot is generated in SPSS through the procedures under the menu marked **Graphs**. Once you click on this procedure, do the following:

- Click on the **Scatter . . .** label.

- Click on **Simple**.

- Click on **Define**.

- From the list of variables, select your dependent variable and click on the box to the right of **Y axis** to put your dependent variable in this space.

- From the list of variables, select your independent variable and click on the box to the right of **X axis** to put your independent variable in this space.

- Click **OK** to generate this scatterplot.

Correlation

A bivariate correlation is generated in SPSS through the procedure called **Correlation** under the **Analyze** menu. Once you click on the **Analyze** menu, do the following:

- Click on **Correlation**.

- Click on **Bivariate**.

- Select two variables from the list of variables and click them into the box under the label **Variable**.

- Click on the box in front of the name **Pearson** to get the Pearson's correlation coefficient.

- To have your correlation tested with a two-tailed test, check the radial button on the line marked **Two-Tailed Test**. For a one-tailed test, check that radial button.

- Click **OK** to generate the correlation for these two variables.

Bivariate Regression

A bivariate regression analysis is generated in SPSS through the procedure called **Regression** under the **Analyze** menu. Once you click on the **Analyze** menu, do the following:

- Click on **Regression**.

- Click on **Linear**.

- Select a variable from the list of variables to be your dependent variable, and click it into the box under the word **Dependent**.

- Select a variable from the list of variables to be your independent variable, and click it into the box under the word **Independent**.

- Click **OK** to generate the regression coefficient and statistical tests of these coefficients.

Other types of regression analysis (e.g., binary logistic and nonlinear) are also available in SPSS under the **Analyze → Regression** menus. Within this same command sequence, SPSS also provides the options for analyzing the effects of multiple independent variables (called *multiple regression analysis*).

APPLYING WHAT YOU HAVE LEARNED

1. It is important to look at scatterplots because

   a. they give a visual image of the strength of the relationship between the variables.

   b. they give an idea of whether the relationship is linear.

   c. they help identify outliers and other influential points in the analysis.

   d. all of the above are true.

2. In a graph in which both the X and Y variables are arranged from low to high scores, a strong positive relationship between these variables would involve a scattergram that looks like

   a. a skinny cigar, moving from the bottom left to top right of the graph.

   b. a skinny cigar, moving from the top left to bottom right of the graph.

   c. a straight line, moving from the top left to bottom right of the graph.

   d. a shotgun blast pattern.

3. Which of the following is the strongest correlation between two variables?

    a. $r = +.54$

    b. $r = -.68$

    c. $r = +.22$

    d. $r = -.15$

4. Correlation analysis is most appropriate for exploring the relationship between

    a. two quantitatively measured variables.

    b. two qualitatively measured variables.

    c. two nominal variables.

5. Outliers may influence the visual image of a scatterplot, but they do not affect the calculated value of the correlation coefficient.

    a. True

    b. False

6. A linear relationship is defined by a straight line in which

    a. a unit increase in X has the same effect on Y for all values of Y.

    b. a unit increase in X has a stronger effect on Y at larger values of Y.

    c. a unit increase in X has a weaker effect on Y at large values of Y.

7. Which of the following statistical techniques assumes a linear relationship between Y and X?

    a. Pearson's correlation coefficient.

    b. regression analysis.

    c. ANOVA.

    d. All of the above are true.

    e. Only a and b are true.

8. The regression coefficient (b or the slope) represents

    a. how a unit change in the independent variable influences the dependent variable.

    b. the value of Y when X is 0.

    c. the proportion of variation in Y explained by X.

    d. the difference between the expected and observed sample means.

9. Once a researcher knows the slope and y-intercept term, he or she can use the regression equation to compute predicted values for the dependent variable on the basis of any value of the independent variable.

    a. True

    b. False

10. The variation of scores around the regression line is

    a. unexplained variation.

    b. total variation.

    c. explained variation.

    d. standard deviation.

11. A major problem with bivariate correlation and regression analyses is that this relationship may change dramatically once other variables are taken into account.

    a. True

    b. False

12. The number of prior arrests (P) ranges from 0 to 10 or more prior arrests, and the length of prison sentences (S) ranges from 1 year to 99 years. If the correlation between these two variables is $-.02$, this would indicate which of the following patterns?

    a. An increase in P is associated with an increase in S.

    b. A decrease in P is associated with a decrease in S.

    c. An increase in P is strongly associated with a decrease in S.

    d. A decrease in P is strongly associated with an increase in S.

    e. There is basically no relationship between P and S.

13. Explain in words the direction and the magnitude of the correlations between the following sets of quantitative variables:

    a. income and education ($r = +.67$) _____

b. exposure to pornography and the number of sex offenses ($r = +.13$) _____

c. number of prior arrests and length of prison sentence ($r = +.40$) _____

d. number of police officers and the city's crime rate ($r = -.08$) _____

e. teen drug use rate and the age of the population ($r = -.35$) _____

14. Use the scatterplot below to answer the following questions:

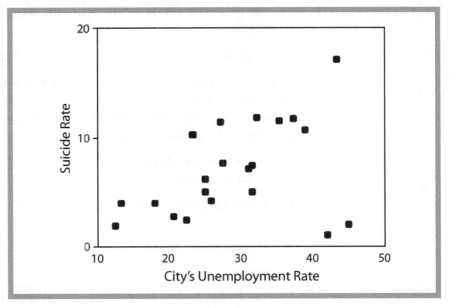

a. What variable is the dependent variable in this scatterplot, the suicide rate or the unemployment rate? _____

b. What is the independent variable in this scatterplot? _____

c. Is this a positive or negative relationship? _____

d. Is this a weak, moderate, or strong relationship? _____

e. Draw the least squares regression line on the scattergram that you think would "fit" this data on suicide and unemployment rates. _____

f. Describe in words what this scatterplot tells you about the relationship between these variables. _____
_____

15. Suppose you conducted an analysis of the relationship between the number of prison disturbances (Y) and the number of guard infractions against inmates (X) in 30 maximum security institutions.

Your regression analysis resulted in the following regression equation and summary statistics:

$$Y_{disturbances} = 5 + .1X_{g\text{-infractions}} \qquad r = +.40 \qquad N = 30$$

a. Interpret the nature and magnitude of the correlation in this case. _____

b. Interpret the regression coefficient (the slope) in this example. _____

c. Interpret the value of the y-intercept in this example. _____

d. How much of the variation in prison disturbances is explained by the number of guard infractions against inmates? Identify and calculate the appropriate statistical procedure to derive this answer from the above summary statistics. _____

e. How many prison disturbances would you expect at the following prisons:

1. A maximum security prison with 100 guard infractions? _____

2. A maximum security prison with 1,000 guard infractions? _____

3. A maximum security prison with 10,000 guard infractions? _____

4. A maximum security prison with no guard infractions? _____

5. A prison with 500 guard infractions? _____
(Caution: Think about this one before you answer.)

f. Some statistician asked you to test the null hypothesis about the relationship between prison disturbances and number of guard infractions at these 30 maximum security prisons. The null hypothesis is *Ho:* $r = 0$, and the statistician wants you to use a two-tailed test and a .05 significance level.

1. What test statistics are you going to use? A z-, t-, χ^2, or F-test? _____

2. How many degrees of freedom are associated with this test?
   _____

3. What is the critical value for this test statistic? _____

4. Using the appropriate test of significance, what is your obtained test statistic? _____

5. Do you reject or not reject the null hypothesis that there is no correlation between these variables? _____ Justify your answer. ✦

14

Introduction to Multivariate Analysis

*R*ather than focusing on the relationship between two variables, criminologists are often concerned about identifying multiple causes of criminal behavior and assessing the impact of one particular risk factor after adjusting or taking into account other variables that affect crime and this risk factor. The means by which this task is accomplished is through the use of techniques of multivariate analysis.

The techniques of contingency table analysis, analysis of variance (ANOVA), correlation, and regression discussed in the previous chapters have focused on bivariate relationships. This means that they are concerned with assessing the relationship between two variables. Unfortunately, as I have suggested throughout these chapters, many of these basic bivariate relationships may be misleading because they are influenced by some other variable(s). Once we take into account these other variables, the basic bivariate relationship between X and Y may strengthen, weaken, or remain the same. However, what is important is that these other "contaminating factors" have been controlled for so that we can make clearer inferences about the "true" nature and magnitude of the relationship between our primary variables of X and Y. We control for these factors by conducting various types of multivariate (i.e., multiple variable) analyses.

This chapter provides a brief introduction to the logic of **multivariate analysis**. I will discuss why multivariate analysis is important and illustrate its use within the context of contingency table analysis, correlation, and regression. My discussion of these multivariate methods will be more intuitive than statistical because the computational details become too intense for most undergraduate students in the social sciences. Let us begin with the big "why" question.

WHY DO MULTIVARIATE ANALYSIS?

There are two fundamental reasons why multivariate analysis is important in numerous areas of social research and social life. These primary reasons involve the ideas of multiple causes and statistical control.

Exploring Multiple Causes

This may not be profound, but it is true that human behavior is complex. There is not one single cause of any type of behavior. As discussed in Chapter 2, there are both proximate and distal causes, spurious associations, and developmental causal chains that describe the interrelationships among variables. These types of **multiple causes** and multiple causal chains suggest that the mere focus on the $X \rightarrow Y$ causal path may oversimplify and misrepresent the true relationship among these variables.

When you assume that behavior has multiple causes, the obvious next question is which of these variables (e.g., x_1, x_2, x_3, . . .) is most important in understanding or explaining variation in another variable (Y). The only way to answer this question is by conducting a **multivariate analysis** to assess the relative importance of these variables. Multivariate analysis answers the question of relative importance by including each of these variables within the same analysis to isolate their unique contributions.

Statistical Control

One of the most important concepts in multivariate analysis is the notion of statistical control. **Statistical control** involves the use of analytical techniques to adjust for or purge the influence of other variables from the primary relationship of interest. It is often stated in the form of "What effect does X have on Y after controlling for the effects of Z on both X and Y?"

By controlling for the effects of other variables, it should be obvious that statistical control is crucial for evaluating the mediating effects or spurious associations among these variables. For example, if the correlation between X and Y reduces to 0 after controlling for other variables, then this basic XY relationship is not a direct causal path. It may be due to an indirect causal path (i.e., $X \rightarrow Z \rightarrow Y$) or a spurious association (i.e., $X \leftarrow Z \rightarrow Y$). In either case, controlling for Z is important because it better specifies the net impact of X on Y.

Statistical control is also important in the context of evaluating the relative importance of multiple causes. In particular, by adjusting for the effects of other variables in the statistical model, each variable is purged of its joint variation with the other variables, thereby providing a more level "playing field" for assessing the relative importance of the variables.

I recognize that this discussion of statistical control is a bit obtuse, jargon ridden, and/or vague. Hopefully, after it is illustrated within the following techniques (i.e., contingency tables, correlation, and regression), you will gain a better understanding of this concept and why it is such a crucial element of multivariate analysis.

TYPES OF MULTIVARIATE ANALYSIS

The logic of multivariate analysis, multiple causes, and statistical control can be easily illustrated by applying them to some of the bivariate statistical procedures discussed in previous chapters. Multivariate analyses involving contingency tables, correlation, and regression techniques are described below.

Multivariate Contingency Table Analysis

Multivariate analysis is conducted within the context of contingency tables through the inclusion of additional variables. For example, assume that the variables of interest to you have two categories. The analysis of the relationship between X and Y would involve a 2×2 contingency table. The addition of another variable (Z) would expand the analysis to a $2 \times 2 \times 2$ contingency table. The dimensions would be a $2 \times 2 \times 2 \times 2$ table if you were interested in the multivariate analysis of four variables.

Any cross-tabulation that explores the interrelationships among three or more variables is called a **multivariate contingency table**. Multivariate tables can have any number of dimensions and categories for each variable. For example, a $4 \times 2 \times 3$ table has three dimensions (variables) and different numbers of categories within them (four, two, and three, respectively).

To illustrate the application of multivariate analysis to contingency tables, suppose you are interested in the sources of support and opposition to gun control. You expect both gender and age to be important predictors of these attitudes. All variables are coded into three categories: *gun control attitude* (Support, Oppose), *gender* (Male, Female), and *age* (< 30, ≥ 30). Further assume that gun control attitude is your dependent variable and that both gender and age are your independent variables. A 2 × 2 × 2 contingency table of joint frequencies and column percentages for examining these independent and dependent variables is presented in Table 14.1.

TABLE 14.1	Gender and Age Differences in Gun Control Support (hypothetical data for 800 people)					
	Table of Joint Frequencies					
Gun Control	**< 30 Years Old**			**≥ 30 Years Old**		
	M	**F**	**Total**	**M**	**F**	**Total**
Support	156	180	336	96	120	216
Oppose	44	20	64	104	80	184
Total	200	200	400	200	200	400
	Table of Column Percents					
Gun Control	**< 30 Years Old**			**≥ 30 Years Old**		
	M (%)	**F (%)**	**Total**	**M (%)**	**F (%)**	**Total**
Support	78	90	336	48	60	216
Oppose	22	10	64	52	40	184
Total%	100	100	400	100	100	400

Now, to understand how multivariate analysis is done in contingency table analysis, notice how the variables are arranged in Table 14.1. The independent variables (*gender* and *age*) are included as column variables, whereas the dependent variable (*gun control attitude*) is the row variable. You should also notice that this table is set up in such a way that separate 2 × 2 tables for gun control and gender are presented for each category of age. In the language of multivariate tabular analysis, the categories of age (< 30 or ≥30) are considered "levels" of the third or subsequent variables.

I have set up the tables in this format because it permits an easier interpretation of the gender and gun control relationship for each age group. If you were primarily interested in the age by gun control relationship, you would treat gender as the "level" variable and display separate tables for men and women. However, in either case, the effects of each variable on the dependent variable can be evaluated by looking at the table of column percents.

Now, let's ask some questions about the effects of gender and age on gun control support after we statistically control for the other variable. These questions and answers are summarized below:

- *Are there gender differences in gun control support?* Yes, the column percents in the bottom panel of Table 14.1 indicate that females are more supportive of gun control than males for both persons under 30 (90% support for females versus 78% support for males) and persons 30 or older (60% support for females vs. 48% support for males). Because these gender differences are identical for each age group (i.e., there is a 12% point difference between males and females for each age group), statistically controlling for age by doing separate analyses for each age does not change this basic relationship between gender and gun control support.

- *Are there age differences in gun control support?* Yes, within each gender group, there are large differences between persons under 30 and those older in their gun control support. Among females, younger women are far more supportive than older women (90% versus 60%). Among men, the level of support is lower, but the younger men are also more supportive than older men (78% versus 48%). The constant 30% point differences between younger and older persons for both females and males indicate that controlling for gender does not affect the basic relationship between age and gun control support.

- *Which variable, gender or age, is most important in accounting for differences in gun control support?* Age. Why? Look at the magnitude of age differences within gender groups versus the magnitude of gender differences within age groups. In particular, the bottom panel of Table 14.1 indicates a 30% point difference in gun control support by age groups for each gender group, but only a 12% point difference in gun control support by gender groups for each age group. Under these conditions, both age and gender are important factors in understanding gun control attitude, but age is the most important factor.

This example of gender and age differences in gun control attitude illustrates the basic principles underlying a multivariate contingency table analysis. By comparing bivariate relationships within levels of other variables, we are able to determine whether this basic relationship is the same or different across levels of another variable. When there is no difference in the basic bivariate relationship in these "level" tables (i.e., like the pattern found in Table 14.1), we conclude that this relationship is not conditioned or influenced by this other variable(s). The same logic applies to situations in which the number of variables increases, but the interpretation of the tables becomes more cumbersome, especially when the effects are not consistent across levels of these other variables.

To formally test for statistical significance, the multivariate contingency table analysis reduces to a series of χ^2 tests of independence in each of the bivariate tables. More advanced statistical approaches for assessing the conditional relationships between categorical variables involve multivariate logistic regression analysis. This latter technique is described in more advanced statistics books and is available for use within the SPSS statistical package.

Partial Correlation Coefficients

Another way to illustrate how statistical control works in multivariate analysis is to examine the computational details for assessing what is called the **partial correlation coefficient**. This partial correlation coefficient represents the correlation between two variables (r_{xy}) once controls are introduced for other variables. Under the symbolic form of the partial correlation coefficient ($r_{xy.z}$), the variables that follow the "dot" notation (.z) represent the control variables.

The partial correlation between X and Y controlling for Z is given by the following formula:

$$r_{xy.z} = \frac{r_{xy} - r_{xz}r_{yz}}{\sqrt{1 - r_{xz}^2}\sqrt{1 - r_{yz}^2}}, \text{ where}$$

r_{xy} is the correlation between X and Y, r_{xz} is the correlation between X and Z, and r_{yz} is the correlation between Y and Z.

A close examination of the structure of this formula should give you a clear idea of how the principle of statistical control for another variable (Z in this case) works in the case of the partial correlation coefficient. Specifically, the effect of Z on the bivariate correlation between X and Y (r_{xy}) is essentially purged by subtracting out the variation it shares with X (i.e., r_{xz}) and the variation it shares with Y (r_{yz}). The net result is the correlation between X and Y once the "contaminating" effects of Z have been removed (i.e., $r_{xy.z}$). It removes the variance that Z has in common with both X and Y. The stronger Z is correlated with both X and Y, the more dramatically the bivariate correlation between X and Y will be reduced by controlling for Z.

How the value of the partial correlation coefficient ($r_{xy.z}$) is influenced by the magnitude of intercorrelations among the variables can be demonstrated by examples. In fact, assume that the bivariate correlation between X and Y is the same ($r_{xy} = .50$), but the intercorrelation between these variables and Z varies in four different ways. These four different scenarios and their impact on the value of $r_{xy.z}$ are summarized below. The values for $r_{xy.z}$ in each case are found by simply plugging into the equation for the partial correlation the values of the bivariate correlations provided in each scenario.

- *Scenario 1: Z is uncorrelated with both X and Y.*

  $r_{xy} = .50; \, r_{xz} = .00; \, r_{yz} = .00 \Rightarrow r_{xy.z} = .50$

- *Scenario 2: Z is weakly correlated with both X and Y.*

  $r_{xy} = .50; \, r_{xz} = .10; \, r_{yz} = .20 \Rightarrow r_{xy.z} = .49$

- *Scenario 3: Z is strongly correlated with both X and Y.*

  $r_{xy} = .50; \, r_{xz} = .60; \, r_{yz} = .80 \Rightarrow r_{xy.z} = .04$

- *Scenario 4: Z is uncorrelated with X but strongly correlated with Y.*

  $r_{xy} = .50; \, r_{xz} = .00; \, r_{yz} = .80 \Rightarrow r_{xy.z} = .83$

So, what is the lesson learned here about how statistical control for another variable influences the magnitude of a bivariate correlation? Here are the "bottom line" principles:

- When other variables (Z) are uncorrelated with both X and Y, controlling for Z will have no effect on the correlation between X and Y. This situation is illustrated in Scenario 1, above. In these types of situations, $r_{xy.z} = r_{xy}$.

- When other variables (Z) are correlated with both X and Y, controlling for Z will reduce the magnitude of the correlation between X and Y. The stronger the correlation between Z and the other variables (X and Y), the greater the reduction in the correlation between X and Y. When Z is weakly correlated with these variables (see Scenario 2), controlling for Z has a minimal impact. However, when Z is strongly related to both variables (see Scenario 3), controlling for Z will dramatically reduce the bivariate correlation between X and Y. So, when Z is correlated with the other variables, the partial correlation will be less than the bivariate correlation (i.e., $r_{xy.z} < r_{xy}$).

- When a variable (Z) has a correlation with X or Y, but has a zero correlation with one of these variables, the partial correlation between X and Y will be larger than the bivariate correlation between X and Y. This situation is depicted in Scenario 4 above. In these types of situations, Z is called a *suppressor variable* because it suppresses the variance that either X or Y has in common with Z but that is not part of the other variable. When Z suppresses the correlation between X and Y, statistically controlling for Z will result in the partial correlation being larger than the bivariate correlation (i.e., $r_{xy.z} > r_{xy}$).

The extension of partial correlation to multiple control variables follows this same line of reasoning, but the hand computations of these correlation coefficients become a nightmare. However, if you understand the logic of this three-variable example, you will have no problem grasping the principles of statistical control in a more complicated case of multivariate analysis using multiple control variables.

Multivariate Regression Analysis

Multivariate regression analysis involves the extension of the bivariate regression equation to incorporate more than one independent variable. The term **multiple regression** is most often used to convey this type of multivariate analysis.

Similar to bivariate regression, multiple regression analysis uses the method of least squares to derive estimates of the y-intercept term (a) and the regression coefficient (b) that minimize the sum of the squared errors of prediction (i.e., the residual sum of squares). However, in multivariate applications, there are separate regression coefficients (designated as b_1, $b_2, b_3 \ldots b_n$) linked to multiple independent variables (designated as X_1, $X_2, X_3 \ldots X_n$). Thus, the general form of the multiple regression equation is given by the following formula:

$$Y = a + b_1 X_1 + b_2 X_2 + b_3 X_3 + \ldots b_n X_n, \text{ where}$$

$b_1 =$ the partial regression coefficient for the effects of X_1 on Y controlling for all other independent variables,

b_2 = the partial regression coefficient for the effects of X_2 on Y controlling for all other independent variables,

b_3 = the partial regression coefficient for the effects of X_3 on Y controlling for all other independent variables, and

n = the number of independent variables.

The astute reader should notice that this stuff about **partial regression coefficients** sounds a lot like **partial correlation coefficients**. Well, you are right. They are actually quite comparable except that regression coefficients are interpreted in terms of the net "effect" of an independent variable on a dependent variable, whereas partial correlations are non-causal statements about net "association" between two variables after controlling for other variables.

The math involved in estimating OLS (i.e., *Ordinary Least Squares*) regression coefficients is mind-numbing, especially when it involves more than two independent variables. For these situations, knowledge of matrix algebra is essential. Because of the computational morass, hand calculations are almost always replaced by computer software programs to conduct multivariate regression analyses.

To illustrate how statistical control works within the context of partial regression coefficients, consider the linear regression equation for two independent variables. This equation has the following form:

$$Y = a + b_{1.2}X_1 + b_{2.1}X_2$$

The least squares estimates of the partial regression coefficients ($b_{1.2}$, $b_{2.1}$) and y-intercept (a) are based on the following formulas:

$$b_{1.2} = \frac{cov(x_1 y) \times var(x_2) - cov(x_2 y) \times cov(x_1 x_2)}{var(x_1) \times var(x_2) - cov(x_1 x_2)}$$

$$b_{2.1} = \frac{cov(x_2 y) \times var(x_1) - cov(x_1 y) \times cov(x_1 x_2)}{var(x_1) \times var(x_2) - cov(x_1 x_2)}$$

$$a = \overline{Y} - b_{1.2}\overline{X}_1 - b_{2.1}\overline{X}_2$$

Although these formulas are somewhat intimidating to look at, what is important to derive from them is how statistical control works in multivariate regression analysis. In particular, notice how the $b_{1.2}$ partial regression coefficient associated with X_1 is derived by purging from the covariation of X_1 and Y the "contaminating" effects of X_2 on both X_1 and Y. The comparable situation characterizes the $b_{2.1}$ partial regression coefficient associated with X_2 except that the "corrupting" effect of X_1 is removed. Although the calculations are a bit more complicated, the logic of statistical control is identical in the case of partial correlation and partial regression coefficients.

To get a general idea of the interpretation of these partial regression coefficients, consider the hypothetical regression equation relating individuals' income (Y) to their years of education (X_1) and the dollar amount of their inherited wealth (X_2). The regression equation is $Y = 10,000 + 500\,X_1 + .67\,X_2$.

Given this regression equation, the slope coefficient for education (X_1) suggests that for each additional year of education, one's income will increase by $500 after you control for the effect of inherited wealth on both educational achievement and earned income. Similarly, the regression coefficient for inherited wealth (X_2) implies that each additional dollar of inherited wealth will result in a 67-cent increase in earned income once the effects of education on income and inherited wealth are taken into account. The y-intercept term in this example indicates that even if a person had no education and no inherited income, he or she would still make $10,000.

Similar to bivariate regression, the overall fit of the regression model can be statistically evaluated by computing the coefficient of determination (R^2). In this case, however, the R^2 is computed on the basis of the residual sum of squared errors in predicting of Y from X_1, X_2, and any other independent variables in the regression analysis.

If the independent variables explain a sufficient proportion of variation in the dependent variable, you can also use the obtained multiple regression equation to predict values of the dependent variable. For our example on income, if a person had 16 years of education and inherited $100,000, his or her predicted income would be $85,000 ($\hat{Y} = 10,000 + 500[16] + .67[100,000] = \$85,000$).

For purposes of evaluating the relative importance of independent variables in a multiple regression analysis, the social analyst must examine what are referred to as **standardized partial regression coefficients**. These standardized coefficients are also called *beta (β) coefficients*. These standardized coefficients are found by taking the original regression coefficients (the b's or, more accurately, the **unstandardized partial regression coefficients**) and dividing them by their respective standard deviations for the independent and dependent variables. This standardization process places all of the variables in the same standard units, thereby permitting a better basis for evaluating what variable is most important.

The logic and need for computing standardized partial regression coefficients can be easily demonstrated with our example on predicting income. In this particular case, the unstandardized partial regression coefficient for the effect of education ($b_{1.2} = 500$) is far superior in size to the unstandardized partial regression coefficient for inherited wealth ($b_{2.1} = .67$). Unfortunately, you cannot conclude that education is over 500 times more important than inherited wealth because these variables are not measured in the same unit. However, by adjusting these unstandardized coefficients by their respective standard deviations, you can produce standardized partial regression coefficients that allow for direct comparisons of the relative importance of the variables. Both unstandardized and standardized regression coefficients are part of the regular output from SPSS and other statistical packages for multivariate analyses.

SUMMARY OF MAJOR POINTS

This brief chapter was designed to provide an overview of several techniques for conducting multivariate analysis. The inclusion of multiple independent variables in any substantive analysis is important for purposes of statistical control and for assessing the relative importance of different variables. More advanced statistics courses and books will describe multivariate contingency table analysis, partial correlation, and multiple regression in greater detail. I hope this brief overview arouses your curiosity about learning more about these more advanced statistical procedures.

KEY TERMS

Multiple Causes

Multiple Regression

Multivariate Analysis

Multivariate Contingency Tables

Partial Correlation Coefficient

Standardized Partial Regression
  Coefficients (Betas [β])

Statistical Control

Unstandardized Partial
  Regression Coefficients (b's)

MAJOR FORMULAS

The Partial Correlation Between X and Y Controlling for Z:

$$r_{xy.z} = \frac{r_{xy} - r_{xz}r_{yz}}{\sqrt{1 - r_{xz}^2}\sqrt{1 - r_{yz}^2}}$$

The General Form of the Multiple Regression Equation:

$$Y = a + b_1 X_1 + b_2 X_2 + b_3 X_3 + \ldots b_n X_n$$

The Multiple Regression Equation for Two Independent Variables:

$$Y = a + b_{1.2} X_1 + b_{2.1} X_2$$

The Partial Regression Coefficients ($b_{1.2}$, $b_{2.1}$) for Two Independent Variables:

$$b_{1.2} = \frac{cov(x_1 y) \times var(x_2) - cov(x_2 y) \times cov(x_1 x_2)}{var(x_1) \times var(x_2) - cov(x_1 x_2)}$$

$$b_{2.1} = \frac{cov(x_2 y) \times var(x_1) - cov(x_1 y) \times cov(x_1 x_2)}{var(x_1) \times var(x_2) - cov(x_1 x_2)}$$

The y-Intercept (a) in Multiple Regression Equation for Two Independent Variables:

$$a = \overline{Y} - b_{1.2} \overline{X}_1 - b_{2.1} \overline{X}_2$$

SPSS Applications (*Optional Section*)

Multivariate analyses in SPSS for contingency tables, correlation, and regression are simply extensions of the procedures used in bivariate analysis. For example, to perform a multivariate contingency table in SPSS, do the following steps:

- Under the **Analyze** menu, click on **Descriptive Statistics**.

- Select the procedure **Crosstab**.

- Select a particular variable as the **Row Variable** and **Column Variable**.

- Select the other variables that you want to serve as control variables, and insert them under the option labeled **Layers**.

- The first control variable will be referred to as *Layer 1 of 1*. If you then insert another control variable under **Layers**, it will be called *Layer 2 of 2*.

- Any number of control variables can be added through the **Layers** option.

- Follow the remaining steps in the bivariate **Crosstabs** to define various cell options (e.g., show row percentages, column percentages, and expected values) and statistical tests (e.g., chi-square) for these contingency tables.

To perform a partial correlation analysis through SPSS, all that is required is to select a different option within the procedure called Correlation. The basic steps include the following:

- Click on **Analyze**.

- Click on **Correlation**.

- Click on **Partial**.

- Insert the names of your primary variables under the **Variables** box.

- Insert your control variables under the **Controlling for . . .** box.

Finally, multiple regression analysis in SPSS is also an easy extension of bivariate regression. The major difference is that multiple independent variables are listed under the menu marked **Independent(s)**.

APPLYING WHAT YOU HAVE LEARNED

1. Multivariate analysis involves statistical applications of three or more variables.

    a. True

    b. False

2. A major goal of multivariate analysis is

    a. to explore multiple causes of a dependent variable.

    b. to control for other variables that influence a bivariate relationship.

    c. to explore mean differences between three groups.

    d. all of the above are true.

    e. only a and b are true.

3. In a multivariate contingency analysis, a 3 × 4 × 2 table has

    a. 3 cells.

    b. 9 cells.

    c. 24 cells.

4. Statistical controls within contingency table analysis are conducted by examining the bivariate relationship between two variables for different categories of third or additional variables.

    a. True

    b. False

5. If the relationship between X and Y is totally spurious, controlling for Z will

    a. increase the magnitude of the correlation between X and Y.

    b. decrease the bivariate correlation between X and Y to a value of 0.

    c. have no effect on the correlation between X and Y.

6. If Z is uncorrelated with X and Y, controlling for Z will

    a. increase the magnitude of the correlation between X and Y.

    b. decrease the bivariate correlation between X and Y to a value of 0.

    c. have no effect on the correlation between X and Y.

7. The unstandardized partial regression coefficient in a multivariate analysis represents the impact of the effect of one particular independent variable on the dependent variable once adjustments or controls are made for the other independent variables.

    a. True

    b. False

8. In a multivariate regression analysis, the y-intercept represents the

    a. value of Y when X_1 is 0 and all other independent variables have values greater than 0.

    b. value of Y when X_1 is greater than 0 and all other independent variables have values greater than 0.

    c. value of Y when X_1 and all other independent variables are equal to 0.

9. In most criminological research, there will be no differences between the results of bivariate and multivariate analyses.

    a. True

    b. False

10. When determining the most important variable in a multivariate regression analysis, the analyst should look at the relative size of the

    a. standardized partial regression coefficients.

    b. unstandardized partial regression coefficients.

    c. Y-intercept term.

11. Assume the following multivariate regression equation was obtained from a study of the risk factors for chronic delinquency ($Y_{del\text{-}acts}$):

    $$Y_{del\text{-}acts} = 1.5 + .25\,(\text{age}) + .00001\,(\text{city size})$$

    a. How many delinquent acts would be predicted for a 16-year-old juvenile who lives in a city of 10,000 people? _____

    b. How many delinquent acts would be predicted for a 16-year-old juvenile who lives in a city of 100,000 people? _____ ✦

Table of Area Under the Normal Curve (Select Values)

Column A	Column B	Column C	Column A	Column B	Column C
z-Score	z to Mean	Area > z	z-Score	z to Mean	Area > z
0.00	.0000	.5000	1.95	.4744	.0256
.10	.0398	.4602	1.96	.4750	.0250
.15	.0596	.4404	2.00	.4772	.0228
.20	.0793	.4207	2.05	.4798	.0202
.25	.0987	.4013	2.10	.4821	.0179
.30	.1179	.3821	2.15	.4842	.0158
.35	.1368	.3632	2.20	.4861	.0139
.40	.1554	.3446	2.25	.4878	.0122
.45	.1736	.3264	2.30	.4893	.0107
.50	.1915	.3085	2.33	.4901	.0099
.55	.2088	.2912	2.35	.4906	.0094
.60	.2257	.2743	2.40	.4918	.0082
.65	.2422	.2578	2.45	.4929	.0071
.70	.2580	.2420	2.50	.4938	.0064
.75	.2734	.2266	2.55	.4946	.0054
.80	.2881	.2119	2.58	.4951	.0049
.85	.3023	.1977	2.60	.4953	.0047
.90	.3159	.1841	2.65	.4960	.0040
.95	.3289	.1711	2.70	.4965	.0035
1.00	.3413	.1587	2.75	.4970	.0030
1.05	.3531	.1469	2.80	.4974	.0026
1.10	.3643	.1357	2.85	.4978	.0022
1.15	.3749	.1251	2.90	.4981	.0019
1.20	.3849	.1151	2.95	.4984	.0016
1.25	.3944	.1056	3.00	.4987	.0013
1.28	.3997	.1003	3.10	.4990	.0010
1.30	.4032	.0968	3.20	.4993	.0007
1.35	.4115	.0885	3.30	.4995	.0005
1.40	.4192	.0808	3.40	.4997	.0003

Column A	Column B	Column C		Column A	Column B	Column C
z-Score	z to Mean	Area > z		z-Score	z to Mean	Area > z
1.45	.4265	.0735		3.50	.4998	.0002
1.50	.4332	.0668		3.60	.49984	.00016
1.55	.4394	.0606		3.70	.49989	.00011
1.60	.4452	.0548		3.80	.49993	.00007
1.64	.4495	.0505		3.90	.49995	.00005
1.65	.4505	.0495		4.00	.49997	.00003
1.70	.4554	.0446		>4.01	≈ .50000	≈ .00000
1.75	.4599	.0401				
1.80	.4641	.0359				
1.85	.4678	.0322		*Note:* Widely used z's areas are highlighted.		
1.90	.4713	.0287				

Source: Adapted and adridged from: C. Frankfort-Nachmias and A. Leon-Guerrero, *Social Statistics for a Diverse Society*, 3rd ed. Copyright © 2002 by Sage Publications. Used with permission.

B Critical Values of t-Distribution

	One-Tailed Test				
$\alpha =$	.10	.05	.025	.01	.005
	Two-Tailed Test				
$\alpha =$	.20	.10	.05	.02	.01
df					
1.	3.078	6.314	12.706	31.821	63.657
2.	1.886	2.920	4.303	6.965	9.925
3.	1.638	2.353	3.182	4.541	5.841
4.	1.533	2.132	2.776	3.747	4.604
5.	1.476	2.015	2.571	3.365	4.032
6.	1.440	1.943	2.447	3.143	3.707
7.	1.415	1.895	2.365	2.998	3.499
8.	1.397	1.860	2.306	2.896	3.355
9.	1.383	1.833	2.262	2.821	3.250
10.	1.372	1.812	2.228	2.764	3.169
11.	1.363	1.796	2.201	2.718	3.106
12.	1.356	1.782	2.179	2.681	3.055
13.	1.350	1.771	2.160	2.650	3.012
14.	1.345	1.761	2.145	2.624	2.977
15.	1.341	1.753	2.131	2.602	2.947
16.	1.337	1.746	2.120	2.583	2.921
17.	1.333	1.740	2.110	2.567	2.898
18.	1.330	1.734	2.101	2.552	2.878
19.	1.328	1.729	2.093	2.539	2.861
20.	1.325	1.725	2.086	2.528	2.845
21.	1.323	1.721	2.080	2.518	2.831
22.	1.321	1.717	2.074	2.508	2.819
23.	1.319	1.714	2.069	2.500	2.807
24.	1.318	1.711	2.064	2.492	2.797
25.	1.316	1.708	2.060	2.485	2.787

	One-Tailed Test				
$\alpha =$	.10	.05	.025	.01	.005
	Two-Tailed Test				
$\alpha =$	.20	.10	.05	.02	.01
df					
26.	1.315	1.706	2.056	2.479	2.779
27.	1.314	1.703	2.052	2.473	2.771
28.	1.313	1.701	2.048	2.467	2.763
29.	1.311	1.699	2.045	2.462	2.756
30.	1.310	1.697	2.042	2.457	2.750
31.	1.309	1.696	2.040	2.453	2.744
32.	1.309	1.694	2.037	2.449	2.738
33.	1.308	1.692	2.035	2.445	2.733
34.	1.307	1.691	2.032	2.441	2.728
35.	1.306	1.690	2.030	2.438	2.724
36.	1.306	1.688	2.028	2.434	2.719
37.	1.305	1.687	2.026	2.431	2.715
38.	1.304	1.686	2.024	2.429	2.712
39.	1.304	1.685	2.023	2.426	2.708
40.	1.303	1.684	2.021	2.423	2.704
41.	1.303	1.683	2.020	2.421	2.701
42.	1.302	1.682	2.018	2.418	2.698
43.	1.302	1.681	2.017	2.416	2.695
44.	1.301	1.680	2.015	2.414	2.692
45.	1.301	1.679	2.014	2.412	2.690
46.	1.300	1.679	2.013	2.410	2.687
47.	1.300	1.678	2.012	2.408	2.685
48.	1.299	1.677	2.011	2.407	2.682
49.	1.299	1.677	2.010	2.405	2.680
50.	1.299	1.676	2.009	2.403	2.678
51.	1.298	1.675	2.008	2.402	2.676
52.	1.298	1.675	2.007	2.400	2.674
53.	1.298	1.674	2.006	2.399	2.672
54.	1.297	1.674	2.005	2.397	2.670
55.	1.297	1.673	2.004	2.396	2.668
56.	1.297	1.673	2.003	2.395	2.667
57.	1.297	1.672	2.002	2.394	2.665
58.	1.296	1.672	2.002	2.392	2.663
59.	1.296	1.671	2.001	2.391	2.662
60.	1.296	1.671	2.000	2.390	2.660

One-Tailed Test				
$\alpha =$	.10	.05	.025	.01	.005

Two-Tailed Test				
$\alpha =$	.20	.10	.05	.02	.01

df					
70.	1.294	1.667	1.994	2.381	2.648
80.	1.292	1.664	1.990	2.374	2.639
90.	1.291	1.662	1.987	2.368	2.632
100.	1.290	1.660	1.984	2.364	2.626
200.	1.284	1.657	1.978	2.355	2.613
∞	1.282	1.645	1.960	2.326	2.576

Source: R.A. Fisher and F. Yates. 1963. *Statistical Tables for Biological, Agricultural and Medical Research*. 6th Edition. Adapted from Table III. Permission granted from Pearson Education Limited.

C

Critical Values of Chi-Square Test (χ^2)

		Significance Level (α)			
df	**.10**	**.05**	**.025**	**.01**	**.001**
1	2.706	3.841	5.024	6.635	10.828
2	4.605	5.991	7.378	9.210	13.816
3	6.251	7.815	9.348	11.345	16.266
4	7.779	9.488	11.143	13.277	18.467
5	9.236	11.070	12.833	15.086	20.515
6	10.645	12.592	14.449	16.812	22.458
7	12.017	14.067	16.013	18.475	24.322
8	13.362	15.507	17.535	20.090	26.125
9	14.684	16.919	19.023	21.666	27.877
10	15.987	18.307	20.483	23.209	29.588
11	17.275	19.675	21.920	24.725	31.264
12	18.549	21.026	23.337	26.217	32.910
13	19.812	22.362	24.736	27.688	34.528
14	21.064	23.685	26.119	29.141	36.123
15	22.307	24.996	27.488	30.578	37.697
16	23.542	26.296	28.845	32.000	39.252
17	24.769	27.587	30.191	33.409	40.790
18	25.989	28.869	31.526	34.805	42.312
19	27.204	30.144	32.852	36.191	43.820
20	28.412	31.410	34.170	37.566	45.315
21	29.615	32.671	35.479	38.932	46.797
22	30.813	33.924	36.781	40.289	48.268
23	32.007	35.172	38.076	41.638	49.728
24	33.196	36.415	39.364	42.980	51.179
25	34.382	37.652	40.646	44.314	52.620
26	35.563	38.885	41.923	45.642	54.052
27	36.741	40.113	43.195	46.963	55.476
28	37.916	41.337	44.461	48.278	56.892
29	39.087	42.557	45.722	49.588	58.301
30	40.256	43.773	46.979	50.892	59.703
31	41.422	44.985	48.232	52.191	61.098

Significance Level (α)

df	.10	.05	.025	.01	.001
32	42.585	46.194	49.480	53.486	62.487
33	43.745	47.400	50.725	54.776	63.870
34	44.903	48.602	51.966	56.061	65.247
35	46.059	49.802	53.203	57.342	66.619

Source: R.A. Fisher and F. Yates. 1963. *Statistical Tables for Biological, Agricultural and Medical Research*. 6th Edition. Adapted from Table IV. Permission granted from Pearson Education Limited.

D

Critical Values of F-Test at .05 Alpha Level

df1	1	2	3	4	5	6	7	8	9	10
df2										
1	161	199	216	225	230	234	237	239	241	242
2	18.5	19.0	19.2	19.3	19.3	19.3	19.4	19.4	19.4	19.4
3	10.1	9.55	9.28	9.12	9.01	8.94	8.89	8.85	8.81	8.79
4	7.71	6.94	6.59	6.39	6.26	6.16	6.09	6.04	6.00	5.96
5	6.61	5.79	5.41	5.19	5.05	4.95	4.88	4.82	4.77	4.74
6	5.99	5.143	4.757	4.534	4.387	4.284	4.207	4.147	4.099	4.060
7	5.59	4.737	4.347	4.120	3.972	3.866	3.787	3.726	3.677	3.637
8	5.32	4.459	4.066	3.838	3.687	3.581	3.500	3.438	3.388	3.347
9	5.12	4.256	3.863	3.633	3.482	3.374	3.293	3.230	3.179	3.137
10	4.96	4.103	3.708	3.478	3.326	3.217	3.135	3.072	3.020	2.978
11	4.84	3.982	3.587	3.357	3.204	3.095	3.012	2.948	2.896	2.854
12	4.75	3.885	3.490	3.259	3.106	2.996	2.913	2.849	2.796	2.753
13	4.67	3.806	3.411	3.179	3.025	2.915	2.832	2.767	2.714	2.671
14	4.60	3.739	3.344	3.112	2.958	2.848	2.764	2.699	2.646	2.602
15	4.54	3.682	3.287	3.056	2.901	2.790	2.707	2.641	2.588	2.544
16	4.49	3.634	3.239	3.007	2.852	2.741	2.657	2.591	2.538	2.494
17	4.45	3.592	3.197	2.965	2.810	2.699	2.614	2.548	2.494	2.450
18	4.41	3.555	3.160	2.928	2.773	2.661	2.577	2.510	2.456	2.412
19	4.38	3.522	3.127	2.895	2.740	2.628	2.544	2.477	2.423	2.378
20	4.35	3.493	3.098	2.866	2.711	2.599	2.514	2.447	2.393	2.348
21	4.32	3.467	3.072	2.840	2.685	2.573	2.488	2.420	2.366	2.321
22	4.30	3.443	3.049	2.817	2.661	2.549	2.464	2.397	2.342	2.297
23	4.28	3.422	3.028	2.796	2.640	2.528	2.442	2.375	2.320	2.275
24	4.26	3.403	3.009	2.776	2.621	2.508	2.423	2.355	2.300	2.255
25	4.24	3.385	2.991	2.759	2.603	2.490	2.405	2.337	2.282	2.236
26	4.22	3.369	2.975	2.743	2.587	2.474	2.388	2.321	2.265	2.220
27	4.21	3.354	2.960	2.728	2.572	2.459	2.373	2.305	2.250	2.204
28	4.20	3.340	2.947	2.714	2.558	2.445	2.359	2.291	2.236	2.190
29	4.18	3.328	2.934	2.701	2.545	2.432	2.346	2.278	2.223	2.177
30	4.17	3.316	2.922	2.690	2.534	2.421	2.334	2.266	2.211	2.165
31	4.16	3.305	2.911	2.679	2.523	2.409	2.323	2.255	2.199	2.153

df1	1	2	3	4	5	6	7	8	9	10
df2										
32	4.15	3.295	2.901	2.668	2.512	2.399	2.313	2.244	2.189	2.142
33	4.14	3.285	2.892	2.659	2.503	2.389	2.303	2.235	2.179	2.133
34	4.13	3.276	2.883	2.650	2.494	2.380	2.294	2.225	2.170	2.123
35	4.12	3.267	2.874	2.641	2.485	2.372	2.285	2.217	2.161	2.114
36	4.11	3.259	2.866	2.634	2.477	2.364	2.277	2.209	2.153	2.106
37	4.10	3.252	2.859	2.626	2.470	2.356	2.270	2.201	2.145	2.098
38	4.10	3.245	2.852	2.619	2.463	2.349	2.262	2.194	2.138	2.091
39	4.09	3.238	2.845	2.612	2.456	2.342	2.255	2.187	2.131	2.084
40	4.08	3.232	2.839	2.606	2.449	2.336	2.249	2.180	2.124	2.077
41	4.08	3.226	2.833	2.600	2.443	2.330	2.243	2.174	2.118	2.071
42	4.07	3.220	2.827	2.594	2.438	2.324	2.237	2.168	2.112	2.065
43	4.07	3.214	2.822	2.589	2.432	2.318	2.232	2.163	2.106	2.059
44	4.06	3.209	2.816	2.584	2.427	2.313	2.226	2.157	2.101	2.054
45	4.06	3.204	2.812	2.579	2.422	2.308	2.221	2.152	2.096	2.049
47	4.05	3.195	2.802	2.570	2.413	2.299	2.212	2.143	2.086	2.039
48	4.04	3.191	2.798	2.565	2.409	2.295	2.207	2.138	2.082	2.035
49	4.04	3.187	2.794	2.561	2.404	2.290	2.203	2.134	2.077	2.030
50	4.03	3.183	2.790	2.557	2.400	2.286	2.199	2.130	2.073	2.026
51	4.03	3.179	2.786	2.553	2.397	2.283	2.195	2.126	2.069	2.022
52	4.03	3.175	2.783	2.550	2.393	2.279	2.192	2.122	2.066	2.018
53	4.02	3.172	2.779	2.546	2.389	2.275	2.188	2.119	2.062	2.015
54	4.02	3.168	2.776	2.543	2.386	2.272	2.185	2.115	2.059	2.011
55	4.02	3.165	2.773	2.540	2.383	2.269	2.181	2.112	2.055	2.008
56	4.01	3.162	2.769	2.537	2.380	2.266	2.178	2.109	2.052	2.005
57	4.01	3.159	2.766	2.534	2.377	2.263	2.175	2.106	2.049	2.001
58	4.01	3.156	2.764	2.531	2.374	2.260	2.172	2.103	2.046	1.998
59	4.00	3.153	2.761	2.528	2.371	2.257	2.169	2.100	2.043	1.995
60	4.00	3.150	2.758	2.525	2.368	2.254	2.167	2.097	2.040	1.993
61	4.00	3.148	2.755	2.523	2.366	2.251	2.164	2.094	2.037	1.990
62	4.00	3.145	2.753	2.520	2.363	2.249	2.161	2.092	2.035	1.987
63	3.99	3.143	2.751	2.518	2.361	2.246	2.159	2.089	2.032	1.985
64	3.99	3.140	2.748	2.515	2.358	2.244	2.156	2.087	2.030	1.982
65	3.99	3.138	2.746	2.513	2.356	2.242	2.154	2.084	2.027	1.980
66	3.99	3.136	2.744	2.511	2.354	2.239	2.152	2.082	2.025	1.977
67	3.98	3.134	2.742	2.509	2.352	2.237	2.150	2.080	2.023	1.975
68	3.98	3.132	2.740	2.507	2.350	2.235	2.148	2.078	2.021	1.973
69	3.98	3.130	2.737	2.505	2.348	2.233	2.145	2.076	2.019	1.971
70	3.98	3.128	2.736	2.503	2.346	2.231	2.143	2.074	2.017	1.969
71	3.98	3.126	2.734	2.501	2.344	2.229	2.142	2.072	2.015	1.967
72	3.97	3.124	2.732	2.499	2.342	2.227	2.140	2.070	2.013	1.965
73	3.97	3.122	2.730	2.497	2.340	2.226	2.138	2.068	2.011	1.963

df1	1	2	3	4	5	6	7	8	9	10
df2										
74	3.97	3.120	2.728	2.495	2.338	2.224	2.136	2.066	2.009	1.961
75	3.97	3.119	2.727	2.494	2.337	2.222	2.134	2.064	2.007	1.959
76	3.97	3.117	2.725	2.492	2.335	2.220	2.133	2.063	2.006	1.958
77	3.96	3.115	2.723	2.490	2.333	2.219	2.131	2.061	2.004	1.956
78	3.96	3.114	2.722	2.489	2.332	2.217	2.129	2.059	2.002	1.954
79	3.96	3.112	2.720	2.487	2.330	2.216	2.128	2.058	2.001	1.953
80	3.96	3.111	2.719	2.486	2.329	2.214	2.126	2.056	1.999	1.951
81	3.96	3.109	2.717	2.484	2.327	2.213	2.125	2.055	1.998	1.950
82	3.96	3.108	2.716	2.483	2.326	2.211	2.123	2.053	1.996	1.948
83	3.96	3.107	2.715	2.482	2.324	2.210	2.122	2.052	1.995	1.947
84	3.95	3.105	2.713	2.480	2.323	2.209	2.121	2.051	1.993	1.945
85	3.95	3.104	2.712	2.479	2.322	2.207	2.119	2.049	1.992	1.944
86	3.95	3.103	2.711	2.478	2.321	2.206	2.118	2.048	1.991	1.943
87	3.95	3.101	2.709	2.476	2.319	2.205	2.117	2.047	1.989	1.941
88	3.95	3.100	2.708	2.475	2.318	2.203	2.115	2.045	1.988	1.940
89	3.95	3.099	2.707	2.474	2.317	2.202	2.114	2.044	1.987	1.939
90	3.95	3.098	2.706	2.473	2.316	2.201	2.113	2.043	1.986	1.938
95	3.94	3.092	2.700	2.467	2.310	2.196	2.108	2.037	1.980	1.932
100	3.94	3.087	2.696	2.463	2.305	2.191	2.103	2.032	1.975	1.927

Source: R.A. Fisher and F. Yates. 1963. *Statistical Tables for Biological, Agricultural and Medical Research*. 6th Edition. Adapted from Table VI. Permission granted from Pearson Education Limited.

Answers to "Applying What You Have Learned" Problems

Chapter 1

1. Descriptive statistics are summary measures of variables like their means and standard deviations. Inferential statistics involve the same measures except these summary statistics are used to estimate population parameters and/or test statistical hypotheses about these parameters.

2. Sample statistics are summary measures of a variable that are based on a sample of results. Population parameters are these summary measures based on the population of all possible cases. We use sample data to estimate the numerical value of these population parameters.

3. This statistic on support for legalizing marijuana is based on a sample. Without knowing anything about the sample (e.g., how it was selected, whether it is a random sample of the entire U.S. population, and how large the sample was), we really can't say much about what this sample statistic of 34% tells us about Americans' views about legalizing marijuana. The actual proportion of American adults who favor legalization may be far higher or lower than this sample value.

4. Most students learn about descriptive statistics in the sixth grade and again in high school algebra class.

5. When watching TV news, you should notice how graphs and charts are used to convey statistical information. You should also notice that this information is presented in a largely "factual" manner—that is, broadcasters and reporters rarely challenge the accuracy of the numbers they report.

6. True: Greek symbols are used in statistics to represent population parameters.

Chapter 2

1. b

2. d

3. a

4. d

5. e

6. d

7. b

8. d

9. b (under the assumption that there will be pressure on police departments in these cities to show a low crime rate so that tourists are not scared away)

10. d

11. No, we can't conclude that eating a lot of ice cream causes people to be criminal under these conditions for the following reasons: (1) Such an inference would result in the commission of the *ecological fallacy* (because a strong association between ice cream consumption and crime rates of cities doesn't necessarily mean that the ice cream eaters are committing criminal offenses—we just don't know because we haven't collected data on individuals, only cities), and (2) the basic relationship between ice cream consumption and crime rates is also spurious because both variables are influenced by common factors (e.g., seasonality affects ice cream consumption and crime rates [both are more common in summer months and lower during winter months]).

12. No, we cannot make the inference that castration reduces the likelihood of sex offending for the following reasons: (1) People who volunteer to be castrated may be quite different from those who do not and (2) a wide variety of other factors should be taken into account (e.g., how *sex offender* is measured, whether large and random probability-based samples were used, and whether these differences were due to cultural differences between Scandinavian countries and the United States).

13. No, we cannot tell that drug courts are more effective than other courts in dealing with substantive abuse without knowing about (1)

the measurement of key concepts (e.g., what constitutes a drug court or recidivist?), (2) sampling design (e.g., are the samples randomly selected from all drug offenders?), and (3) research design (e.g., was an experimental design employed in which offenders were randomly assigned to experimental and control groups?). Given that these results are provided by the Drug Court Clearinghouse, it is also possible that some political interests may be involved in the obtained results (e.g., does this national organization have a vested interest in finding that drug court is more effective than other courts?).

14. No, you cannot conclude that the threat of capital punishment is not a general deterrent for homicide from these results because (1) you need to control for other variables that may influence this relationship (e.g., socioeconomic characteristics of states), and (2) the temporal ordering may be incorrect in that states with high homicide rates pass death penalty laws to reduce the number of murders.

15. No, racial profiling cannot be inferred from these findings. For example, it could be the case that blacks are given more severe prison sentences because they have longer criminal records or commit more serious crimes than whites. In this case, these findings would not necessarily mean that criminal justice officials are singling out black offenders for disparate treatment. You would have to control for other factors related to arrest practices and race before concluding a causal link between minority group membership and racist practices.

Chapter 3

1. a

2. b

3. e

4. b

5. b

6. Examples of nominal, ordinal, and interval or ratio measures of anger:

Nominal: Are you angry? ☐ No ☐ Yes

What label best represents how you feel right now? ☐ Angry
☐ Bitter ☐ Happy ☐ Sad ☐ Bored ☐ Other

Ordinal: How often do you get angry?   ☐ Never   ☐ Rarely   ☐ Sometimes   ☐ Always

How many times in the last year have you hit someone with your fist in anger?   ☐ 0   ☐ 1 to 5 times   ☐ 5 to 10 times   ☐ More than 10 times

Interval or Ratio: How many anger management classes have you taken?   ☐ 0   ☐ 1   ☐ 2   ☐ 3   ☐ 4   ☐ 5   ☐ 6, . . . etc.

7. Examples of nominal, ordinal, and interval or ratio measures of employment:

Nominal: Are you current employed outside the home?
☐ No   ☐ Yes

Ordinal: What is your employment status?   ☐ Not Employed   ☐ Part-time Employed   ☐ Full-time Employed

Interval or Ratio: How many hours do you work per week?
☐ 0–9   ☐ 10–19   ☐ 20–29   ☐ 30–39   ☐ 40–49
☐ 50–59   ☐ 60–69   ☐ 70–79   ☐ 80–89   ☐ 90–99
(Notice that each category is of equal width, so it is an interval scale.)

8. Examples of nominal, ordinal, and interval or ratio measures of income:

Nominal: Do you make over $100,000 per year?   ☐ No   ☐ Yes

Ordinal: How much money did you make last year?   ☐ < $25,000   ☐ $25,000 to $50,000   ☐ $50,001 to $100,000   ☐ over $100,000

Interval or Ratio: How much money did you make last year?
_____ (insert dollar value to the closest $1,000)

9. Examples of nominal, ordinal, and interval or ratio measures of drug use:

Nominal: Which of these illegal drugs have you most recently used?
☐ Marijuana   ☐ Cocaine   ☐ Meth   ☐ Heroin   ☐ Other

Ordinal: How often have you used illegal drugs in the last year?
☐ Never   ☐ Once or Twice   ☐ About Once a Month   ☐ Once a Week   ☐ Daily

Interval or Ratio: How many pounds of marijuana were in your possession when you were busted by the police? _____ (fill in value)

10. The categories are not mutually exclusive (someone who is between 40 and 45 years old would fit into two different categories), and the categories are not collectively exhaustive (e.g., people aged 61 to 69 are excluded).

Chapter 4

1. a. Frequency distribution with proper labels:

TABLE 1a   Race of 20 Individuals

Race	Frequency
1 = Black	7
2 = White	11
3 = Other	2
Total N	20

b. Percentage distribution with proper labels:

TABLE 1b   Race of 20 Individuals

Race	Percent
1 = Black	35
2 = White	55
3 = Other	10
Total Percent	100
	(N = 20)

c. Interpretation of Table 1: The majority of people are white, about one-third are black, and only about 10% are of "other" races.

2. a. Frequency distribution for traffic tickets for teenage drivers:

TABLE 2a   Number of Traffic Tickets for Teenage Drivers (N = 30 Drivers)

Number of Tickets	Frequency
0	15
1	9
2	3
4 or More	3
Total N	30

b. Percentage distribution for number of traffic tickets:

TABLE 2b   Number of Traffic Tickets for Teenage Drivers (*N* = 30 drivers)

Number of Tickets	Percent
0	50.0
1	30.0
2	10.0
4 or More	10.0
Total Percent	100
	(*N* = 30)

c. Summary: Half of the teenage drivers do not have a traffic ticket, about one-third have one ticket, and the remaining 20% have two or more tickets.

3. Here is one example of a mutually exclusive, collectively exhaustive, and culturally sensitive classification of educational attainment:

< High School Graduate
High School Graduate or GED
Some College
College Graduate
Post-College Graduate Education

4. You use a cumulative distribution when you have ordinal or interval or ratio measures of variables arranged in a frequency distribution.

5. Here is the completed table involving the *Cumulative % < Than:*

City Size	%	Cumulative % < Than
< 10,000	10	10
10,001–20,000	5	15
20,001–50,000	15	30
50,001–100,000	25	55
100,001–1 million	22	77
Over 1 million	23	100

a. Summarize findings: Most common size city was 50,001–100,000. 30% of cities have 50,000 or fewer residents. About one-fourth of cities have over 1 million residents.

    b. 30% of cities have 50,000 or less residents.

    c. 77% of cities have 1 million or less residents.

    d. 33% of the cities have < 10,000 or greater than 1 million people (10% + 23% = 33%).

6. The biggest problem with this table of the victim's age is that it is too busy. You do not need to have frequency and percentage distributions in the same table and the percentage less than or greater than in the same table. So, one clear fix would be to just include the percentage column (%) and the cumulative percentage less than column (*c*%<).

7. This bar chart tells you that the number of gang members reported in Las Vegas newspapers has generally increased over time. However, it doesn't really tell you anything about the number of gang members in Las Vegas because newspapers tend to sensationalize and distort the number of gang members (so the sample of newspaper stories is dubious), and it is unclear how gang members are defined in this study (e.g., members of motorcycle gangs and groups like the Hell's Angels are not usually counted).

8. This table tells you that the dominant weapon in Washington, DC, homicides in 1999 was a firearm. Firearms were used in over three-fourths of these homicides.

9. The revised table provides a more succinct summary of the lethal weapons in homicides. It maintains the crucial distinction from the original table that the vast majority of homicides involved firearms and that knives were the next most prevalent weapon.

10. There are too many tables within the one table, and you don't need to include both the number (frequency) and the percentage distributions in the same table. So, develop separate tables for gender, race, and age, *and* include only the percentage distributions in the table (and put the sample size [*n*] within parentheses at the bottom of the 100% total).

11. These line graphs show that the number of prisoners under sentences of death increased dramatically from 1980 to 1989 and has steadily increased for both racial groupings. For each year, more whites than blacks and other racial groups were given death sentences.

12. a. The execution rate in China per 100,000 is .26 ([3,400 executions / 1,300,000,000 population] × 100,000 = .26). The execu-

tion rate in the United States is .02 per 100,000 ([58 executions / 294,000,000 population] × 100,000 = .02).

    b.   The China-to-U.S. execution ratio is 13 (.26 execution rate for China / .02 execution rate for United States = 13). Interpretation: China's execution rate is 13 times higher than the U.S. rate.

13. a.   Robbery rate of 60 per 1,000 residents. Computed as (30 / 500) × 1000 = 60.

    b.   Robbery rate of 6,000 per 100,000 residents. Computed as (30 / 500) × 100,000 = 6,000.

Chapter 5

1. d

2. c

3. a

4. e

5. a

6. b

7. a

8. a

9. c

10. c

11. Means, medians, and modes are considered magic numbers because they are used to represent an entire distribution of scores. If one number could represent all numbers, they would be magic numbers.

12. Bush got the most votes but did not get the majority of votes in the election. He therefore represents the modal minority.

13. Two is the mode (there are two 2's but only one of the other numbers).

14. The modal robbery target is *Street/Highway Mugging.*

15. Median score is 5. Note: Make sure you first arrange numbers from low to high before you figure out the median ➜ 2, 4, 5, 7, 9 ➜ median = 5.

16. Median score is 6. Note: Make sure you first arrange numbers from low to high before you figure out the median. → 2, 4, 5, 7, 9, 11 → median = (5 + 7) / 2 = 6. Note: You take the average of the third (5) and fourth (7) scores because you have an even number of observations.

17. Using the formula for the refined median, the median age is 21.23. This is found by plugging the following values into the formula for the refined median: md = L + [(n / 2) – F / f] × w → : 20.5 + [(550 / 2 – 261) / 191] × 10 = 21.23.

18. The U.S. Census Bureau uses the median family income rather than mean family income because income is highly skewed (i.e., there are a few people like millionaires and billionaires who adversely affect the mean). The median is the best measure of central tendency when you have a skewed distribution.

19. The mean is 3.

20. a.   The average percent victimized per city was 5% (i.e., 15 / 3 = 5).

    b.   The average percent victimized per population is 8.49%. Use the formula for the weighted mean = [4 (100,000) + 2 (10,000) + 9 (1,000,000)] / 1,110,000 = 8.49.

21. An average marijuana consumption of one pound may be influenced by extreme marijuana users and depends on how it is measured. You would also want to know if marijuana consumption is normally distributed, as well as the median, the mode, and whether there are extreme scores or outliers. Also, is this a random sample of all American households or just those who smoke a lot of dope?

Chapter 6

1.   e

2.   b (because 200 is the mean in this example, so adding a single score that is the same value as the mean will reduce the overall variability from the mean, thereby reducing the variance and standard deviations)

3.   e (because the mode has nothing to do with the variance and its computation)

4. a (This is true by the very definition of the variance and standard deviations as representing the sum of the squared deviations from the mean.)

5. d

6. a

7. a

8. d

9. The range is an unstable measure of dispersion because it is based solely on the two most extreme scores. The most extreme high scores and the most extreme low scores are often exceptional cases.

10. The range is 8 because the high score is 9 and the low score is 1. Thus, $9 - 1 = 8$.

11. The 25th percentile is found by plugging in the following values: $1.5 + [(25 - 12.5) / 25] \times 1 = 2.0$. The 75th percentile is found by plugging in the following values: $6.5 + [(75 - 68.8) / 31.2] \times 3 = 7.1$, where 6.5 represents the true lower limit of the interval that contains the 75th percentile case, 68.8 is the cumulative percentage up to but not including the interval that contains the 75th percentile case, 31.2 is the percentage of cases in the interval that contains the 75th percentile case, and 3 is the width of the interval that contains the 75th percentile case. So, the intermediate range in this example ranges from 2.0 to 7.1.

12. Extreme scores affect the mean (i.e., they move the mean toward them). Because the standard deviation and variance represent deviations from the mean, extreme scores will also affect these measures. In other words, extreme scores will increase the size of both the standard deviation and variance.

13. The sample variance is 7 ($\sum (x - \bar{x})^2 / n - 1 = 42 / 6 = 7$), and the sample standard deviation is 2.65 (i.e., $\sqrt{7} = 2.65$).

14. The population variance is 6 ($\sum (x - \bar{x})^2 / n = 42 / 7$), and the population standard deviation is 2.45 (i.e., $\sqrt{6} = 2.45$).

15. Using only the information provided, you should take the job with the smaller standard deviation ($sd = 100$). This tells you that salaries are relatively closer to the average of $40,000 compared to the situation in which the standard deviation is $10,000. The safe bet would be to take the job with the lower standard deviation.

16. The standard deviation and variance in this example are both 0. There is no variation because all of the scores have the same value of 5.

17. The standard deviation and variance are related (sd = $\sqrt{\text{var}}$), but we prefer to use the standard deviation because it is expressed in the same units as the original variable.

18. The variance for a binary variable is given by p × q, where *p* is the proportion of cases in one category and *q* is the proportion of cases in the other category. So, in this example, the variance is .16 (.80 × .20). The standard deviation is found by taking the square root of the variance. Thus, the standard deviation is .4 (i.e., $\sqrt{.16}$).

Chapter 7

1. d

2. a

3. e

4. b

5. a

6. b

7. d

8. b

9. d

10. a

11. Sampling distributions are important because they provide a comparative standard. In hypothesis testing, we compare our sample value(s) with what is expected based on the sampling distribution of all possible outcomes of that test statistic to reach our substantive conclusion about rejecting or not rejecting the original hypothesis.

12. Use the formula for z-scores ($z = [x - \bar{x}]/\text{sd}$) to find the following answers:

   a. $z = 0$

   b. $z = +1.0$

c. $z = -2.00$

d. 34.13%

e. 47.72%

f. 95.44%

g. .64%

h. .64%

i. 114.56 arrests (found by converting top 5% into a z-score of +1.64 and then plugging in the values for the mean and standard deviation to solve for x—i.e., $+1.64 = [x - 108] / 4 \rightarrow x = 114.56$ arrests)

j. 101.44 arrests. Use the same formula as in problem 12i, except that the lowest 5% is represented by a z-score of −1.64. Thus, $-1.64 = (x - 108) / 4 \rightarrow x = 101.44$ arrests.

k. Z-score that corresponds to the middle 80% is $z = \pm 1.28$. So, the middle 80% is represented by daily arrests ranging from 102.88 to 113.12.

13. Top 1% of the dangerous years would have 55.1 terrorist attacks. Found by converting top 1% into a z-score of +2.33 (look for .01 in Column C of Appendix A). Then solve for x in the formula for z-scores: $+2.33 = (x - 31.8) / 10 \rightarrow x = 55.1$.

14. To answer these questions, you need to use the binomial expansion. If you follow the logic of the binomial expansion as shown in Table 7.3, you will find the following answers to these questions:

a. Probability of 3 rehabilitated = .312.

b. Three or more rehabilated = .312 (3 rehab) + .156 (4 rehab) + .031 (5 rehab) = .499 (i.e., the probability is about .5 that you will get 3 or more rehabilitated drug offenders in 5 drug court participants).

c. Probability of 0 rehabilitated = .031.

d. Probability of 5 rehabilitated = .031.

e. The two most unlikely outcomes are 0 rehabilitated and 5 rehabilitated in 5 drug court participants.

15. Probability of five successes when $p = 3/4 \rightarrow (3/4)(3/4)(3/4)(3/4)(3/4)$ = .237. Note that there is only one way to get five successes on five trials, so $(1)(.237) = .237$.

Chapter 8

1. c

2. a

3. a

4. d

5. c

6. a

7. d

8. b

9. d

10. c

11. Without random sampling from the population, you cannot estimate sampling error, and thus you have no idea whether or not your sample is representative of that underlying population.

12. Large samples that are random samples of the population are associated with small sampling error. The smaller the magnitude of sampling error, the more closely your sample estimates will converge on the true population value(s).

13. With a random sample of 61 U.S cities and a population standard deviation of 1.2 and a mean homicide rate of 6.8 per 100,000 in your sample:

   a. 6.8 per 100,000 is your single best guess of the average homicide rate in all U.S. cities.

   b. The 68% confidence interval $= 6.8 \pm 1.0\,(1.2\,/\,\sqrt{61}) = 6.65$ to 6.95. We are 68% confident that the true homicide rate of U.S. cities falls somewhere between 6.65 and 6.95 per 100,000.

   c. The 90% confidence interval $= 6.8 \pm 1.64\,(1.2\,/\,\sqrt{61}) = 6.55$ to 7.05. We are 90% confident that the true homicide rate of U.S. cities falls somewhere between 6.55 and 7.05 per 100,000.

d. The 95% confidence interval $= 6.8 \pm 1.96 \,(1.2 \,/\, \sqrt{61}) = 6.50$ to 7.10. We are 95% confident that the true homicide rate of U.S. cities falls somewhere between 6.5 and 7.1 per 100,000.

e. The 99% confidence interval $= 6.8 \pm 2.58 \,(1.2 \,/\, \sqrt{61}) = 6.40$ to 7.20. We are 99% confident that the true homicide rate of U.S. cities falls somewhere between 6.4 and 7.2 per 100,000.

f. As you increase the confidence level, you increase the width of the confidence interval.

14. When the population standard deviation is unknown, the appropriate comparison distribution involves t-scores.

a. 6.8 per 100,000 is your best guess of the average homicide rate in all U.S. cities.

b. The 90% confidence interval $= 6.8 \pm 1.671 \,(1.2 \,/\, \sqrt{61}) = 6.54$ to 7.06. We are 90% confident that the true homicide rate of U.S. cities falls somewhere between 6.54 and 7.06 per 100,000.

c. The 95% confidence interval $= 6.8 \pm 2.00 \,(1.2 \,/\, \sqrt{61}) = 6.49$ to 7.11. We are 95% confident that the true homicide rate of U.S. cities falls somewhere between 6.49 and 7.11 per 100,000.

d. The 99% confidence interval $= 6.8 \pm 2.66 \,(1.2 \,/\, \sqrt{61}) = 6.39$ to 7.21. We are 99% confident that the true homicide rate of U.S. cities falls somewhere between 6.39 and 7.21 per 100,000.

15. Drunk driving among random sample of 15 people, $p = .30$ (proportion who said they drove drunk), sample standard deviation $= .46$. Thus,

a. 30% is our single best guess of the proportion of adult Americans who have driven while drunk.

b. The 95% confidence interval $= .30 \pm 2.145 \,(.46 \,/\, \sqrt{15}) = .05$ to .55. We are 95% confident that the true percentage of U.S. adults who drink and drive falls somewhere between 5% and 55%. Notice how wide this interval is (from 5% to 55%) because the sample size is small ($n = 15$) and thus you have a large standard error.

c. The 90% confidence interval $= .30 \pm 1.761 \,(.46 \,/\, \sqrt{15}) = .09$ to .51. We are 90% confident that the true percentage of U.S. adults who drink and drive falls somewhere between 9% and 51%.

    d. Issues to consider involve how drunk driving is measured (i.e., are people truthful in their reports of drinking and driving, and what constitutes drinking [e.g., one drink or multiple drinks]?). There are probably issues about sampling bias as well (e.g., those who respond to surveys about drunk driving are probably different from people who do not respond to surveys).

Chapter 9

1. d
2. e
3. d
4. d
5. d
6. e
7. a
8. a
9. d
10. a
11. a
12. e
13. a (*Note:* c is an expression about two population means, *not* a population mean.)
14. b
15. e

Chapter 10

1. a
2. b
3. d
4. b

5. b

6. d

7. a. $H_o: p_{relapse} = .40$

   b. $H_o: p_{success} = 40\%$

   c. $H_o: \mu_{lsat} = 150$

   d. $H_o: \mu_{alcohol} = 50$

   e. $H_o: \mu_{west} - \mu_{nonwest} = 0$

   f. $H_o: p_{male} - p_{female} = 0$

   g. $H_o: p_{am} - p_{can} = 0$

   h. $H_o: \mu_{IQ} = 0$

8. a. $z = \pm 1.96$

   b. $z = +1.64$

   c. $z = -1.64$

   d. $z = \pm 1.96$

   e. $z = -1.64$

   f. $t = \pm 2.086$

   g. $t = +1.725$

   h. $t = -1.725$

   i. $t = \pm 2.015$

   j. $t = +1.680$

   k. $t = -1.680$

   l. $z = \pm 2.58$

   m. $z = -2.33$

   n. $z = +2.33$

   o. $z = +2.33$

   p. $t = \pm 2.756$

   q. $t = -2.423$

9. a. Reject H_o because the observed z-score is greater than the critical value of our test statistic.

   b. Reject H_o because the observed z-score is greater than the critical value of our test statistic.

   c. Do not reject H_o because the observed z-score is not greater than the critical value of our test statistic. An observed z-score of -2.40 is a rare outcome, but it does not fall in the zone of rejection established on the basis of our one-tailed test.

   d. Reject H_o because the observed z-score is greater than the critical value of our test statistic.

   e. Reject H_o because the observed t-score is greater than the critical value of our test statistic.

   f. Do not reject H_o because the observed t-score is not greater than the critical value of our test statistic.

   g. Reject H_o because the observed t-score is greater than the critical value of our test statistic.

   h. Do not reject H_o because the observed z-score is greater than the critical value of our test statistic.

   i. Reject H_o because the observed t-score is greater than the critical value of our test statistic.

   j. Reject H_o because the observed t-score is greater than the critical value of our test statistic.

10. Sample size primarily affects hypothesis testing by decreasing the size of the standard error. So, as you increase the sample size, you decrease the standard error, and thus, all other things constant, you increase the chances of rejecting the null hypothesis (i.e., you increase the chances of finding a statistically significant difference).

Chapter 11

1. e

2. a

3. c

4. a

5. a

6. c

7. d

8. a

9. a

10. b

11. c

12. c

13. d

14. d

15. b

16. a

17. a

18. a. R1 = 130, R2 = 165, C1 = 95, C2 = 80, C3 = 120.

   b. r1c1 = 60, r1c2 = 50, r1c3 = 20, r2c1 = 35, r2c2 = 30, r2c3 = 100.

   c. Dependent variable = property crime victimization; independent variable = place of residency.

   d. "Column percent" is the table you would interpret in this example because the independent variable is the column variable and the dependent variable is the row variable.

   e. Interpretation: The majority of people have been a property crime victim, and the modal resident in the sample is a city dweller (these are interpretations of the marginal frequencies). About 83% of city residents compared to only about one-third of the other types of residents reported being victims of property crime (this is the interpretation of the joint frequencies).

   f. The visual method would suggest a "strong" relationship. There is about a 46 percentage point difference in the victimization experiences of city dwellers and other residents.

   g. The degrees of freedom in this example are equal to $(r - 1)(c - 1) = (2 - 1)(3 - 1) = 2$ degrees of freedom.

h. The critical value of chi-square for 2 degrees of freedom at a .05 alpha level is 5.991. (See Appendix C for chi-square values for different degrees of freedom and significance levels.)

i. Chi-square value is 61.6. This is found by subtracting the observed from the expected score in each cell, squaring this difference, dividing this squared difference by the expected cell frequency, and summing across all cells. See the example in Table 11.6 and related discussion for help in figuring out how to derive this chi-square value.

j. Conclusion: The chi-square value of 61.6 exceeds the critical value of 5.991, so we reject the null hypothesis that the two variables are not related. When the visual method is combined with the chi-square results, it indicates that place of residency and property victimization are strongly related. City residents are far more likely to be property crime victims than both town and suburban residents.

Chapter 12

1. a

2. a

3. d

4. c

5. d

6. Strong

7. Moderate or strong

8. Weak

9. Strong (due to group 4 being different than other groups)

10. Weak

11. a

12. c

13. c

14. e

15. b

16. a. Dependent variable = bribes.

    b. Independent variable = political party.

    c. Minor differences, because most of the scores are about the same for each group except the odd case of 15 bribes for one Republican.

    d. $SS_{total} = 132$.

    e. $SS_{between} = 10$.

    f. $SS_{within} = 122$.

    g. The ANOVA summary table for the bribery data:

Source	Sum of Squares	df	Mean Sum of Squares	F-Value
Between Groups	10	1	10.00	.656
Within Groups	122	8	15.25	
Total	132	9		

    h. F critical value = 5.32 at 1 and 8 degrees of freedom.

    i. There is no major difference in the number of bribes taken by Democrats and Republicans.

    j. Eta square = Bet SS / Total SS = 10 / 132 = .076 → 7.6% of the variation in number of bribes is explained by political party.

    k. 7.6% of the variation in number of bribes is explained by knowledge of one's political party affiliation.

Chapter 13

1. d

2. a

3. b

4. a

5. b

6. a

7. e

8. a

9. a

10. a

11. a

12. e

13. a. A strong positive linear relationship, such that increases in income are associated with increases in education and vice versa.

b. A weak positive linear relationship, such that as the amount of exposure to pornography increases, the number of sex offenses also tends to increase.

c. A moderate positive linear relationship, such that as the number of prior arrests increases, the length of the prison sentence also increases.

d. Basically no linear relationship between the number of police officers and the city's crime rate. Increasing the number of police officers in a city has only a weak association with decreasing crime rates.

e. A moderate negative linear association such that higher rates of teen drug use are associated with younger age of the population.

14. a. *Suicide rate* is the dependent variable (note: we usually put the dependent variable on the Y-axis).

b. The city's unemployment rate is the independent variable.

c. The relationship is positive (i.e., it goes from the left bottom to the right top of the graph).

d. The visual display in the graph suggests a moderate to weak relationship. The points generally fall along an expanded straight line, but there are some exceptions that will reduce the magnitude of the correlation.

e. If you draw the "least square" line, it will basically run through the middle of most points at about a 45 degree angle.

f. This graph shows a positive relationship between these variables and that there are some departures. Increasing unemployment rates are associated with increasing suicide rates.

15. a. There is a moderate positive linear relationship between the number of prison disturbances and the number of guard infractions. Increases in the number of guard infractions are associated with increases in the number of prison disturbances.

b. The *slope* means that a unit change in the number of guard infractions increases by one-tenth the number of prison disturbances.

c. The y-intercept means that if you had no guard infractions at a maximum security prison (i.e., X = 0), you would still have five prison disturbances.

d. $R^2 = r^2 = .40^2 = .16$ → 16% of the variation in prison disturbances is accounted for by the number of guard infractions.

e. 1. 100 guard infractions → y = 5 + .1(100) = 15 prison disturbances.

2. 1,000 guard infractions → y = 5 + .1(1,000) = 105 prison disturbances.

3. 10,000 guard infractions → y = 5 + .1 (10,000) = 1,005 prison disturbances.

4. Maximum security prisons with 0 guard infractions → y = 5 + .1(0) = 5 prison disturbances.

5. A prison with 500 guard infractions → do not know because this analysis is based solely on maximum security prisons, not all prisons.

f. 1. You would do a t-test because of the small sample size (*n* = 30 maximum security prisons).

2. *n* – 2 = 28 degrees of freedom.

3. critical value of t-statistic at 28 degrees of freedom and alpha of .05 for a two-tailed test → t = ±2.048.

4. $t = r\sqrt{n-2/1-r^2} = .40 \times \sqrt{28/.84} = 2.31.$

5. Reject H_o that there is no correlation between these variables because the obtained t-value of 2.31 exceeded the expected

t-value of ±2.048 under the null hypothesis and our decision rule (two-tailed test and .05 alpha level).

Chapter 14

1. a
2. e
3. c
4. a
5. b
6. c
7. a
8. c
9. b
10. a
11. a. 5.6
   b. 6.5 ✦

References

Amnesty International. 2005. *The Death Penalty: Death Penalty Statistics.* http://www.amnesty.org.

Archer, Dane, and Rosemary Gartner. 1987. *Violence and Crime in Cross-National Perspective.* New Haven, CT: Yale University Press.

Block, Carolyn Rebecca, Richard L. Block, and the Illinois Criminal Justice Information Authority. 2005. *Homicides in Chicago, 1965–1995* [Computer file]. ICPSR06399-v5. Chicago, IL: Illinois Criminal Justice Information Authority [producer], 1998. Ann Arbor, MI: Inter-University Consortium for Political and Social Research [distributor], 2005-07-06.

Bonczar, Thomas P. 2003. *Prevalence of Imprisonment in the U.S. Population, 1974–2001.* NCJ 197976, October. Washington, DC: Bureau of Justice Statistics.

Bonczar, Thomas P., and Tracy L. Snell. 2005. *Capital Punishment 2004.* NCJ 211345. Washington, DC: Bureau of Justice Statistics.

Bowling, Michael, Gene Lauver, Matthew J. Hickman, and Devon B. Adams. 2005. *Background Checks for Firearm Transfers, 2004.* NCJ 210117. Washington, DC: U.S. Department of Justice, Bureau of Justice Statistics.

Catalano, Shannon. 2005. *Criminal Victimization, 2004.* NCJ 210674. Washington, DC: Bureau of Justice Statistics, National Crime Victimization Survey.

Centers for Disease Control and Prevention (CDC). 1997. *Youth Risk Behavior Study.* Atlanta, GA: CDC.

Central Intelligence Agency. 2005. *The World Factbook.* Washington, DC: http://www.odci.gov/cia/publications/factbook/geos/us.html.

Cohen, Thomas H., and Brian Reaves. 2006. *Felony Defendants in Large Urban Counties, 2002.* NCJ 210818. Washington, DC: U.S. Department of Justice, Bureau of Justice Statistics.

Durose, Matthew R., and Patrick Langan. 2004. *Felony Sentences in State Courts, 2002.* NCJ 206916. Washington, DC: Bureau of Justice Statistics.

Espy, M. Watt, and John Ortiz Smykla. 1991. *Executions in the United States, 1608–1991: The Espy File* [data file]. Inter-University Consortium for Social and Political Research. Ann Arbor: University of Michigan.

Federal Bureau of Investigation (FBI). 1935–2005. *Crime in the United States.* Washington, DC: U.S. Government Printing Office.

Frankfort-Nachimas, Chava, and Anna Leon-Guerrero. 2002. *Social Statistics for a Diverse Society*, 3rd ed. Thousand Oaks, CA: Sage.

Gallup Poll. 2004. *The Gallup Poll*. http://poll.gallup.com. June 28. Princeton, NJ: Gallup Organization.

———. 2006. *The Gallup Poll*. http://poll.gallup.com. February 3. Princeton, NJ: Gallup Organization.

Greenfeld, Lawrence A. 1997. *Sex Offenses and Offenders: An Analysis of Data on Rape and Sexual Assault*. NCJ 163392. Washington, DC: Bureau of Justice Statistics.

Hickman, Matthew J., and Brian Reaves. 2003. *Local Police Departments 2000*. NCJ 196002. Washington, DC: Bureau of Justice Statistics.

Jenkins, Philip. 1994. *Using Murder: The Social Construction of Serial Homicide*. New York: Aldine de Gruyter.

Kinsey, Alfred C., Wardell B. Pomeroy, Clyde E. Martin, and Paul H. Gebhard. 1953. *Sexual Behavior in the Human Female*. Philadelphia: W. B. Saunders.

Klaus, Patsy. 2006. *Crime and the Nation's Households, 2004*. NCJ 211511. Washington, DC: Bureau of Justice Statistics.

Koppel, Herbert. 1987. *Lifetime Likelihood of Victimization*. Washington, DC: Bureau of Justice Statistics.

Langan, Patrick A., and John M. Dawson. 1995. *Spousal Murder Defendants in Large Urban Counties*. NCJ 153256. Washington, DC: Bureau of Justice Statistics.

McCorkle, Richard C., and Terance D. Miethe. 2002. *Panic: The Social Construction of the Street Gang Problem*. Upper Saddle River, NJ: Prentice Hall.

Miethe, Terance D., and Hong Lu. 2005. *Punishment: A Comparative Historical Perspective*. Cambridge: Cambridge University Press.

Miethe, Terance D., Jodi Olson, and Ojmarrh Mitchell. 2006. "Specialization and Persistence in the Arrest Histories of Sex Offenders: A Comparative Analysis of Alternative Measures and Offense Types." *Journal of Research in Crime and Delinquency* 43(2): 1–26.

Miethe, Terance D., and Wendy C. Regoeczi. 2004. *Rethinking Homicide: Exploring the Structure and Process Underlying Deadly Situations*. Cambridge: Cambridge University Press.

Mosher, Clayton J., Terance D. Miethe, and Dretha M. Phillips. 2002. *The Mismeasure of Crime*. Thousand Oaks, CA: Sage.

National Center for Health Statistics. *Vital Statistics*. http://www.cdc.gov/nchs.

National Crime Victimization Survey (NCVS). 2002. *Criminal Victimization in the United States, 2002, Statistical Tables, March 3, 2004*. NCJ 200561. Washington, DC: National Institute of Justice. http://www.ojp.usdoj.gov/bjs/pub/pdf/cvus02.pdf.

National Vital Statistics Reports. 2004. *Trends in Health and Aging*. Washington, DC: National Center for Health Statistics, U.S. Department of Public Health.

Plate, Thomas. 1975. *Crime Pays*. New York: Simon & Schuster.

Regoeczi, Wendy C., and Marc Reidel. 2003. "The Application of Missing Data Estimation Models to the Problem of Unknown Victim/Offender Relationships in Homicide Cases." *Journal of Quantitative Criminology* 19(3): 155–183.

Schmitt, Erica Leah, Patrick A. Langan, and Matthew R. Durose. 2002. *Characteristics of Drivers Stopped by Police, 1999*. NCJ 191548. Washington, DC: Bureau of Justice Statistics.

Snell, Tracy. 2001. *Capital Punishment 2000*. NCJ 190598. Washington, DC: Bureau of Justice Statistics.

Sourcebook of Criminal Justice Statistics. 2003. *Federal Drug Seizures*. Table 4.36. NCJ 208756. Washington, DC: Bureau of Justice Statistics.

Sullivan, Michael. 2005. *Fundamentals of Statistics*. Upper Saddle River, NJ: Pearson Prentice Hall.

U.S. Census Bureau. 2004. *American Factfinder*. Washington, DC: U.S. Census Bureau.

U.S. Department of Health and Human Services (DHHS). 2004. *Results from the 2003 National Survey on Drug Use and Health: National Findings*. Rockville, MD: U.S. Department of Health and Human Services, Substance Abuse and Mental Health Services Administration.

Washington, DC, Metropolitan Police Department. http://mpdc.dc.gov/mpdc.

Weinrott, Mark R., and Maureen Saylor. 1991. "Self-Report of Crimes Committed by Sex Offenders." *Journal of Interpersonal Violence* 6: 286–300.

Wilbanks, William. 1984. *Murder in Miami: An Analysis of Homicide Patterns and Trends in Dade County (Miami), Florida, 1917–1983*. Lanham, MD: University Press of America.

Zahn, Marjorie, Coramae Mann, and Nancy Rodriquez. 2006. *Images of Color, Images of Crime*, 3rd ed. Los Angeles, CA: Roxbury. ✦

Glossary of Key Terms

Alpha Level (α) The probability of making a Type I error (i.e., rejecting a true hypothesis). It is also called the *significance level of a test statistic.* Common alpha levels in social science research are .05 and .01.

Alternative Hypothesis (Hₐ) The research or substantive hypothesis that you really expect when testing the null hypothesis. The alternative hypothesis is derived from existing theory, previous research, and/or sound logical reasoning. Ha, Ha! The alternative hypothesis is no joke.

Analysis of Variance (ANOVA) A statistical procedure used with a quantitatively measured dependent variable and a nominal or ordinal independent variable. It partitions the total variation in the dependent variable into two components: between-group variation and within-group variation. ANOVA provides a technique for evaluating how much variation in a dependent variable is accounted for by knowledge of the independent variable.

Bar Charts A visual display of a qualitative variable or attributes. The length of the bars is proportional to the frequency of the category. Categories with more observations in them have longer bars.

Between-Group Variation Variation between the group means and the overall or grand mean in ANOVA applications. It is computed as the sum of the squared deviations from the mean for each category of the independent variable from the grand mean.

Binomial Distribution A probability sampling distribution of r successes on N trials. It requires a binary variable (e.g., success or failure) and becomes very close in shape to the normal curve when the number of trials or observations is greater than 50.

Bivariate Analysis Analyses that focus on the joint occurrence and/or association between two variables. Examples include basic two-way cross-tabulations or contingency tables, correlation, and one-way ANOVA.

Bivariate Association The observed relationship between two variables that is found by doing a bivariate analysis.

"Canned" Data Sets Term applied in secondary data analysis to refer to situations in which the researcher does not have to do a lot of data collection or initial coding of the data because someone else has already done it. The data is in the "can," meaning it is already preserved and ready to eat, consume, or crunch.

Causal Validity The ability to say that X causes Y because the three major factors associated with causal inferences have been satisfied (i.e., temporal ordering, empirical association, and nonspuriousness). Experiments with random assignment to experimental and control groups are the best research designs for assessing this type of validity associated with causal inferences.

Central Limit Theorem A very useful statistical principle that states that the sampling distribution of repeatedly large random samples will approach a normal distribution as the sample size increases. This theorem is the basis for why the normal curve is often used as the comparative standard for parameter estimation and hypothesis testing.

Chi-Square Distribution A sampling distribution that is often used in the analysis of the relationship between two qualitative variables. The shape of this distribution depends on the degrees of freedom. In the analysis of a contingency table between two qualitative variables, the degrees of freedom are found by multiplying the number of rows minus one $(R - 1)$ and the number of columns minus one $(C - 1)$.

Chi-Square Test A statistical test of independence between two categorical variables. The critical values of this test depend on the significance level (α) and the degrees of freedom.

Codebook A document that contains the names of variables, their possible values, and specific rules for translating words and numbers into numerical codes. You really cannot do any type of primary data collection or secondary data analysis without some type of codebook to tell you how particular variables were classified or coded and the meaning of particular numerical codes in the data file.

Coding The physical process of translating verbal or written words or numbers into other numerical or alphanumerical values that are more readable by various computer software programs. Examples include translating one's gender into the numerical coding system of 1 = Male and 2 = Female. Coding is a necessary step in data preparation.

Coefficient of Determination (R²) A measure of the proportion of variation in a dependent variable that is accounted for by the independent variable(s). It also measures the proportional reduction in error in predicting a dependent variable on the basis of the independent variable rather than solely based on the mean of the dependent variable.

Collectively Exhaustive Categories for a variable cover all possibilities for that variable. For example, for the variable *biological sex*, you are male, female, or both (i.e., hermaphrodites). Those are all the possibilities.

Column Percentages Within a contingency table, the percentage distribution within each category of the column variable.

Computer Software Technology that is used to input, analyze, and represent data for purposes of statistical analysis. SPSS and Microsoft Excel are the primary types of computer software that are described in this book.

Confidence Intervals A range of scores that is likely to capture an unknown population parameter. Confidence intervals include a point estimate of the population parameter and a margin of error (i.e., a *give-and-take component*) around this point estimate for the population mean or proportion.

Confidence Level A probability statement of the likelihood of capturing the true population value within a confidence interval. Common confidence levels in the social sciences involve z-scores or t-scores whose combined probability of occurrence is 68%, 90%, 95%, or 99%.

Content Analysis A qualitative research method that involves the analysis of the content of any written or verbal form of communication. To do this type of analysis, the research needs to establish rules for coding the content of this information.

Contingency Table A tabular display of the relationship between two categorical variables. The size of this cross-tabulation of variables is based on the number of categories of the row variable and the number of categories of the column variable. It is called a *contingency table* under the assumption that the value on some variable is contingent upon the value on some other variable.

Correlation Coefficient (r) A measure of the strength of a linear relationship between two quantitative variables. It is the most commonly used measure of statistical association in criminology and other types of social science research.

Critical Values The boundaries of a sampling distribution that define what constitutes a rare or common outcome under a null hypothesis and the particular decision rule used by the researcher. The actual values are determined by the type of sampling distribution (e.g., t- or normal distribution), the alpha level of the test, and the nature of the alternative hypothesis (e.g., if it is nondirectional, there are two critical values; if the alternative hypothesis is directional [< or >], there is only one critical value). These critical value(s) are defined as *critical* because they establish the boundary of the zone of rejection for rejecting the null hypothesis. The confidence level in confidence intervals provides a related type of "critical value."

Cumulative Distributions A frequency or percentage distribution of a quantitative variable that shows the number or percentage of observations that are above or below a particular category.

Data The information that is collected, coded, and analyzed in a research study or report. Social data may include information on individuals, groups, neighborhoods, and other larger ecological units (e.g., states or nations).

Degrees of Freedom An important concept in parameter estimation and hypothesis testing. It represents the number of scores that are "free" to vary when estimating a population value.

Dependent Variable The "effect" or outcome variable in a cause–effect chain. It is the variable whose outcome depends on some other variable. It is the Y in the $X \rightarrow Y$ chain.

Descriptive Statistics Summary measures that are used for purposes of data description and reduction. Common descriptive statistics include various measures of central tendency or location (e.g., means, medians, and modes), dispersion and variation (e.g., standard deviation and variances), and association (e.g., correlations and regression coefficients).

Developmental Chain The type of causal relationship between variables in which A causes B, B causes C, C causes D, and so on. It is graphically illustrated as $A \rightarrow B \rightarrow C \rightarrow D$. In this particular chain, the variable A does not affect the variable D directly. A influences D only through B and C. Confused? Just think of a chain reaction when thinking of developmental chains.

Distal Causes The remote causal factors in a developmental chain. In the causal chain $A \rightarrow B \rightarrow C \rightarrow D$, both variables A and B are distal causes of D. Think *distance* or *far away* when thinking distal.

Ecological Fallacy The error in causal inference that occurs as the result of trying to make inferences about the behavior of individuals from data on aggregate or ecological data. For example, if states with higher rates of *Playboy* magazine subscriptions also have higher rates of pot smoking, you cannot say that individuals who "read" *Playboy* smoke more dope because you did not collect the information on individuals. You can only say that states with high *Playboy* readership have high rates of dope smoking. Period. Saying anything about individual users or readers is the ecological fallacy.

Empirical Association An observable relationship between two variables (e.g., as X goes up, Y goes down). An observable relationship between two variables is a necessary condition for the causal inference that X causes Y. However, just because two variables are associated does not mean they are causally related.

Eta Squared (η^2) A measure of association in the analysis of variance (ANOVA). It is also called the *correlation ratio*. It is interpreted as the proportion of error reduction when the means of each category of the independent variable are used to predict scores on the dependent variable rather than just using the grand mean for these predictions. It is also interpreted as the proportion of variation in the dependent variable that is accounted for by the particular categories of the independent variable(s).

Expected Cell Frequencies The number of observations in a particular cell of a contingency table that are expected if the two variables are independent. The chi-square test of independence is based on the differences between these expected cell frequencies and the observed cell frequencies.

Experimental Designs The type of research method that is used primarily to evaluate causal relationships between a treatment (i.e., the "cause") and the outcome or "effect." The classical experimental design involves two groups (a treatment group and a control group) and random assignment to these groups.

F-Ratio or F-test The ratio of the mean squared between-group variance and the mean squared within-group variance. This ratio is used in hypothesis testing within ANOVA applications to test the hypothesis that the population means are identical. Critical values of the F-sampling distribution are used to reach decisions about rejecting or not rejecting hypotheses within this ANOVA framework. It is also used to test the significance of the coefficient of determination (R^2) in a regression analysis.

Frequency Distributions A numerical representation of the relative distribution of scores on a variable.

"Garbage In, Garbage Out" (GIGO) The idea that statistical analysis is basically worthless if you have a bad sample, bad measurement of concepts, errors in information processing, and political agendas underlying the data analysis. If you have garbage coming into the earlier stages of data analysis, you are guaranteed to have garbage come out.

Generalizability The ability to generalize your substantive conclusions to some other context. Usually we talk about generalizing from our sample results to some wider population. A major threat to generalizability is sampling (i.e., your sample does not represent the population). Within the context of experiments, generalizability is also referred to as *external validity*. Experimental results in a particular study sometimes do not generalize to a wider population because of the artificiality of the setting in which the original experiments take place. In other words, people may behave in a particular way in a very controlled environment, but they are totally different in another context. This would be an example of low generalizability.

Grand Mean It is the mean across all observations. The term is also called the *overall mean*. It is used within the ANOVA tradition and is the basis of the total variation (i.e., the total variation is variation around the grand mean).

Histograms A visual representation of the distribution of scores for a quantitative variable. There is often no blank space between the categories of a histogram to indicate that the variable has a continuous distribution. A histogram is a visual equivalent to a bar chart for qualitative variables, except that the bar chart often has space between the bars to indicate that the variable is not continuous.

Independent Variable The variable that causes or influences another variable. It is called the *treatment variable* in experimental designs. In the simple causal chain $X \rightarrow Y$, X is the independent variable. It is that variable that precedes the outcome variable in time.

Inferential Statistics The type of statistical methods that is used to estimate population values from the observations and analyses of a sample. Hypothesis testing and developing confidence intervals are two contexts in which inferential statistics are used.

Informed Consumers These are people who have a good grasp of the logic of statistical thinking and use this information to become more astute and valuable employees and citizens.

Interval Measurement The level of quantitative measurement involving the properties of differences in magnitude and equal distance between the response categories. Examples include one's age (coded in years [1, 2, 3, 4, 5, . . .] or in equal 10-year intervals [0–9, 10–19, 20–29, . . .]) or number of gallstones passed per year (using the same response categories as the age example).

Joint Distributions The distribution of marijuana cigarettes or, in statistics, the intersection of any two categories of two variables in a contingency table. The cells within a contingency table reflect the joint distributions of these two categories of the two variables.

"Least Squares" Method The type of regression analysis in which the y-intercept and slope coefficients are estimated in such a way that they minimize the sum of the squared deviations from the observed and predicted values of the dependent variables. This method is often referred to as *ordinary least squares (OLS) regression analysis*.

Linear Relationship A functional relationship between two variables that is expressed as a straight line. The regression equation $Y = a + b\,X$ is a specification of the linear relationship between variable X and Y.

Line Graphs A representation that plots the points on a graph and connects them with lines.

Marginal Distributions The distribution of the two variables of a contingency table when the variables are treated separately. Two types of marginal distributions involve the row frequencies and column frequencies.

Margin of Error The component of a confidence interval that is the product of the confidence level and the standard error. It is also called the "give-and-take" component in loose statements about confidence intervals (e.g., "The mean age is 30, give or take 3 years"). In the formula for a confidence interval $\mu \pm z_{cl}\,se$, the margin of error is the $\pm z_{cl}\,se$ component.

Mean The statistical average that is computed by summing up all scores and dividing by the number of scores. It is the most commonly used summary measure of central tendency and typicality in statistics. It is not an angry statistic.

Measurement The outcome of the process of operationalization (i.e., the outcome of the process of attaching specific meaning to abstract concepts). Measurement is a necessary condition for statistical analysis (i.e., if you have not measured a variable or attribute, you cannot compute statistics on it because a variable or attribute does not exist without measurement).

Measurement Validity Situations in which you are really measuring what you think you are measuring. Having bad measures of concepts (e.g., using police data on known offenses as a measure of the true extent of crime) is a major contributor to the "garbage in, garbage out" syndrome.

Median The middle score in an ordered array of scores. It is similar to the thing that divides a highway in half that you should not be driving on. 50% of the scores fall above it, and 50% fall below it.

Missing Data It is data that is missing!!! Missing data often occurs because some information is simply not available, people space out and skip questions during interviews, they refuse to respond to personal questions, or they give weird answers that we end up throwing out in our analysis. In studies of homicide, about 50% of the data on the victim–offender relationship is missing because the police do not have any idea who the offender is. When you have a lot of missing data by acts of omission or commission (e.g., errors in information processing, or coding errors), you've got problems!!!

Modal Interval In a quantitative frequency distribution, it is the interval that contains the largest number of observations.

Mode The most frequently occurring score or category in a distribution. The mode may or may not be representative of the majority of cases in a distribution.

$MS_{Between}$ Versus MS_{Within} The two major components of variance that are used in the F-ratio. They represent the sum of the squares of the between-group and within-group components of the total variation that are adjusted by their respective degrees of freedom.

Multiple Causes The recognition that human behavior is complex and has multiple causes is a primary reason for doing multivariate analysis. By including multiple variables and using statistical controls, various statistical techniques allow researchers to identify the most important variables within this context of multiple causes.

Multiple Regression A multivariate analysis procedure that is designed to assess the net impact of multiple independent variables on a dependent variable. The dependent variable is assumed to be measured on an interval or ratio scale when the regression coefficients are estimated using the method of ordinary least squares (OLS).

Multivariate Analysis Research strategies and data analytic techniques that involve the investigation of more than two variables at the same time or within the same statistical analysis. Examples include multiple regression analysis in which the effects of two or more independent variables are assessed in terms of their impact on a dependent variable.

Mutually Exclusive The property of measurement categories that do not overlap. Examples include *number of arrests* (coded 0, 1, 2, 3, or more). If you used some overlapping categories in this example (0, 1, 2–3, 3 or more), you violated this sacred property because a person with 3 arrests could be put in more than one category. A good indication that you have violated this property is when you add up the percent of cases or people in each category and it sums to a value greater than 100%. Either your math is bad or you are counting some people twice because the categories are not mutually exclusive.

N (number of observations) The number of scores from which statistics are computed. When used to describe the number of observations in a sample or population, it is often presented as $N = some value$.

Naturalistic Observation Studies that involve watching or observing people in natural settings. Just think of bird watching. This is also called "field" studies.

Nominal Measurement Measures of qualitative attributes that are different in type, kind, or form. Although numbers are often assigned to nominal measures, the numbers do not refer to distance—they just represent differences between categories. Examples include one's race (coded 1 = Black, 2 = White, or 3 = Other), gender (M or F), or bored with these examples (coded 0 = No, 1 = Yes, or 9 = Don't Know). Remember that the actual numbers assigned to nominal variables are arbitrary and essentially meaningless—what matters is they tell us that the people or objects in the different categories are simply different from each other.

Nonprobability Sampling Sampling designs in which elements are selected for inclusion in a sample on the basis of some factor other than probability. Examples include convenience or availability sampling, and snowball sampling.

Normal Distribution The most commonly used and assumed sampling distribution in statistical analysis. It is also called the *standard normal probability distribution* or, more simply, the *normal curve*. When a variable is normally distributed, it has many well-defined properties (i.e., it is symmetrical around its mean, bell-shaped, and unimodal, and a constant proportion of cases fall within given standard deviations from the mean).

A variable that is normally distributed or approximates a normal distribution is symbolized as x ≈ *Norm* (μ, σ), where μ = the population mean and σ = the population standard deviation.

Null Hypothesis (H_o) The hypothesis that is tested in the process of statistical inference. The null hypothesis may involve a particular population parameter (e.g., the population mean or the population proportion) or a difference between two or more population parameters (e.g., whether two population means are identical).

Observed Cell Frequencies The number of observations that are found jointly by the intersection of each column *and* each row of a contingency table. For example, in a contingency table of race and gender, the number of black males would be one of these observed cell frequencies.

One-Tailed or Two-Tailed Tests The terms used to describe the situation in which the alternative hypothesis is either directional (i.e., one-tailed) or nondirectional (i.e., two-tailed). Rare outcomes that lead to the rejection of the null hypothesis occur in one or two tails of sampling distributions. In a one-tailed test, the region of the comparison distribution that establishes when the null hypothesis would be rejected is all on one side (i.e., tail) of the distribution. In a two-tailed test, the region is spread out in the tails of both sides of the sampling distribution.

One- Versus Two- Versus N-Way ANOVA Different types of analysis of variance that are defined by the number of independent variables in the analysis. One-way ANOVA has one independent variable, two-way ANOVA has two independent variables, and so forth. The term *N-way* is the generic way to designate the number of independent variables (e.g., if N = 5 independent variables, it would be called a five-way ANOVA).

Operationalization The process by which particular meaning is attached to abstract concepts for purposes of developing observable indicators and measures of these concepts.

Ordinal Measurement Measures of quantitative variables whose categories can be arranged in order (from low to high or vice versa), but the actual distance between them is either unknown or unequal. Examples include self-reported happiness (coded *never, rarely, sometimes,* and *always happy*) or your social class (coded *low, middle,* and *upper class*).

Outliers Influential points and otherwise weird observations that seriously distort the calculated values of many descriptive statistics. Having Bill Gates included in a random sample of 100 people to estimate the average income of all U.S. residents is an example of an outlier. Generally, outliers are people who are extremely deviant in a statistical way—they have the consequence of inflating or deflating particular statistics. After we identify outliers and influential points in a data file, we try to understand why the particular case is strange, and then usually delete it from our analyses. So, Bill Gates would be excluded because his astronomical income would really distort our sample statistics.

Partial Correlation A type of multivariate analysis involving the investigation of the bivariate correlation between two variables once controls are introduced for other variables. In the case of three variables, the partial correlation between X and Y controlling for Z is symbolized as $r_{xy.z}$.

Percentage Distributions The distribution of scores that have been standardized by dividing the number of cases in each category by the total number of observations (N). The sum of percentages within each category will add up to 100% in a properly constructed percentage distribution.

Pie Chart A visual representation of the relative frequency distribution of observations across categories. The entire set of observations is represented by the entire pie, while the size of the individual "slices" indicates the relative frequency of observations within the particular categories.

Population Parameters Numbers and statistical information that we are trying to estimate from samples of data. Usually these values are unknown and are represented by Greek symbols (e.g., μ and σ). Sample statistics are used to estimate the values of these population parameters.

Probability Sampling A sampling procedure in which each element in the population has a known probability of being included in the sample. It is the type of sampling that is widely assumed in any type of statistical inference.

Proximate Causes The immediate or closest direct causal factor in a causal chain. In the example $A \rightarrow B \rightarrow C$, A is the proximate cause of B and B is the proximate cause of C. Think *proximity* when thinking proximate causes.

Qualitative Variables The measurement of attributes (e.g., gender, race, or country of birth) that differ in their qualities, type, and/or kind. Nominal measures are qualitative variables.

Quantitative Variables The measurement of characteristics of objects or people that vary in their quantity, magnitude, intensity, and/or duration. Whenever you see the words *how often* or *how much*, you are talking about a quantitative variable. Ordinal, interval, and ratio variables are quantitative variables.

Random Assignment The process used in the assignment of people or objects into groups so that weird and normal factors should be equally dispersed across the groups. By assigning group membership at random (flipping coins, with heads in group 1, tails in group 2), the two groups should not differ on any characteristic other than the one that is the ultimate focus on the research. To make solid inferences about the effects of a particular "treatment" in an experimental design, it is really important that, if possible, people are assigned by a random process to the experimental and control groups.

Random Samples The basic type of sample that is assumed in statistical inference. You cannot provide reasonable estimates of population parameters or test statistical hypotheses about these population parameters from a sample of data unless that sample is randomly selected from that population.

Range A measure of the dispersion of scores. The range represents the difference between the lowest and highest scores in an ordered array. Because these two extreme points are often exceptional cases, intermediate ranges (like the interquartile range) are often used to further gauge the dispersion of scores.

Rate A particular type of ratio that is conveyed as a number per given standard units. For example, crime rates are often expressed as the number of offenses per 100,000 residents.

Ratio A measure of the relative frequency of one category of a variable compared to another. For example, if 10 males and 2 females were included in a sample, the male-to-female ratio would be 5:1 (10 / 2 = 5).

Ratio Measurement Measures of quantitative variables that have a nonarbitrary zero point and equal distance between the categories. When expressed in equal-width intervals, variables such as your *age*, *years of formal education*, and *number of arrests for drug use* are examples of ratio measures because the value *0* is meaningful.

Refined Median This is the median that is derived from data that is grouped into categories. It is an estimated value that is computed by the interpolation of scores across the class interval that contains the median case.

Regression Coefficient The slope in the regression equation, symbolized as *b* (when talking about unstandardized regression coefficients) or β (*beta*, when referring to standardized regression coefficients). It represents the change in Y for a unit change in X in the general linear model of the form $Y = a + b\,X$.

Regression Equation A formal statement of the relationship between a dependent variable (Y) and an independent variable (X). The linear form of this regression equation is $Y = a + b\,X$.

Residual Sum of Squares The sum of the squared errors in predicting a dependent variable (Y) on the basis of the independent variable(s) (X). These errors in prediction are found by estimating a regression equation ($Y = a + b\,X$) and then calculating the discrepancies between the observed Y values and expected Y values based on the estimates of the slope and y-intercept term in the regression equation. In the tradition of ANOVA, the residual sum of squares is the same as the within-group sum of squares.

Row Percentages Within a contingency table, the percentage distribution within each category of the row variable.

Sample Statistics The numbers that are crunched or calculated from a sample of observations. Common sample statistics include means and standard deviations. We use sample statistics to estimate population values. Latin letters are used to symbolize sample statistics (e.g., sd = standard deviation).

Sampling Bias The problem that occurs when sample statistics do not accurately represent population parameters due to basic flaws in the sampling design. Major sources of sampling bias include the use of outdated or ordered lists from which the sample is drawn and nonresponse by survey respondents that is associated with particular characteristics of the sample elements. Sampling bias is one of the major threats to the external validity and generalizability of a study's results.

Sampling Distributions Theoretical and hypothetical distributions of all possible outcomes of a test statistic. Sampling distributions are used for comparative purposes to establish the likely outcomes under particular conditions (e.g., the null hypothesis is true). Within the area of statistical inference, the sampling distribution is used to make a decision about whether the observed sample values are a rare or common outcome under a null hypothesis and the expected distribution of possible outcomes that derives from it. The most commonly used sampling distributions in social statistics are the normal curve, the t-distribution, the chi-square (χ^2) distribution, and the F-distribution.

Sampling Error The discrepancy between sample statistics and population parameters that is due solely to random chance. The magnitude of sampling error can be reduced by taking larger random samples from the respective population.

Scatterplot or Scatter Diagram A visual representation of the relationship between two quantitative variables. The data points on this graph are the joint intersection of the X and Y scores for each individual or case. A good idea of the general direction and relative magnitude of association between two quantitative variables can be determined by simply looking at this graphic distribution of data points in Cartesian coordinates (x, y).

Secondary Data Analysis The type of research design that involves the analysis of data that has already been collected by someone else. Examples include analyses based on preexisting government documents and historical records. Compared to collecting your own data (called *primary data analysis*), secondary analysis is quick, cheap, and relatively painless.

Significance Level Another name for alpha (α) or the probability of making a Type I error in statistical inference. The researcher decides what particular significance level to use in a given problem. The most commonly used significance levels are .05 and .01 for either one-tailed or two-tailed tests.

Skewed Distributions A distribution of scores that is not symmetrical around the mean. A "right" or positive skewed distribution is one in which the mean is larger than the median and mode because a few extreme scores pull the mean to the right of median. A "left" or negative skewed distribution is one in which the mean is smaller than the median and mode value because a few extremely low scores pull down the mean to the left of the median. When distributions are skewed, the median is a better measure of typicality and central tendency than the mean.

Slope (b) or Regression Coefficient The value in a regression equation that represents how a unit change in the independent variable influences the dependent variable. In high school math books' discussions of linear equations, the slope is described as the "rise over the run" in a $Y - X$ graph.

Social Statistics Groups of statistics that hang out together in bars, nightclubs, and other social settings? No. This term refers to the general kinds of statistical analysis that are done by people trained in the social and behavioral sciences to represent patterns and/or trends on various aspects of human behavior. In contrast to "pure" statistics, the term *social* is also sometimes used to indicate that they are less mathematically rigorous and more consumer friendly.

Spreadsheets A format or platform for inputting data into a computer program for subsequent analyses. Microsoft Excel is an example of a spreadsheet program.

SPSS This acronym stands for Statistical Package for the Social Sciences. It is the most widely used computer software program for analyzing data in the social and behavioral sciences.

Spuriousness The condition in which two variables appear to be causally related but they are not because another variable is the common cause of both of them. A necessary condition for asserting that variable X causes variable Y is that this relationship is nonspurious.

Standard Deviation A measure of average dispersion of scores around the mean. It is computed as the square root of the sum of average squared deviations from the mean. Along with the mean and sample size, the standard deviation is a sufficient statistic for nearly all calculations in social statistics. The larger the standard deviation, the greater the spread of scores around the mean.

Standard Error of the Estimate The standard error is the standard deviation of a sampling distribution. It is a measure of sampling error (i.e., the discrepancy between sample statistics and population parameters that is due exclusively to random sampling). This measure of dispersion in a sampling distribution is reduced in magnitude when the sample size is increased.

Standardized Partial Regression Coefficients (β's) Regression coefficients in a multiple regression analysis that have been adjusted by the ratio of the standard deviations in the X and Y variables. The conversion of unstandardized partial regression coefficients (b's) into standardized regression coefficients permits clearer comparisons of the relative importance of different variables in predicting the dependent variable.

Standardized Scores Scores that are adjusted to a common (i.e., standard) metric or scale. The most widely used standard score is the z-score, which converts a raw score into a standard score by (1) subtracting the mean from the raw score and (2) dividing this difference by the standard deviation. Standard scores are often preferred over raw scores because they make comparisons of different groups easier due to their use of the same metric or scale.

Statistical Association The relationship between two or more variables. When the two variables are qualitative variables, statistical association is measured by the joint occurrence of attributes. For quantitative variables, the measure of statistical association involves the principle of covariation between these variables. Correlations are the most common measure of a statistical association for quantitative variables, whereas the chi-square test is a widely used test of the significance of a statistical association in a contingency table analysis of categorical variables.

Statistical Control Statistical adjustments made in multivariate analysis to remove the influence of other variables on the basic relationship between X and Y. Once statistical controls are introduced in a multivariate analysis, the social analyst can speak about the conditional or net effects of some independent variable on a dependent variable when the "contaminating" effects of some other variable (Z) are removed or taken into account.

Statistical Inference The process of using sample data to estimate unknown population parameters and to test statistical hypotheses.

Statistical Versus Substantive Significance The potential dilemma that arises when large samples are used to test statistical hypotheses. Due to the fact that the likelihood of achieving statistically significant differences (i.e., rejecting the null hypothesis) increases as the sample size increases, one may question the substantive importance of these differences. Good practices require a focus on both the formal statistical conclusions and the substantive meaning attached to the magnitude of these differences.

Table of Column Percentages A type of contingency table in which the cell entries are derived by dividing each joint frequency $(r_i c_j)$ by the total number of observations in a particular column $(\mathbf{C}_j)$.

Table of Row Percentages A type of contingency table in which the cell entries are derived by dividing each joint frequency $(r_i c_j)$ by the total number of observations in a particular row $(\mathbf{R}_i)$.

Table of Total Percentages A type of contingency table in which the cell entries are derived by dividing each joint frequency $(r_i c_j)$ by the total number of observations (N).

t-Distribution A sampling distribution that more closely resembles the normal probability distribution when the size of the sample increases. This distribution is used in constructing confidence intervals and hypothesis testing when the population standard deviation is unknown and the sample size(s) is less than 50 $(N < 50)$.

Temporal Ordering The necessary condition for causal inference that the causal variable (X) must precede in time the effect variable (Y). Temporal ordering is established in experimental designs by introducing the experimental treatment (the cause or X variable) before measuring the outcome variable (the effect or Y variable).

Total Percentages Within a contingency table, the percentage distribution that represents the percentage of the total sample (N) that is contained within each cell of the table.

Total Variation The sum of the squared deviation of each individual's score from the overall or grand mean. Within ANOVA, this variation is decomposed or partitioned into between-group and within-group variation. The total variation is what we are trying to explain by knowledge of group membership or other independent variables in a statistical analysis.

t-Tests Statistical tests of population parameters from sample data that use the t-distribution as the comparative basis for parameter estimation and hypothesis testing.

Type I Error The error in statistical inference that derives from the decision to reject a true null hypothesis. This is also called the *alpha level* (α) or *significance level* of a test.

Type II Error The error in statistical inference that derives from the decision to accept a false null hypothesis (i.e., failing to reject the null hypothesis when in fact it is false). By minimizing the possibility of making a Type II error, you increase the probability of a Type I error, and vice versa.

Univariate Analysis An analysis of one variable. Common statistics used in univariate analyses include various descriptive statistics like means, medians, modes, standard deviations, and variances.

Unstandardized Regression Coefficients (b) The slope of the regression equation linking one or more independent variables (X) with a dependent variable. They are "unstandardized" coefficients because they are expressed in the same units as the independent and dependent variables.

Variable Something that varies in magnitude, duration, and/or intensity. Ordinal, interval, and ratio measurement correspond to the measurement of quantitative variables. In contrast, nominal measures of concepts are called *attributes* or *qualitative variables*.

Variance A measure of dispersion of scores around the mean. It is computed as the sum of the average squared deviations from the mean. The larger the variance, the greater the spread of scores around the mean.

Weighted Means Means that are computed from frequency distributions in which more importance (i.e., weight) is given to some observations than others. For example, a student's grade point average (GPA) is figured as a weighted mean because courses with more credit value are given more importance in the computation of your overall GPA.

Within-Group Variation Variation between the individual's score and the mean score for their respective group. It also represents the remainder or error in prediction that is left when we use the group means to explain the total variation.

Y-Intercept (a) The estimated value in a regression equation that represents the point where the regression line intersects the y-axis. In other words, in the regression equation $Y = a + b X$, the y-intercept (a) is the value of Y when $X = 0$.

Zone of Rejection The area(s) of a sampling distribution that designate the sample outcomes that will lead to the rejection of the null hypothesis in favor of the alternative hypothesis. There are two zones of rejection in the tails of the sampling distribution when the alternative hypothesis is nondirectional. One zone of rejection (i.e., in either the left [lower] or right [upper] tail of the distribution) is established when the alternative hypothesis specifies a particular direction.

z-scores A standardized score that converts a distribution to have a mean of 0 and a standard deviation of 1. Z-scores are also called *normal deviates* to designate their use for normal distributions. Raw scores are converted to z-scores by the following formula: $z = (x - \mu) / \sigma$. Positive z-scores represent scores that are greater than the mean, and negative z-scores designate scores that are below the mean.

z-Tests Tests of statistical significance and parameter estimation that use the normal probability distribution for comparative purposes of defining rare and common outcomes. ✦

Subject Index